gas not
2 0/=

LIFE IN THE ROMAN WORLD
OF NERO AND ST. PAUL

THE MACMILLAN COMPANY
NEW YORK · BOSTON · CHICAGO
SAN FRANCISCO

MACMILLAN & CO., Limited
LONDON · BOMBAY · CALCUTTA
MELBOURNE

THE MACMILLAN CO. OF CANADA, Ltd.
TORONTO

VIEW INTO FORUM FROM TEMPLE OF VESTA, A.D. 64. *Frontispiece.*

From extreme left — above : Palace of Caligula on Palatine ; on level : Temple of Vesta, Temple of Castor, Basilica Julia, Arch of Tiberius, Temple of Saturn ; above : Temple of Jupiter on Capitol. In background : Record Office, with (in front) Golden Milestone, Rostra, and Temple of Concord. In right foreground : back of Temple of Julius. The Arch of Augustus has been omitted to allow of the view. (Reconstruction after Auer, Hülsen, Tognetti, etc.)

LIFE IN
THE ROMAN WORLD

OF NERO AND ST. PAUL

BY

T. G. TUCKER

Litt.D., Camb. ; Hon. Litt.D., Dublin

PROFESSOR OF CLASSICAL PHILOLOGY IN THE UNIVERSITY OF MELBOURNE

AUTHOR OF 'LIFE IN ANCIENT ATHENS,' ETC.

New York
THE MACMILLAN COMPANY
1911

Norwood Press
J. S. Cushing Co. — Berwick & Smith Co.
Norwood, Mass., U.S.A.

PREFACE

THE reception accorded to my *Life in Ancient Athens*
has led me to write the present companion work
with an eye to the same class of readers. In the
preface to the former volume it was said : " I have
sought to leave an impression true and sound, so
far as it goes, and also vivid and distinct. The style
adopted has therefore been the opposite of the
pedantic, utilizing any vivacities of method which are
consistent with truth of fact." The same principles
have guided me in the present equally unpretentious
treatise. I agree entirely with Mr. Warde Fowler
when he says: " I firmly believe that the one great
hope for classical learning and education lies in the
interest which the unlearned public may be brought
to feel in ancient life and thought."

For the general reader there is perhaps no period
in the history of the ancient world which is more
interesting than the one here chosen. Yet, so far
as I know, there exists no sufficiently popular work
dealing with this period alone and presenting in
moderate compass a clear general view of the matters
of most moment. My endeavour has been to represent as faithfully as possible the Age of Nero, and

nowhere in the book is it implied that what is true
for that age is necessarily as true for any other. The
reader who is not a special student of history or
antiquities is perhaps as often confused by descriptions of ancient life which cover too many generations
as by those — often otherwise excellent — which include too much detail.

I have necessarily consulted not only the Latin
and Greek writers who throw light upon the time,
but also all the best-known standard works of
modern date. It is perhaps scarcely necessary to
state that in matters of contemporary government,
administration, and public life my guides have been
chiefly Mommsen, Arnold, and Greenidge; for social
life Marquardt, Friedländer, and Becker-Göll; for
topography and buildings Jordan, Hülsen, Lanciani,
and Middleton; nor that the Dictionaries of Smith
and of Daremberg and Saglio have been always at
hand, as well as Baumeister's *Denkmäler*, and Guhl
and Koner's *Life of the Greeks and Romans*. The
admirable *Pompeii* of Mau-Kelsey has been, of course,
indispensable. I have also derived profit from the
writings of Prof. Sir W. M. Ramsay in connexion
with St. Paul, and from Conybeare and Howson's *Life
and Epistles* of the Apostle. Useful hints have been
found in Mr. Warde Fowler's *Social Life in Rome
in the Age of Cicero*, and in Prof. Dill's *Roman
Society from Nero to Marcus Aurelius*. A personal
study of ancient sites, monuments, and objects of
antiquity at Rome, Pompeii, and elsewhere has
naturally been of prime value. Those intimately

acquainted with the immense amount of the available material will best realize the difficulty there has been in deciding how much to say and how much to " leave in the inkstand."

For the drawings other than those of which another source is specified I have to thank Miss M. O'Shea, on whom has occasionally fallen the difficult task of giving ocular form to the mental visions of one who happens to be no draughtsman. For the rest I make acknowledgment to those books from which the illustrations have been directly derived for my own purposes, without reference to more original sources.

I am especially grateful for the permission to use so considerable a number of illustrations from the *Pompeii* of Mau-Kelsey, from Professor Waldstein's *Herculaneum*, and from Lanciani's *New Tales of Old Rome*.

T. G. T.

October 1909.

CONTENTS

xi

ILLUSTRATIONS

XV

MAPS AND PLANS

INTRODUCTION

THE subject of this book is "Life in the Roman World of Nero and St. Paul." This is not quite the same thing as "Life in Ancient Rome" at the same date. Our survey is to be somewhat wider than that of the imperial city itself, with its public and private structures, its public and private life. The capital, and these topics concerning it, will naturally occupy the greater portion of our time and interest. But it is quite impossible to realise Rome, its civilisation, and the meaning of its monuments, unless we first obtain some general comprehension of the empire — the Roman world — with its component parts, its organisation and administration. The date is approximately anno Domini 64, although it is not desirable, even if it were possible, to adhere in every detail to the facts of that particular year. In A.D. 64 the Emperor Nero was at the height of his folly and tyranny, and, so far as our information goes, the Apostle Paul was journeying about the Roman world in the interval between his first and second imprisonments in the capital.

One cannot, perhaps, achieve a wholly satisfying

picture in a treatise of the present dimensions. It would require a very bulky volume to realise with any adequateness the ideal aim. It would be well if, in the first instance, we could imagine ourselves standing somewhere far aloft over the centre of the empire, and possessing as wide-ranging a vision as that of the Homeric gods. From that exalted stand-point we might gaze upon the active life of towns, upon the labourers working their lands from the Atlantic to the Euphrates, and upon the men who go down to the sea in ships and do their business in great waters. We should perceive their occupations and amusements, their material surroundings, their various dress and manners, their methods of travel, the degree of their personal safety and liberty. Then we should descend to earth in the middle of Rome itself, and become for the time being inhabitants of that city, privileged to take part in its public business and its public pleasures, to enter the houses of what may be called its representative citizens, to share in the various elements of its social day, and to estimate the moral, intellectual, and artistic cultivation of Roman society.

Such would be the ideal. Here it must suffice to select the most essential or interesting matters, and to present them with such vividness as the necessary brevity will permit. Very little preliminary knowledge will be taken for granted; the use of Latin or technical terms will be shunned, and every topic will be dealt with, as far as possible, in the plainest of English.

Nevertheless, while aiming at entire lucidity, the following chapters will aim even more scrupulously at telling the truth. There are doubtless a number of matters — though generally of relatively small moment — about which we are, and probably always shall be, uncertain. The best way to deal with these, in a work which is descriptive rather than argumentative, is to omit them. For the rest it must be expected of any one whose professional concern it has been to saturate himself for many years in the literature of the times, and to study carefully their monumental remains, that he should occasionally make some statement, drop some passing remark or judgment, which may appear to be in conflict with assertions made in other quarters. If a few examples are met with in the present book, they may be taken as made with all deference, but with deliberation.

It is perhaps well to say this with some emphasis, in view of the blunders often innocently committed by those who happen to be speaking of this period. There are those who know it almost only through the medium of the *Acts of the Apostles*, and who entertain the most erroneous notions concerning Gallio or Festus, concerning Roman justice, Roman taxation, or Roman moral and religious attitudes. There are those, again, who know it almost only through the manuals of history; that is to say, they know the dates and facts of the reigns of the emperors, but have never realised, not to say visualised, the contemporary Roman as a human being. There exist denunciations of the morals of the Roman world of this date which would lead one to believe that every man was a Nero and every woman a Messalina : denunciations so lurid that, if they were a third part true, the continuance of the Roman Empire, or even of the Roman race, for a single century would be simply incomprehensible. On the other hand there have been accounts of the material glory of Rome which have conjured up visions of splendour worthy only of the *Arabian Nights;* and sometimes the comment is added that it was all won from the blood and sweat heartlessly wrung from a world of miserable slaves. It is not too much to say that none of these descriptions could come from a writer or speaker who knew the period at first hand.

The most dangerous form of falsehood is that which contains some portion of truth. The life of many a Roman was deplorably dissolute ; the splendour of Rome was beyond doubt astonishing; of oppression there were too many scattered instances ; but we do not judge the civilisation of the British Empire by the choicest scandals of London, nor the good sense of the United States by the freak follies of New York. We do not take it that the modern satirist who vents his spleen on an individual or a class is describing each and all of his contemporaries, nor even that what he says is necessarily true of such individual or class. Nor is the professional moralist himself immune from jaundice or from the disease of exaggeration.

The endeavour here will be to realise more

veraciously what life in the Roman world was like.
For those who are familiar with the political history
and the escapades of Nero there may be some filling
in of gaps and adjusting of perspective. For those
who are familiar with the journeyings and experiences
of St. Paul there may be some correction of errors
and misconceptions. For those who have any thought
of visiting the ruins of Rome and Pompeii, it may
prove helpful to have secured some comprehension of
this period. Pompeii was destroyed only fifteen
years after our date, and all those houses, large
and small, were occupied in the year 64 by
their unsuspecting inhabitants. Meanwhile mansions,
temples, and halls stood in splendour above those
platforms and foundations over which we tread amid
the broken columns in the Roman Forum or on the
Palatine Hill.

CHAPTER I

EXTENT AND SECURITY OF THE EMPIRE

THE best means of realising the extent of the Roman Empire in or about the year 64 is to glance at the map. It will be found to reach from the Atlantic Ocean to the Euphrates, from the middle of England — approximately the river Trent — to the south of Egypt, from the Rhine and the Danube to the Desert of Sahara. The Mediterranean Sea is a Roman lake, and there is not a spot upon its shores which is not under Roman rule. In round numbers the empire is three thousand miles in length and two thousand in breadth. Its population, which, at least in the western parts, was much thinner then than it is over the same area at present, cannot be calculated with any accuracy, but an estimate of one hundred millions would perhaps be not very far from the mark.

Beyond its borders — sometimes too dangerously near to them and apt to overstep them — lay various peoples concerning whom Roman knowledge was for the most part incomplete and indefinite. Within its own boundaries the Roman government carefully collected every kind of information. Such precision

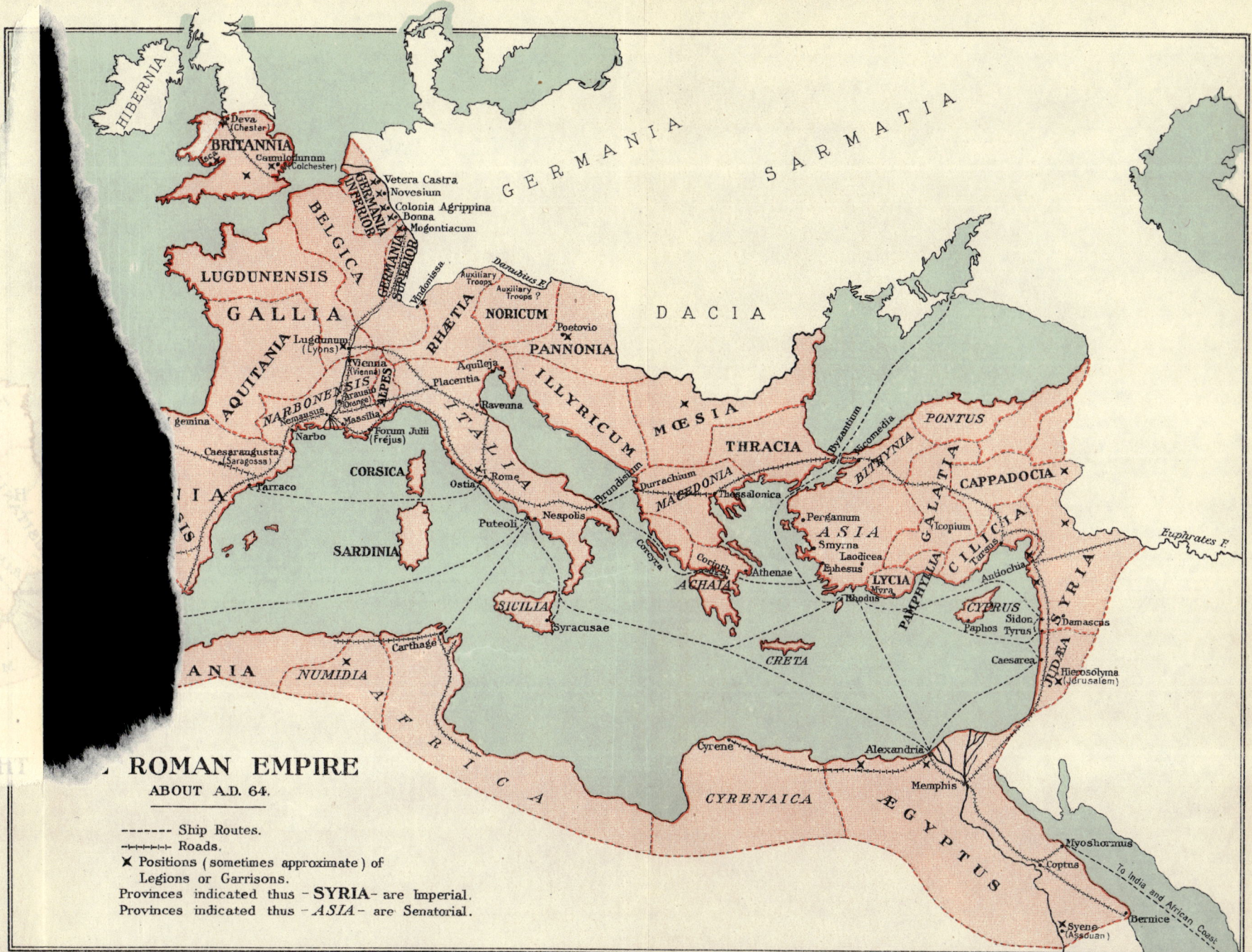

ROMAN EMPIRE

ABOUT A.D. 64.

- - - - - - Ship Routes.
- +++++ Roads.
✗ Positions (sometimes approximate) of Legions or Garrisons.
Provinces indicated thus - **SYRIA** - are Imperial.
Provinces indicated thus - *ASIA* - are Senatorial.

HIBERNIA

BRITANNIA

Deva (Chester)

Camulodunum (Colchester)

GERMANIA

SARMATIA

Vetera Castra
Novesium
Colonia Agrippina
Bonna
Mogontiacum

GERMANIA INFERIOR
GERMANIA SUPERIOR

BELGICA

LUGDUNENSIS

GALLIA

Vindonissa

Auxiliary Troops
Danubius F.
Auxiliary Troops ?

RHÆTIA

NORICUM

DACIA

Poetovio

AQUITANIA

Lugdunum (Lyons)

Vienna (Vienne)
Arausio (Orange)
Nemausus
Narbo
Massilia
Forum Julii (Fréjus)

NARBONENSIS

ALPES

PANNONIA

Aquileja

Placentia

Ravenna

ILLYRICUM

MŒSIA

THRACIA

Byzantium

Nicomedia

PONTUS

gemina

Caesaraugusta (Saragossa)

Tarraco

CORSICA

ITALIA

Roma
Ostia

Neapolis

Puteoli

SARDINIA

Brundisium

Durrachium

MACEDONIA

Thessalonica

Pergamum

ASIA

Smyrna
Laodicea
Ephesus

BITHYNIA

GALATIA

Iconium

CAPPADOCIA

CILICIA

Tarsus

Antiochia

SYRIA

Euphrates F.

SICILIA

Syracusae

Corcyra

ACHAIA

Corinth
Athenae

Rhodus

LYCIA
Myra

PAMPHYLIA

CYPRUS

Sidon
Paphos Tyrus

Damascus

CRETA

Caesarea

JUDÆA

Hierosolyma (Jerusalem)

Carthage

NUMIDIA

ANIA

AFRICA

Cyrene

CYRENAICA

Alexandria

Memphis

ÆGYPTUS

Myoshormus

Coptus

To India and African Coast

Bernice

Syene (Assouan)

E. & R. Clark, Ltd. Printers, Edin.

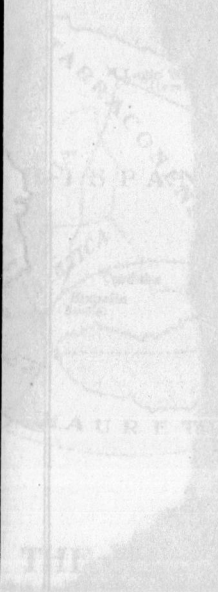

was indispensable for the carrying out of those Roman
principles of administration which will be described
later. But of the nations or tribes beyond the
frontiers only so much was known as had been
gathered from a number of more or less futile
campaigns, from occasional embassies sent to Rome
by such peoples, from the writings of a few venturous
travellers bent on exploration, from slaves who had
been acquired by war or purchase, or from traders
such as those who made their way to the Baltic in
quest of amber, or to Arabia, Ethiopia, and India in
quest of precious metals, jewels, ivory, perfumes, and
fabrics.

There had indeed been sundry attempts to annex
still more of the world. Roman armies had crossed
the Rhine and had twice fought their way to the
Elbe; but it became apparent to the shrewd
Augustus and Tiberius that the country could not be
held, and the Rhine was for the present accepted as
the most natural and practical frontier. In the East
the attempts permanently to annex Armenia, or a
portion of Parthia, had so far proved but nominal or
almost entirely vain.

On the Upper Euphrates at this date there was a
sort of acknowledgment of vague dependence on
Rome, but the empire had acquired nothing more
solid. Forty years before our date a Roman expedi-
tion had penetrated into South-west Arabia, of which
the wealth was extravagantly over-estimated, but it
had met with complete failure. Into Ethiopia a

punitive compaign had been made against Queen
Candace, and a loose suzerainty was claimed over
her kingdom, but the Roman frontier still stopped
short at Elephantine. Over the territories of the
semi-Greek semi-Scythian settlements to the north
of the Black Sea Rome exercised a protectorate,
which was for obvious reasons not unwelcome to
those concerned. Along or near the eastern frontier
she well understood the policy of the "buffer state,"
and, within her own borders in those parts, was ready
to make tools of petty kings, whose own ambitions
would both assist her against external foes and
relieve her of administrative trouble.

At no time did the Roman Empire possess so
natural or scientific a frontier as at this, when it was
bounded by the Rhine, the Danube, the Black Sea,
the Euphrates, the Desert, and the Atlantic. The
only exception, it will be perceived, was in Britain,
but the Roman idea there also was to annex the whole
island, a feat which was never accomplished. Two
generations after our chosen date Rome had conquered
as far as the Firths of Clyde and Forth; it had
crossed the Southern Rhine, and annexed the south-
west corner of Germany, approximately from Cologne
to Ratisbon; it had passed the Danube, and secured
and settled Dacia, which is roughly the modern
Roumania; and it had pushed its power somewhat
further into the East. But it had not thereby
increased either its strength or its stability.

At the period then with which we are to deal,

the Roman Empire included the countries now known as Holland, Belgium, France, Spain and Portugal, Switzerland, Italy, the southern half of the Austrian Empire, Greece, Turkey, Asia Minor, Syria and Palestine, Egypt, Tripoli and Tunis, Algeria, Marocco, and also the southern two-thirds of England. Within these borders there prevailed that greatest blessing of the Roman rule, the *pax Romana,* or "Roman peace." Whatever defects may be found in the Roman administration, on whatever abstract grounds the existence of such an empire may be impugned, it cannot be questioned that for at least two centuries the whole of this vast region enjoyed a general reign of peace and security such as it never knew before and has never known since. That peace meant also social and industrial prosperity and development. It meant an immense increase in settled population and in manufactures, and an immense advance — particularly in the West — in civilised manners and intellectual i terests.

Peoples and tribes which had been at perpetual war among themselves or with some neighbour were reduced to quietude. Communities which had been liable to sudden invasion and to all manner of arbitrary changes in their conditions of life, in their burdens of taxation, and even in their personal freedom, now knew exactly where they stood, and, for the most part, perceived that they stood in a much more tolerable and a distinctly more assured position than before. If there must sometimes be a tyrant, it would be the Roman tyrant, and he,

as we shall find, affected them but little. All
irresponsible local tyrannies, whether of kings or
parties, were abolished.

On the high seas within the empire you might
voyage with no fear whatever of pirates. If you
looked for pirates you must look beyond the Roman
sphere to the Indian Ocean. There might also be
a few to be found in the Black Sea. On the high
road you might travel from Jerusalem to Rome,
and from Rome to Cologne or Cadiz, with no fear
of any enemy except such banditti and footpads as
the central or local government could not always
manage to put down. On the whole there was nearly
everywhere a clear recognition of the advantages
conferred by the empire.

It is quite true that during these two centuries we
meet with frequent trouble on the borders and with
one or two local revolts of more or less strength. At
our chosen date the Jews were being stirred by their
fanatical or "zealot" party into an almost hopeless
insurrection; within two years the rebellion broke
out. Three years later still, certain ambitious semi-
Romans took advantage of a troubled time to make
a determined but futile effort to form a Gaulish or
German-Gaulish empire of their own. Half a century
after Nero the Jews once again rose, but were
speedily suppressed. But apart from these abortive
efforts — made, one by a unique form of religious zeal,
one by adventurous ambition, at opposite extremities

of the Roman world — there was established a general,
and in most cases a willing, acceptance of the situation and a proper recognition of its benefits.

The only serious war to be feared within the
empire itself was a civil war, begun by some aspiring leader when his chance seemed strong of ousting
the existing emperor or of succeeding to his throne.
Four years from the date at which we have placed
ourselves such a war actually did break out. Nero
was driven from the throne in favour of Galba,
and the history of the year following is the history
of Otho murdering Galba, Vitellius overthrowing
Otho, and Vespasian in his turn overthrowing
Vitellius. Yet all this is but the story of one entirely exceptional year, the famous "year of four
emperors." Take out that year from the imperial
history; count a hundred years before and more
than a hundred years after, and it would be impossible to find in the history of the world any period
at which peace, and probably contentment, was
so widely and continuously spread. Think of all
the countries which have just been enumerated as
lying within the Roman border; then imagine that,
with the exception of one year of general commotion,
two or three provincial and local revolts, and
occasional irruptions and retaliations upon the
frontier, they have all been free from war and its
havoc ever since the year 1700. In our year of
grace 64, although the throne is occupied by a
vicious emperor suffering from megalomania and

enormous self-conceit, the empire is in full enjoyment
of its *pax Romana.*

Another glance at the map will show how secure
this internal peace was felt to be. The Roman
armies will be found almost entirely upon the
frontiers. It was, of course, imperative that there
should be strong forces in such positions — in Britain
carrying out the annexation; on the Rhine and
Danube defending against huge-bodied, restless
Germans and their congeners; on the Euphrates to
keep off the nimble and dashing Parthian horse and
foot; in Upper Egypt to guard against the raids of
"Fuzzy-Wuzzy"; in the interior of Tunis or Algeria to keep the nomad Berber tribes in hand.
In such places were the Roman legions and their
auxiliary troops regularly kept under the eagles, for
there lay their natural work, and there do we find
them quartered generation after generation.

It is, of course, true that they might be employed
inwards as well as outwards; but it must be manifest
that, if there had been any widespread disaffection,
any reasonable suspicion that serious revolts might
happen, there would have been many other large bodies
of troops posted in garrison throughout the length and
breadth of the provinces. In point of fact the whole
Roman military force can scarcely have amounted
to more than 320,000 men, while the navy consisted
of two small fleets of galleys, one regularly posted at
Misenum at the entrance to the Bay of Naples, the
other at Ravenna on the Adriatic. To these we may

add a flotilla of boats operating on the Lower Rhine
and the neighbouring coasts. Except during the
year of civil war the two fleets have practically no
history. They enjoyed the advantage of having
almost nothing to fight against. If pirates had become dangerous — as for a brief time they threatened
to do during the Jewish revolt — the imperial ships
would have been in readiness to suppress them. They
could be made useful for carrying despatches and
imperial persons or troops, or they might be used
against a seaside town if necessary. Beyond this
they hardly correspond to our modern navies. There
was no foreign competition to build against, and no
"two-power standard" to be maintained.

The Roman troops, it has already been said, were
almost wholly on the frontier. So far as there are
exceptions, they explain themselves. It was found
necessary at all times to keep at least one legion
regularly quartered in Northern Spain, where the
mountaineers were inclined to be predatory, and
where they were skilful, as they have always been,
at carrying on guerilla warfare. We may, if we
choose, regard this comparatively small army as
policing a lawless district. In but few other places
do we find a regular military force. Rome itself had
both a garrison and also a large body of Imperial
Guards. The garrison, consisting of some 6000
men, was in barracks inside the city, and its purpose was to protect the wealth of the metropolis
and the seat of government from any sudden riot

or factious tumult. It must be remembered that
among the Romans it was soldiers who served as
police, whether at Rome or in the provinces. The
Imperial Guards, consisting of 12,000 troops, were
stationed just outside the gates, in order to secure
the safety and position of the emperor himself, if
any attempt should be made against his person or
authority. The rich and important town of Lugdunum
(or Lyons) had a small garrison of 1200 men, and a
certain number of troops were always to be found in
garrison in those great towns where factious disturbances were either probable or possible. Thus at
Alexandria, where the Jews were fanatical and at
loggerheads with the Greeks, and where the native Egyptians were no less fanatical and might
be at loggerheads with both, it was necessary to
keep a disciplinary force in readiness. Somewhat
similar was the case at Antioch, where the discords
of the Greeks, Syrians, and Jews stood in need of the
firm Roman hand. Nor could a similar regiment be
spared from Jerusalem. The western towns were
generally smaller in size, more homogeneous, and
more tranquil. It was around the Levant that the
popular *émeute* was most to be feared. Doubtless
one may meet, whether in the New Testament or in
Roman and Greek writers, with frequent mention of
soldiers, and we make acquaintance with an occasional
centurion — something socially above a colour-sergeant
and below a captain — or other officer in various
parts of the empire. But it should be understood that,
except in such places as those which have been named,

soldiers were distributed in small handfuls, to act as *gendarmerie*, to deal with brigands, to serve as body-guard and orderlies to a governor, to bear despatches, to be custodians of state prisoners. To these classes belong the centurions of the *Acts of the Apostles*, while Lysias was the colonel of the regiment keeping order in Jerusalem.

What the Roman army was like, whence it was recruited, how it was armed, and what were its operations, are matters to be shown in a later chapter.

Regarded then as a controlling agent, maintaining widespread peace, the Roman Empire answers closely to the British *raj* in India. The analogy could indeed be pressed very much further and with more closeness of detail, but this is scarcely the place for such a discussion.

CHAPTER II

OF the administration in Rome and throughout the provinces enough will be said in the proper place. Meanwhile we may look briefly at one or two questions of interest which will presumably suggest themselves at this stage. Since all this vast region now formed one empire, since Roman magistrates and officers were sent to all parts of it, since trade and intercourse were vigorous between all its provinces, it will be natural to ask, for example, by what means the traveller got from place to place, at what rate of progress, and with what degree of safety and comfort.

In setting forth by land you would elect, if possible, to proceed by one of the great military roads for which the Roman world was so deservedly famous. Not only were they the best kept and the safest; they were also generally the shortest. As far as possible the Roman road went straight from point to point. It did not circumvent a practicable hill, nor, where necessary, did it shrink from cutting through a rock, say to the depth of sixty feet or so. It did not avoid a river, but bridged it with a solid structure such as often remains in use till this day. If it met with a marsh, wooden piles were driven in and the road-bed laid upon them. When it came to a deep narrow valley it built a viaduct on arches.

The road so laid was meant for permanence. A width of ground was carefully prepared, trenches were dug at the sides, three different layers of road

FIG. 1.—THE PONT DU GARD (AQUEDUCT AND BRIDGE).

material were deposited, with sufficient upward curve to throw off the water, and then the whole was paved with closely-fitting many-cornered blocks of stone. In the chief instances there were sidewalks covered with some kind of gravel. The width was not great, but might be anything between ten and fifteen feet. Along such roads the Roman armies marched to their camps, along them the government despatches were carried by the imperial post, and along them were the

C

most conveniently situated and commodious houses of accommodation. For their construction a special grant might be made by the Roman treasury — the cost being comparatively small, since the work, when not performed by the soldiers, was done by convicts and public slaves — and for their upkeep a rate was

FIG. 2. — THE APPIAN WAY BY THE SO-CALLED TOMB OF SENECA.

apparently levied by the local corporations. Besides the paved roads there was, needless to say, always a number of smaller roads, many of them mere strips of four feet or so in width; there were also short-cuts, by-paths, and ill-kept tracks of local and more or less fortuitous creation.

Beside the great highways stood milestones in the shape of short pillars, and generally there were in existence charts or itineraries, sometimes pictured, giving all necessary directions as to the turnings, distances, stopping-places, and inns, and even as to the sights worth seeing on the way. Wherever there were such objects of interest — in Egypt, Syria, Greece, or any other region of art, history, and legend — the traveller could always find a professional guide, whose information was probably about as reliable as that of the modern *cicerone*. In Rome itself there was displayed, in one of the public arcades, a plan of the empire, with notes explaining the dimensions and distances.

The vehicle employed by the traveller would depend upon circumstances. You would meet the poor man riding on an ass, or plodding on foot with his garments well girt ; the better provided on a mule ; a finer person or an official on a horse ; the more luxurious or easy-going either in some form of carriage or borne in a litter very similar to the oriental palanquin. To carriages, which were of several kinds — two-wheeled, four-wheeled, heavy and light — it may be necessary to make further reference ; here it is sufficient to observe that, in order to assist quick travelling, there existed individuals or companies who let out a light form of gig, in which the traveller rode behind a couple of mules or active Gaulish ponies as far as the next important stopping-place, where he could find another jobmaster, or keeper of livery-stables, to send him on further. The rich man, travelling, as he necessarily would, with a train of servants and with full appliances for his comfort, would journey in a coach, painted and gilded, cushioned and curtained, drawn by a team showily caparisoned with rich harness and coloured cloths. This must have presented an appearance somewhat similar to that of the extravagantly decorated travelling-coach of the fourteenth century. The ordinary man of modest means would be satisfied with his mule or horse, and with his one or two slaves to attend him. On the less frequented stretches of road, where there was no proper accommodation for the night, his slaves would unpack the luggage and bring out a plain meal of wine, bread, cheese, and fruits. They would then lay a sort of bedding on the ground and cover it with a rug or blanket. The rich folk might bring their tents or have a bunk made up in their coaches.

Where there was some sort of lodging for man and horse the average wayfarer would make the best of it. In the better parts of the empire and in the larger places of resort there were houses corresponding in some measure to the old coaching-inns of the eighteenth century; in the East there were the well-known caravanserais; but for the most part the ancient hostelries must have afforded but undesirable quarters. They were neither select nor clean. You journeyed along till you came to a building half wine-shop and store, half lodging-house. Outside you might be told by an inscription and a sign that it was the "Cock" Inn, or the "Eagle," or the "Elephant," and that there was "good accommodation." Its keeper might either be its proprietor, or merely a slave or other tenant put into it by the owner of a neighbouring estate and country-seat. Your horses or mules would be put up — with a reasonable suspicion on your part that the poor beasts would be cheated in the matter of their fodder — and you would be shown into a room which you might or might not have to share with someone else. In any case you would have to share it with the fleas, if not with worse.

Perhaps you have brought your food with you, perhaps you send out a slave to purchase it, perhaps you obtain it from the innkeeper. That is your own affair. For the rest you must be prepared to bear with very promiscuous and sometimes unsavoury company, and to possess neither too nice a nose nor too delicate a sense of propriety. Your only consolation is that the charges are low, and that if anything is stolen from you the landlord is legally responsible.

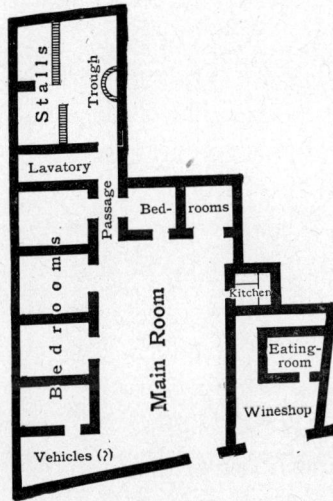

FIG. 3. — PLAN OF INN AT POMPEII.

Doubtless there were better and worse establishments of this kind. There must have been some tolerably good quarters at Rome or Alexandria, and at some of the resorts for pleasure and health, such as Baiae on the Bay of Naples, or Canopus at the Nile mouth. It is true also that for those who travelled on imperial service there were special lodgings kept up at the public expense at certain stations along the great roads. Nevertheless it may reasonably be asked why, in view of the generally accepted standards of domestic comfort and even luxury of the time — what may be called middle-class standards — there was no sufficiency of even creditable hotels. The answer is that in antiquity the class of people who in modern times support such hotels seldom felt the need of their equivalent. In the first place, they commonly trusted to the hospitality of individuals to whom they were personally or officially known, or to whom they carried private or official introductions. If they were distinguished persons, they were readily received, whether in town or country, on their route. In less frequented districts they trusted to their own slaves and to the resources of their own baggage. Their own tents, bedding, provisions and cooking apparatus were carried with them. If they made a stay of any length in a town, they might hire a suite of rooms.

We must not dwell too long upon this topic. Suffice it that travel was frequent and extensive, whether for military and political business, for commerce, or for pleasure. Some roads, particularly that "Queen of Roads," the Appian Way — the same by which St. Paul came from Puteoli to Rome — must have presented a lively appearance, especially near the metropolis. Perhaps on none of these great highways anywhere near an important Roman city could you go far without meeting a merchant with his slaves and his bales; a keen-eyed pedlar — probably

a Jew — carrying his pack; a troupe of actors or
tumblers; a body of gladiators being taken to fight
in the amphitheatre or market-place of some provincial town; an unemployed philosopher gazing sternly
over his long beard; a regiment of foot-soldiers or a
squadron of cavalry on the move; a horseman scouring
along with a despatch of the emperor or the senate;
a casual traveller coming at a lively trot in his hired
gig; a couple of ladies carefully protecting their
complexions from sun and dust as they rode in a kind
of covered wagonette; a pair of scarlet-clad outriders
preceding a gorgeous but rumbling coach, in which a
Roman noble or plutocrat is idly lounging, reading,
dictating to his shorthand amanuensis, or playing
dice with a friend; a dashing youth driving his own
chariot in professional style to the disgust of the
sober-minded; a languid matron lolling in a litter
carried by six tall, bright-liveried Cappadocians; a
peasant on his way to town with his waggon-load of
produce and cruelly belabouring his mule. If you are
very fortunate you may meet Nero himself on one of
his imperial progresses. If so, you had better stand
aside and wait. It will take him a long time to pass;
for, if this is one of his more serious undertakings, there
will be a thousand carriages, many of them resplendent with gold and silver ornament in relief upon the
woodwork, and drawn by horses or mules whose
bridles are gleaming with gold. And, if the beautiful
and conscienceless Poppaea is with him, there may be
also a procession of some five hundred asses, whose
business it is to supply her with the milk in which

she bathes for the preservation of her admirable velvety skin.

There are, of course, many other individuals and types to be met with. If you happen to be traversing certain parts of Spain, the mountains of Greece, the southern provinces of Asia Minor, or the upper parts of Egypt, you will perhaps also meet with a bandit, or even with a band of them. In that case, prepare for the worst. Some of the gang have been caught and crucified : you may have passed the crosses upon your way. This does not render the rest more amiable. St. Paul takes it as natural to be thus "in peril of robbers." Perhaps certain regions of Italy itself were as dangerous as any. We have more than one account of a traveller who was last seen at such-and-such a place, and was never heard of again. It is therefore well, before undertaking a journey through suspected parts, to ascertain whether any one else is going that way. There is sure to be either an official with a military escort or some other traveller with a retinue ; at least there will be some trusty man bearing letters, or some sturdy fellow whom you can hire expressly to accompany you.

After allowing for this occasional embarrassment — which was certainly not greater and almost certainly very much less than you would have encountered in the same parts of the world a century ago — it must be declared that, on the whole, travel by land in the Roman world of the year 64 was remarkably safe. If it was not very expeditious, it was probably on the average quite as much so as in the eighteenth century.

Ordinary travelling by road may not have averaged more than sixty or seventy miles a day, although one hundred miles could be done without much difficulty, while a courier on urgent business could greatly increase that speed.

Next let us suppose that our friend proposes to travel by sea. As a rule navigation takes place only between the beginning of March and the middle of November, ships being kept snug in harbour during the winter months. The traveller may be sailing from Alexandria to the capital or from Rome to Cadiz or to Rhodes. If a trader of sufficient boldness, he may even be proceeding outside the empire as far as India. If so, he will pass up the Nile as far as Coptos, then take either the canal or the caravan route to Myos Hormos on the Red Sea, and thence find ship for India, with a reasonable prospect — if he escapes the Arab pirates — of completing his business and returning home in about six months. Over 120 ships, small and great, leave the above-mentioned harbour each year on the voyage to India, for Alexandria is the great depot for the trade round the Indian Ocean, and the products of India are in lively demand at Rome.

On such a remote course, however, we will not follow. Let us rather suppose that our traveller is proceeding from Alexandria, the second city of the empire, to Rome, which is the first. In this case he may enjoy the great advantage of going on board one of those merchantmen belonging to the imperial service, which sail regularly with a freight of corn to feed the empire city. His port of landing will be Puteoli (Puzzuoli) in the Bay of Naples, which was then the Liverpool of Italy. The rest of the journey he will either make by the Appian Road, or, less naturally, by smaller freight-ship, putting in at

Fig. 4.—Ship beside the Quay at Ostia. (Wolf and twins on mainsail.)

Ostia, the port of Rome recently constructed by the Emperor Claudius at the mouth of the river Tiber. His ship, a well-manned and strongly-built vessel of from 500 tons up to 1100 or more, will carry one large mainsail, formed of strips of canvas strengthened by leather at their joinings, a smaller foresail, and a still smaller topsail. It will be steered by a pair of huge paddles on either side of the stern. There will

be a crow's-nest on the mast, and at the bows a
figurehead of Rome or Alexandria or of some deity,
perhaps of Castor and Pollux combined. A tolerable,
but by no means a liberal, amount of cabin accommodation will be provided. A good-sized ship might
reach 200 feet in length by 50 in breadth. One of
them brought to Rome the great obelisk which now
stands in the Piazza of St. Peter's; another ship had
brought another obelisk, 400,000 bushels of wheat
and other cargo, and a very large number of
passengers. At a favourable season, and with a
quite favourable wind, the ship may expect to reach
the Bay of Naples in as little as eight or nine days:
sometimes it will take ten days, sometimes as many
as twelve. The ship may either proceed directly
south of Crete, or it may run across to Myra in Asia
Minor, or to Rhodes, and thence proceed due west.
As a rule the ancient navigator preferred to keep
somewhat near the shore. Other ships, picking up
and putting down cargo and passengers as they went
along, would pass up the Syrian coast, calling at
Caesarea, Tyre, Sidon, and other places before passing
either north or south of Cyprus. From such a ship
it might be necessary — as it was with St. Paul and
the soldiers to whose care he was committed — to
tranship into another vessel proceeding directly to
Italy. If, as we have imagined, the traveller is on
a cornship of the Alexandria-Puteoli line, he will
reach the Bay one day after passing the straits of
Messina, and his vessel will sail proudly up to port
without striking her topsail, the only kind of ship

which was permitted to do this being such imperial
liners.

There were other famous trade routes of the
period. One is from Corinth; another from the
Graeco-Scythian city at the mouth of the Sea of
Azov, whence corn and salted fish were sent in
abundance; a third from Cadiz, outside the straits
of Gibraltar, by which were brought the wool and
other produce of Andalusia; a fourth from Tarragona
across to Ostia, the regular route for official and
passenger intercourse with Spain. Yet another took
you to Carthage in three days. Across the Adriatic
from Brindisi you would reach in one day either Corfu
or the Albanian coast at Dyrrhachium (Durazzo),
where began the great highroad to the East. Given
a fair wind, your ship might average 125 or 130
miles in the twenty-four hours, and, if you left Rome
on Monday morning, you had a reasonable prospect
of landing in Spain on the following Saturday.
From Cadiz you would probably require ten or
eleven days. There was, it is true, no need to come
by sea from that town. There was a good road all
the way, with a milestone at every Roman mile, or
about 1600 yards. Unfortunately that route would
generally take you nearly a month.

It is not probable that sea travelling was at all
comfortable; but it was apparently quite as much so,
and quite as rapid, as it was on the average a
century ago. Ships were made strong and sound;
nevertheless shipwrecks were very frequent, as they

always have been in sailing days. Wreckers who showed false lights were not unknown. There is also little doubt that the vessels were often terribly overcrowded; one ship, it is said, brought no less than 1200 passengers from Alexandria. That on which St. Paul was wrecked had 276 souls on board, and one upon which Josephus once found himself had as many as 600. It is incidentally stated in Tacitus that a body of troops, who had been both sent to Alexandria and brought back thence by sea, were greatly debilitated in mind and body by that experience. On the other hand, as has been already stated, there was generally no such thing as a pirate to be heard of in all the waters of the Mediterranean.

CHAPTER III

A BRIEF SURVEY OF THE PROVINCES

AFTER thus considering, however incompletely, the manner in which the people of the Roman world contrived to move about within the empire itself, we may proceed to glance at the constituent parts of the world in which they thus travelled to and fro.

And first we must draw a distinction of the highest importance between the western and eastern halves. Naturally enough, Italy itself was before all others the land of the Romans. It was the favoured land, enjoyed the fullest privileges, and was the most completely romanized in population, manners, and sentiment. Besides its larger and smaller romanized towns — of which there were about 1200 — it was dotted from end to end with the country-seats and pleasure resorts of Romans. North and west of Italy were various peoples, differing widely in character, habits, and religion, as well as in physique. East of it were various other peoples differing also from each other in such respects, but for the most part marked by a common civilisation in which the West had but an almost inconsiderable share. Before the Roman con-

quest the nations and tribes of the West had been
in general rude, unlettered, and unorganised. Except
here and there in Spain, where the Phoenicians or
Carthaginians had been at work, and in the Greek
colonies sprung from Marseilles, they had hardly
possessed such a thing as a town. They scarcely
knew what was meant by civic life, with its material
luxuries and graces, its art and literature. They
were commonly small peoples without unity, brave
fighters, but, in all those matters commonly classed
as civilisation, distinctly behind the times. The
superiority of the Roman in these parts was not
merely one of organised strength, military skill, and
political method, it was a superiority also of intellectual life and culture. In Spain, Gaul, Britain,
Switzerland, the Tyrol and southern Austria, and
also in North-West Africa, the Roman proceeded to
organise after his own heart, to settle his colonies, to
impose his language, and to inculcate his ideals. He
was dealing with inferiors; this he fully recognised,
and so for the most part did they.

Meanwhile to the eastward also Rome spread her
conquests. Here, however, she was dealing with
peoples who had already passed under influences in
many respects superior to those brought by the
conqueror, influences which were in a sense only
beginning to educate the conqueror himself. Let us
here, for the sake of clearness, make a brief digression
into previous history.

Throughout the eastern half of the Mediterranean

countries, conquering Rome had been face to face
with an older, a more polished, a more keenly intellectual, and more artistic culture than her own.
This was the civilisation of Greece. We need not
dwell upon the character of Hellenic culture. Anyone who has made acquaintance with the richness
of Greek literature, the clear sureness of Greek art,
the keen insight of Greek science and philosophy, and
the bold experiments of Greek society — especially as
represented by Athens — will understand at once what
is meant. When the Romans, more than two hundred
years before our date, conquered Greece, in so far as
they were a people of letters or of effort in abstract
thought, in so far as they possessed the arts of
sculpture, architecture, painting, and music, they
were almost wholly indebted to Greece. Their own
strength lay in solidity and gravity of character, in
a strong sense of national and personal discipline, in
the gift of law-making and law-obeying. In culture
they stood to the Greeks of that time very much as
the Germans of two centuries ago stood to the French.
After their conquest by the Romans the Greeks per-
force submitted to the rule of might, but the typical
Greek never looked upon the Roman as socially or
intellectually his equal. He became himself the philosophic, artistic, and social teacher of his conqueror.
His own language was richer in literature, and it was
better adapted to every form of conversation. The
Latin of the Romans therefore made no progress in
Greece or the Greek world. It might be made the
language of the Roman courts and of official docu-

ments; but beyond this the ordinary Greek disdained to study it. On the other hand the ordinary well-educated Roman could generally speak Greek. Magistrates and officials were almost invariably thus accomplished, and in Athens or Ephesus they talked Greek as we should naturally talk French in Paris — only better, inasmuch as they learned the language in a more rational and practical way. Nero himself could act, or thought he could act, a Greek play and sing a Greek ode among the Greeks. Most probably the Roman noble had been brought up by a Greek nurse, just as so many English families formerly employed a nurse imported from France. Nor did the Greeks merely ignore the Latin language. They refused to be romanised in any other respect. Even the Roman amusements tended to disgust them, and it is to the credit of his superior refinement that the average Greek was repelled by those brutal exhibitions of gladiatorial bloodshed and slaughter over which the coarser Roman gloated.

When, next, we pass from Greece proper — that is to say, from the Grecian peninsula and the islands and Asiatic shores of the Aegean Sea — into Asia Minor, Syria, and Egypt, we still find the Roman conqueror annexing peoples more versed in the higher arts of life than himself. For ages there had existed in these regions various forms of advanced civilisation. The Assyrian, Babylonian, Phoenician, Hebrew, and Egyptian cultures were old before Rome was born. Later the Persian subjugated all these peoples. And then, four hundred years before the time with which

D

we are dealing, had come the Macedonian Greek, Alexander the Great, and had conquered every one of those provinces which were subsequently to form the eastern part of the Roman Empire as represented on our map. The language and culture of Alexander were Greek, and he carried these and settled them with the most determined policy in every available quarter. After his death his empire broke up into kingdoms, but those kings who succeeded him — every Antiochus of Syria and every Ptolemy of Egypt — were Greek. Their court was Greek, and Hellenism was everywhere the fashion in life, thought, letters, and art. All round the coasts, in all the great cities, on all the main routes, up all the great river valleys of these eastern kingdoms, this graecizing proceeded. Alexander had founded the city of Alexandria, and soon that great and opulent city became more the home of Greek science and literature than Athens itself. His successors founded other great cities, such as Antioch, and there also the civilisation was Greek.

Egyptians, Jews, and Syrians who were possessed of any kind of public, social, or even mercantile ambition therefore naturally spoke Greek, either only, or more often in conjunction with their native tongue. This is the reason why the Septuagint appeared in Greek; why Greek as well as Hebrew and Latin was written over the Cross; why our New Testament was written in Greek; and why Paul could travel about the eastern half of the Roman world and talk fluently wherever he went. He could

address a Roman governor directly at Paphos because
that governor had learned Greek at Rome, either in
school or under his nurse or tutor. He could stand
before the Areopagus at Athens and address that
distinguished body in its own tongue because it was
also one of *his* own tongues.

Not that one could expect the Greek culture, or
even the language, to remain pure when thus spread
abroad. There were blendings of Oriental elements,
Egyptian, Jewish, or Syrian ; but these elements
were themselves derived from advanced and time-
honoured civilisations.

It follows, therefore, that all through the Eastern
half of its domain Rome could not contrive to
romanize. She did not attempt to suppress Greek
ideas; she preferred to utilise them. So long as the
Roman rule was obeyed in its essentials, Rome was
satisfied.

In the main, then, we have, outside Italy, two very
distinct halves of the Roman world: the Eastern,
with its large cities, its active civic life, its high
culture, its contributions to science, art, and luxury —
and, it must be added, its general dissoluteness — with
here and there its pronounced leanings to Oriental
fanaticism ; and the Western, with very few large
towns, with a life more determined by clans and
tribes or country districts, with comparatively little
social culture, contributing almost nothing to art or
science, stronger in its contribution of natural products
and virile men than in those of the more refined or

artificial luxury. Over this half the Roman tongue,
Roman dress, and Roman manners spread rapidly.
In it Roman settlers made .themselves more at home.
The aim of the better classes of the natives was to
render themselves as Roman as possible. It is in
the western part of the empire that you will find
the names which mark systematic Roman settlement,
and which often denote the work of an emperor.
Towns such as Saragossa (Caesarea Augusta), Aosta,
Augsburg, Autun (Augustodunum), and Augst are
foundations of Augustus. Hence the fact that Spain
and France speak a Latin tongue at this day, while
no Latin was ever even temporarily the recognised
language between the southern Adriatic and the
Euphrates.

This prime division made, let us now pass quickly
round the empire, making such brief observations as
may appear most helpful as we go.

In the year 64 the south of Spain, the province of
Baetica — of which we may speak more familiarly as
Andalusia — was prosperous and peaceful, almost completely romanized and latinized. Many of its inhabitants were true Latins, most had made themselves
indistinguishable from Latins. Along the river
Guadalquivir there were flourishing towns, chief
among them being those now known as Seville and
Cordova. The whole region was one of rich pasture
and tillage, and from it the merchant ships from Cadiz
brought to Rome cargoes of the finest wool and of

excellent olives and other fruits. The east of Spain, with Tarragona for its capital, stood next in order for its settled life and steady produce, including wine, salt fish, and sauces, while in the interior the finest steel — corresponding to the Bilbao blades of more modern history — was tempered in the cold streams of the hills above the sources of the Tagus. From Portugal came cochineal and olives. In several parts of the peninsula — in Portugal, in the Asturias, and near Cartagena — were mines of gold and silver, which had been worked by the old Phoenicians and which the Romans had reopened. The chief trouble of Spain, it may be interesting to learn, was the rabbits, and against these there were no guns and no poison, but only dogs, traps, and ferrets. In Gaul there is one province long-established and fully romanized, with its capital at Narbonne, and with flourishing Roman towns, which are now familiar under such names as Arles and Nîmes. This is a region over the coast of which the culture of Greece had managed to stray, centuries before, through the accident of a Greek colony having been founded at Marseilles. In this province a Roman might live and feel that he was still as good as in Italy. But beyond lay what was known as "Long-haired" Gaul, sometimes "Trousered" Gaul, so called from the distinguishing externals of its inhabitants, who wore breeches, let their hair grow long, and on their faces grew only a moustache — three things which no Roman did, and from which, even in these districts, the nobles, who were the first to romanize, were beginning to desist.

The peoples of these Gaulish provinces preferred, like all early Celtic communities, to give their adherence only to clans or tribes, and to unite no further than impulse or expediency dictated, forming no towns larger than a village, living for the most part in poor huts scattered through forests, hills, marshes, and pasture land, and content to sleep on straw, if only they could wear a fine plaid and boast of a gold ornament. The names of many such tribes still remain in the names of the towns which grew up from the chief village of each canton. Such were the Ambiani, who have given us Amiens, and the Remi, who have given us Rheims. Paris and Trèves denote the administrative villages of the Parisii and Treveri. Nevertheless the country had its corn-lands and was rich in minerals and cattle, from which the hides came regularly down the Rhone to be carried to the Mediterranean markets. "Long-haired" Gaul was at this date rude and superstitious, with that weird druidical religion which the Emperor Claudius had done his best to suppress. Its chief vice was that of drunkenness. As with the French, who have largely descended from them, the proverbial passions of the Gauls were for war and for the art of speaking; but at our date the former passion was decaying and the latter gaining ground. The Gaulish provinces united at a point on the Rhone, near which necessarily arose the largest city of that part of the world, namely, Lugdunum, or Lyons, which speedily became not only a seat of administration but a noted school of eloquence.

Of Britain there is as yet little to say. For the last twenty years the Romans had done their best to conquer the Celtic tribes, who suffered, as Celtic tribes were always apt to suffer, from their own disunion. They had now reached the Trent — or rather a line from Chester to Lincoln — had just punished Boudicca (or Boadicea) for her vigorous effort at retaliation and her slaughter of 70,000 Romans or adherents of Rome, and were following the true Roman practice of securing what they had won by building military roads and establishing strong posts of control, as at Colchester, Chester, and Caerleon-on-Usk. Some amount of iron-working was being done in Britain, but its chief exports were, as they had long been, tin, salt, and hides. The British themselves had no towns. The places so called were nothing more than collections of huts, surrounded by rampart and ditch, in some easily defensible spot amid wood or marsh.

Along the Rhine it is enough to note that the Germans were being kept in hand. South of the Danube the region now known as Styria and Carinthia was rich in iron, and both here and all along the mountainous tract of the Tyrol and neighbourhood Rome was steadily pushing her language and habits by means of settlement, trading, and military occupation. It may be remarked by the way that at this date there were in use practically all the Alpine passes now familiar to us — the Mont Genèvre, the Little and Great St. Bernard, the Simplon, the St. Gothard, and the Brenner.

The Upper Balkans were necessarily under
military occupation, but Macedonia was a flourishing
graecized province with Thessalonica — the modern
Salonika — for its capital. Greece proper, known
officially as Achaia, had declined in every respect
since the classical age of Athens. The monuments
of that city were, indeed, as sumptuous as ever; a
number had been added in Roman times, though
generally in inferior taste. Athens was still a sort
of university, but its professors were for the most
part sophists or rhetoricians, beating over again the
old straws of philosophies which had once possessed
a living meaning and exercised a living force. Athens
herself had never properly recovered from the migra-
tion of learning to Alexandria. Delphi, the great
oracular seat of the Greek world, had also declined
in importance, although it could still boast of an
imposing array of buildings and memorials. The
centre of commerce and of official life, a Roman
colony in the midst of Greece, a cosmopolitan and a
dissolute place, was Corinth on the Isthmus. Here
Nero had intended to cut a canal through from sea to
sea — he had turned the first sod with his own hand —
but his personal extravagance caused an insufficiency
of funds, and the project met with the fate of the
first enterprise at Panama. It was, therefore, still
necessary for a traveller proceeding to the East to
cross the Isthmus and reship at Cenchreae. The rest
of Greece was almost all poor and sparsely populated,
and many ancient sites and monuments were already
suffering from neglect and dropping into ruin.

FIG. 6. — THE ACROPOLIS, AT ATHENS. (From D'Ooge.)

Across the Aegean, Asia Minor was in a condition of unprecedented prosperity. It contained no less than five hundred towns of considerable repute, chief among them being Smyrna and Ephesus, with their handsome public buildings, open squares, theatres, gardens, and promenades. Smyrna in particular boasted of its wide marble-paved streets crossing each other at right angles, and provided with arcades running along their sides. Its one defect was the want of proper sewers. Among the sights of the world was the huge temple at Ephesus, dedicated to Artemis, the "Great Diana" of the *Acts of the Apostles*. This temple, the largest in the ancient world, was 425 feet long, 220 wide, and its columns were 60 feet in height and numbered 127.

South-east of the Aegean was situated the opulent Rhodes, the handsomest and strongest port in the Mediterranean, provided with fine harbour buildings, a seat of learning, and so full of art that it contained no less than 3000 statues. In the somewhat desolate interior of Asia Minor were spacious runs for sheep and horses, but wheat also was grown, and the country could at least produce tall and sturdy slaves. In northern Galatia the common people had not yet forgotten the Celtic tongue which they had brought from Gaul over three centuries ago. In the south-east, opposite Cyprus, lay Tarsus, the birth-place of Paul, a city which combined the art of manufacturing goats' hair into tent-cloth with the pursuit of what may be called a university instruction in philosophy, science, and letters. In both these local avocations the apostle employed his youth to good purpose. Across the water Cyprus produced the copper which still bears its name.

Of Syria, rich in corn and fruits, the chief city — the third in the empire — was Antioch, a town splendidly laid out upon the Orontes in a strikingly modern fashion. A broad street with colonnades extended in a straight line through and beyond the

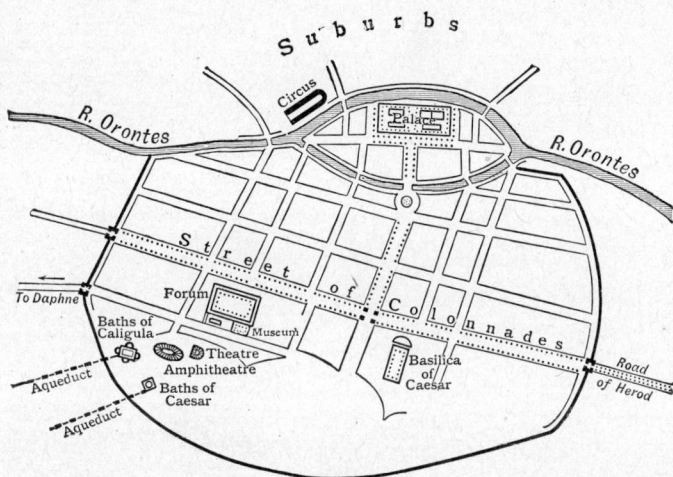

FIG. 7. — PLAN OF ANTIOCH.

city for four miles, and was crossed by others at right angles. This street is said to have been lighted at nights, while the Roman streets remained dark and dangerous. In the neighbourhood of the city was the celebrated park called Daphne, where the voluptuous and almost incredible dissipation of the ancient world perhaps reached its acme. Like Alexandria, Antioch was furiously addicted to horse-racing.

Further down the coast Sidon produced its famous glass, and Tyre its famous purple dye. Inland from these lay the handsome city of Damascus, famed for its gardens and for its work in fine linen. Still farther south was Hierosolyma, or Jerusalem, of which it is perhaps not necessary here to give details. Its population was reckoned at a quarter of a million.

On the coast of Egypt, after you had caught sight, some thirty miles away, of the first glint from the huge marble lighthouse standing 400 feet high upon the island of Pharos, you arrived at Alexandria, the second city of the Roman world and the great emporium for the trade of Egypt, of all Eastern Africa as far as Zanzibar, and of India. From it came the papyrus paper, delicate glass-work, muslin, embroidered cloths, and such additions to luxury as roses out of season. Alexandria, built like Antioch on a rectangular plan, with its chief streets 100 feet in width, contained a Jewish quarter, controlled by a Jewish headman and a Sanhedrin; an Egyptian quarter; and a Greek quarter, in which were the splendid buildings of the Library with its 600,000 volumes, and the University, devoted to all branches of learning and science — including medicine — and provided with botanical and zoological gardens. Here also were the temple of Caesar and the fine harbour buildings. Its population, exceedingly money-loving and pleasure-loving, and comprising representatives of every Oriental people, may have

numbered three-quarters of a million. The circuit
of the city was about thirteen miles, and its chief
street some four miles in length.

Behind it lay Egypt, with its irrigation and traffic
canals kept in good order; with its monuments in
far better preservation than now — the pyramids, for
example, being still coated with their smooth marble
sides, and not to be mounted by the present
steps, from which the marble has been torn; with
its rich corn-lands, its convict mines and quarries,
the Siberia of antiquity; with its string of towns
along the Nile and its seven or eight millions
of inhabitants — mostly speaking Coptic — and full
of strange superstitions and peculiar worship of
animals.

Coming westward we reach the prosperous Cyrene,
and then, by the rather out-
of-the-world Bight of Tripoli,
Africa proper, where once
ruled mighty Carthage, the
colony of Tyre, and where
the Phoenician or Punic
language still survived
among the population of
mixed Phoenicians and
Berbers. Here, too, are
wide and luxuriant stretches
of corn-land, upon which
Rome depends only next,
if next, to those of Alexandria. Further west are

FIG. 8. — EMBLEM OF ANTIOCH.

the Berber tribes of

Mauretania, governed by Rome but hardly yet fully assimilated into the Roman system.

In the Mediterranean Sea lie Crete, a place which had now become of little importance; Sicily, as much Greek as Roman, fertile in crops and possessed of many a splendid Greek temple and theatre; Sardinia, an unhealthy island infested by banditti, and employed

FIG. 9.— EMBLEM OF ALEXANDRIA.

as a sort of convict station, producing some amount of grain and minerals; and Corsica, which bore much the same character for savagery as it did in times comparatively recent, and which had little reputation for any product but its second-rate honey and its wax. The Balearic Islands were chiefly noted for their excellence in the art of slinging, for painters' earth, and for breeding snails for the Roman table.

It remains to say that the feeling of local pride was very strong in the rival towns of the empire. Each gloried in its distinguishing commerce and natural advantages, and the chosen emblems of the greater cities set forth their boasts with much artistic ingenuity. Thus Antioch is symbolised by a female figure seated on a rock, crowned with a turreted

FIG. 10. — EMBLEM OF ROME.
From the Column of Antoninus at Rome.

diadem, and holding in her hand a bunch of ears of corn, while her foot is planted on the shoulder of a half-buried figure representing the river Orontes. Alexandria, with her Horn of Plenty, her Egyptian fruits, and the representations of her elephants, asps, and panthers, as well as of her special deities, appears in relief upon a silver vessel found at Boscoreale near Pompeii and here reproduced.

Such in brief was the Roman Empire. How all this empire was governed, what was meant by emperor, governor, taxation, and justice, is matter for other chapters.

CHAPTER IV

THE IMPERIAL SYSTEM: EMPEROR, SENATE, KNIGHTS, AND PEOPLE

WE have seen, and succinctly traversed, the extent of the Roman world. The next step is to consider, as tersely as possible, its system of government and administration about the year 64. This task is not only entirely necessary to our immediate purpose; it is also one of great interest and profit in itself. If we are either to see in their proper light the experiences of such a man as St. Paul, or to understand the long continuance of so wide an empire, we must observe carefully the principles and methods adopted by the Romans as rulers.

We speak fluently of the "Roman Emperor" and of the "reign of Nero." What was an emperor? What were his powers, and how did he exercise them?

In the first place, it must be noted that, strictly speaking, Rome acknowledged no such thing as an autocrat. It had no monarch; the title "king" was disowned by the Caesars and entirely denied by the people; the emperor was technically not a superior sovereign, but, on the contrary, something inferior to a sovereign. He was the first citizen, the "first man of the state." The state was nominally a commonwealth, and the emperor its most important officer.

He was, to begin with, the representative of Rome as civil and military governor of all provinces containing an army, or apparently calling for an army. "Emperor" means military commander, and he was the commander-in-chief of all the forces of the empire, military or naval, but in a sense far more liberal than would now be intended by such an expression. Of all the fighting forces he had absolute control, determining their numbers, their service, all appointments, their pay, and their discharge. He moved them where he chose, and, beyond this, he possessed the power of declaring war and concluding peace. Wherever there existed an armed force, whether in the far-off field or in garrison, its obedience was due to him. In sign of this every soldier, on the first of January and on the anniversary of the emperor's accession, took a solemn oath — and an oath in those days was felt as no mere matter of form, but as a solemn act of religion — that he would loyally obey the commander-in-chief. The emperor's effigy was conspicuous in the middle of every camp, and, in small, it figured on the standard of every regiment. The sacred obligation of the soldier to an Augustus or a Nero was kept perpetually in evidence, and he was never allowed to forget it. Wherever the emperor appeared or intervened in the provinces, all other powers became subordinate to his.

Theoretically such a commander might always be deposed by the Roman people, acting through

Fig. 11. — Augustus as Emperor.

its Senate. In reality he was master of the situation. If he was ever deposed, or if a new commander was ever appointed, it was by the army. If he proved

a tyrant, there was no other means of getting rid
of him than by the army, unless it were by assassina-
tion. At such times the Senate might make a show
of naming the successor, and the army might make
a show of agreeing with the Senate, but such ex-
pressions, as Tacitus repeats, were "empty and
meaningless words." The madman Caligula had
been assassinated. When, four years after our date,
Nero was compelled to flee from his palace and was
persuaded into committing suicide, it was because
the soldiers had declared against him and had elected
another.

The vast powers of the emperor had come into
the hands of one man simply because the republic
had been found incompetent to handle its empire,
whether from a military or a financial point of view.
It managed neither so consistently nor so honestly
as did the individual.

The emperor, then, by a constitutional fiction,
was an officer of the commonwealth, commanding
its forces, not only with the freedom of action which
Rome had always allowed to its experts in dealing with
the enemy, but with that freedom greatly enlarged,
and with a tenure of the office perpetually renewed.

But to him that hath shall be given — especially
if he is in a position to insist on the gift. The
emperor's military authority, his position as governor
of provinces, could not alone rightfully qualify him
to control Rome itself, with its laws, its magistrates,
its domestic and provincial policy. Theoretically the
Roman emperor never did control these matters.

In practice he did with them very much as he chose. If he seriously wished a certain course to be followed, a certain law to be passed or abolished, even a certain man to be elected to an office, it was promptly done. But how could he thus perpetually interfere and yet appear to remain a constitutional officer? Not through the mere obsequiousness of every one concerned, including the Senate. That would be too transparent, clumsy, and invidious. It was necessary that he should possess some adequate appearance of real authority, and he was therefore ingeniously invested with that authority.

It was thus. There were under the commonwealth certain annual officers of wide and rather indefinite powers called "tribunes of the commons." These persons could veto any measure which they declared to be in opposition to the interests of the people. They could also summon the Senate, and bring proposals before it. Meanwhile their persons were "sacrosanct," or inviolable, during their term of office. Here lay the opportunity. The emperor was invested by the Senate with these "powers of the tribune." He was not actually elected a tribune, for the office was only annual and could not be held along with any other, whereas the emperor must have the prerogatives always, and in conjunction with any other functions which he might choose to hold. He, therefore, only received the corresponding "powers" and privileges. This position enabled him to veto a measure whenever he chose, and with impunity. Naturally therefore it became the custom, as far as possible, to find out his wishes beforehand, and to move accordingly. He could also, in the same right, summon the Senate and bring measures, or get them brought, before it. To make certainty doubly certain, he was granted the right to what we should call "the first business on the notice-paper."

Observe further the shrewdness of the first emperor, Augustus, when he selected this particular position. The "tribunes of the commons" were constitutionally popular champions; they represented the interests of the common people. By assuming a position similar to theirs, the emperor — or commander-in-chief — made it appear to the common people that he was their chief and perpetual representative, and that their interests were bound up with his authority. He took them under his wing, and saw, among other things, that they did not starve or go stinted of amusements. He saw to it that they had corn for their bread, plenty of water, and games in the circus. His "bread and games" kept them quiet.

Supported by the army on one side, with his person secure, enjoying the right of initiative and the right of veto, this officer of the "commonwealth" became indeed the Colossus who bestrode the Roman world. He was invariably made also the Pontifex Maximus, or chief guardian of the religious interests of Rome. He might in addition receive other constitutional appointments — for example, that of supervisor or corrector of morals — whenever these might suit a special purpose. What more could a man desire, if he was satisfied to forego the name of autocrat so long as he possessed the substance? It was quite as much to the purpose to be called *Princeps*, or "head of the state," as to be called a king, like the Parthian or other Oriental monarchs. Among the Romans, therefore, "Princeps" was his regular title. The Graeco-Oriental half of the empire, which had long been accustomed to kings and to treating them almost as gods, frankly styled this head of the state "king" or "autocrat," but no true Roman would forget himself so far as to lapse into this vulgar truth.

One other title, however, the Romans did attach to their "Princeps." Something was still wanting to bring home, to both the Roman and the provincial, the peculiarly exalted position of so great a man; something which should be a recognition of that majesty which made him almost divine, at least with the divinity that doth hedge a king. The title selected for this purpose was *Augustus*, a word for which there is no nearer English equivalent than "His Highness," or perhaps "His Majesty," if we imagine that term applied to one who, by a legal fiction, is not a king. The insane Caligula called himself, or let himself be called, "Lord and Master," and later Domitian temporarily added to this title "God," but even Nero claimed neither of these modest epithets.

Here, then, is the position of Nero: Commander-in-chief of all the forces of Rome by land and sea, and master of its foreign policy; the titular protector of its commons and therefore inviolable of person and virtual controller of laws and resolutions; official head of the state religion; rejoicer in the style of "His Highness the Head of the State." To speak ill of him, or to do anything derogatory to his authority, was *lèse majesté*.

FIG. 12. — COIN OF NERO.
British Museum.

Reference has several times been made to the Senate. It is time now to speak briefly of that body. For the sake of clearness, however, we must include a survey of the recognised constituent elements or "orders" of Roman society.

The body politic consisted nominally of all who where known as "Roman citizens." These included men of every rank, from the artisan, the agricultural labourer, or even the idle loafer — of whom there was more than plenty — up through every grade of the middle classes to the richest and bluest-blooded aristocrat who considered himself in point of birth more than the equal of the emperor. Any such citizen was secured in person and property by the Roman laws. It was a punishable act for the local authorities at Philippi to take Paul, a "Roman citizen," and, before he was condemned, chastise him with rods.

According to the letter of the constitution, the

power of electing all officers of state, and of passing laws, had belonged to this miscellaneous body, the "people," gathered in assembly. Meanwhile the power of determining foreign policy and controlling the finances had lain with a special body, consisting largely of the aristocracy and of ex-officers of state, known as the "Senate." We are not here concerned with the causes of the changes which buried this constitution out of sight, but only with the actual state of things in the year 64.

In point of fact there were, under the emperors, no longer any assemblies of the "people"; the people at large neither elected nor legislated. The chief articles of the constitution had fallen into complete abeyance during the troublous times which preceded the establishment of that poorly disguised monarchy which we know as the empire. All real power of electing and law-making came to be in the hands of the Senate, acting with the emperor. While the emperor dominated the Senate, he was nevertheless glad to fall back upon that body in justification of his own actions and as a means of keeping up the constitutional pretence. He permitted the Senate to pass resolutions, and to exercise authority, just so far as there was no conflict with his own pronounced wishes and interests. It was not his policy to interfere and irritate when there was no occasion. On the other hand, when he desired a piece of legislation or an important administrative novelty, he preferred that it should be backed up by the sanction, or promoted by the apparently spontaneous action, of the Senate. It then bore a better appearance, and was less open to cavil. The people are no longer consulted at all in such matters. They have no say in them, for they have neither plebiscite nor representative government.

It must not be supposed that there never was friction between emperor and Senate. The Senate was often — or rather generally — servile, because it was intimidated. But there were times when it was inclined to assert itself; some of its members occasionally allowed themselves a certain freedom of speech, toward which one emperor might be surprisingly lenient or good-naturedly contemptuous, and another outrageously vindictive. In the year 64 the Senate was outwardly docile enough, although at heart it was anything but loyal to his Highness Nero the Head of the State. It must always be remembered that among the Senate were included many of the highest-born, proudest, and strictest of the Roman nobles or men of eminence. To them the whole succession of emperors was still a series of upstarts — the family of the Caesars — usurping powers which properly belonged to the Senate. You could not expect these persons, aristocrats at heart, and many of them true patriots, bearing names distinguished throughout Roman history, to acquiesce in the spectacle of one who was no better than they, as he passed up to his huge palace on the Palatine Hill, escorted by his guards, or as he entered the Senate-House to give what were practically his orders, perhaps scarcely deigning to recognise men whose families had

been illustrious while his was obscure. At times a
member here or there was calculating his own chances
of supplanting the man who galled him by condescen-
sion, or coldness, or even insult. These aristocrats felt
as the French nobles might feel with Napoleon. And
on his side the emperor, good or bad, never felt quite
safe from a plot to overthrow him. On the whole
these earlier emperors were much engaged in keeping
the Senate in its place, and were inclined, with quite
sufficient reason, to be jealous and suspicious of its
more important members.

It was natural, therefore, that they should keep a
very practical control over the composition of that
body. The situation was much as if a modern nation
were ruled by a virtual autocrat assisted by a House
of Peers. The senators and their families formed a
"senatorial order." So far as the Romans had such
a thing as a peerage under the empire, it is to be
found in the senatorial order. And as a title may
now be either hereditary or conferred by the sovereign
as the "fount of honour," so, under the Roman
emperors, the right to belong to the senatorial order
might come from birth or from the choice of the head
of the state. Normally you belonged to the "order"
if you were the son of a senator; you ranked in that
class of society. To belong to the Senate itself and
to take part in its debates you must then have held
a certain public office and must possess not less than
£8000. The £8000 is the minimum. Most senators
were rich, and some were enormously wealthy. They
are found with a capital of £3,000,000 or £4,000,000

and an income up to £150,000. As for the public
office which you must first hold, you could not even
be a candidate for it unless you were already of the
"order." If, when you are a senator, there is anything serious against you, or if you become impoverished, your name may be expunged from the
list. Otherwise you remain a senator all your life,
and your son in turn is of the "order," and may pass
into the Senate by the same process. If you were a
popular or highly deserving person, and from any
accident had lost your property, the emperor would
frequently make up the deficiency, or your brother
senators would subscribe the necessary amount.

But an emperor could meanwhile raise to the
"order" anyone he chose. He could give him
standing, and so make him eligible as a candidate for
that public office which was preliminary to entering
the actual Senate. Moreover, when it came to the
elections to this office which served as the indispensable stepping-stone to the Senate-House, the
vacancies were limited in number, and the emperor
had the right of either nominating or recommending
the candidates whom he preferred. Needless to say,
those candidates were invariably elected. It was, of
course, monstrous arrogance for Caligula to boast
that he could make his horse a consul if he chose,
but the taunt contained a measure of truth.

Let us then put the case thus. Imagine that a
modern senate is recruited from persons whose
names are in the *Peerage and Baronetage*, and that,

before any scion of such a family can enter the Senate itself, he must go through some sort of under-secretaryship, to which he must first be elected.

But next imagine that the sovereign can raise to the rank of "peerage or baronetage" some favoured person whose family does not yet figure in *Debrett*. Such a man is then entitled to put his name on the list of candidates for the necessary under-secretary-ship, and, when the sovereign reviews that list, he marks the candidate as nominated or recommended by himself. So he passes into the Senate.

Most emperors did this but sparingly. They made the Senate an aristocratic and wealthy body, keeping its numbers at somewhere near 600. We must not be perpetually assuming that the Caesars were either reckless or unscrupulous, because two or three were of that character. Many of them were remarkably capable and sagacious men. They recognised the need of ability and high character in their Senate. They had themselves enough of the old Roman exclusiveness to keep their honours from being made too cheap, and the probability is that under their rule the Senate was quite as honourable and quite as able a body as it was at any time under the republic.

The feeling of *noblesse oblige* was strongly im-planted in this senatorial class. The wealth of most members also put them above the more sordid temptations. The senator was not permitted to undertake any mercantile or financial business. The ancient notion still survived, that the only really honourable occupations for money were war and agriculture. The senator might own land and dispose of its produce or receive its rents, but he could not, for instance, be a money-lender or tax-farmer. Sometimes, no doubt, a senator evaded these provisions by employing a "dummy," but we must not probe too deep under the surface. In compensation for this disability it was from the senatorial class that were drawn all the governors of the important provinces, except Egypt, and all the higher military officers. In these capacities they received salaries. The governor of Africa, for example, was paid £10,000 a year.

Such men were no mere inexperienced aristocrats or plutocrats. They had regularly passed through a military training in youth, and had then held a minor civil appointment, commonly involving some knowledge of public finance. Next they had passed into the Senate and taken part in its business; had then held other public offices which taught them practical administration and probably legal procedure; and had afterwards been put in command of a "legion," that is to say, a brigade or *corps d'armée*. After performing such functions with credit, a senator might be sent to govern Syria or Macedonia or Britain or some other province. He was then a man of varied experience and ripe judgment, trained in official discipline and etiquette, as well as in knowledge. This was the kind of man whom Paul met in Cyprus in the person of the governor Sergius Paulus, •or at Corinth in the person of Gallio.

Certain smaller provinces might be administered by men of another order, who were neither filled with the senatorial traditions nor had passed through the senatorial career. These were but "factors" or "agents" of Caesar, and among them were the Pontius Pilate, Felix, and Festus, who were administrators of Judaea in New Testament times.

Next in rank to the senatorial order stood that of the "Knights." If the senators represent, in a certain sense, the peerage and baronetage, the next order represents — also in a certain sense — the knightage. Generally speaking, it comprehended what we should call the upper middle classes, and particularly those concerned in the higher walks of finance; such persons as, with us, would be the directors or managers of great companies and banks. It also included persons whom the head of the state chose to honour with something less than senatorial standing. Many of these men were extremely wealthy, but the minimum property qualification stood at only £3200, and Roman citizens who possessed that amount were rather apt to pose as knights, and to be commonly spoken of as such by a kind of courtesy title, although their names could not be found upon the authorised rolls. Though several emperors did their best to stop this practice, the endeavour was for the most part fruitless. Once in England the "esquires" were a class with certain recognised claims, but nothing could stop the polite tendency to add "Esq." to the name of a person on a private letter. The case was somewhat similar at Rome, although the practice did not proceed quite so far.

Nevertheless there was a distinct and official roll of "Roman knights," whom the head of the state had honoured with a public present of "the gold ring," a ceremony corresponding to the royal sword-stroke of modern times. This body, mounted on horses nominally presented by the public, and riding in procession through the streets, was reviewed and revised every year. Their roll was called, and if a name was omitted from its proper place, it meant — without explanation necessary — that by the pleasure of the emperor the person in question had ceased to be a knight. Every member of the already-mentioned higher or senatorial order was by right a knight until he actually became a senator, from which time he ceased to enjoy the privileges of a knight because he was enjoying those of the higher order rank. For there were privileges as well as disabilities in each case. As a senator could govern large provinces and command armies, but could not engage in purely financial business; so the knight could — and almost alone did — conduct the large financial enterprises of the Roman world, but could not command armies nor hold any of the great public offices or higher provincial appointments, except the governorship of Egypt. Relatively to the senators the emperor was technically only "first among equals"; he was the first senator, as well as the first man of the state. At this date a senator would

hold a truly public office, civil or military, with or
under this "superior equal," but he would not act
as his personal agent or assistant. The Roman
aristocrat had not yet learned to serve in that
capacity, still less on the "household" staff of the
autocrat. There were as yet no highly placed
Romans serving as Lord High Chamberlain, much
less as Private Secretary. The "knights" stood in
a different position. They were prepared to be the
emperor's personal agents, just as they were prepared
to be the agents of any one else, if sufficiently
remunerated. They would take his personal orders,
whether in managing his estates, collecting his provincial revenues, or relieving him of some routine
portion of his own official labour.

It follows that it was often more lucrative to be
a knight than a senator, and a number of senators
were not unwilling to give up their rank, for the
same reasons which induce a modern peer to serve on
companies or a peeress to open a shop. On the other
hand many a knight would have declined to become
a senator, at least until he had sufficiently feathered
his nest. The inducement to become or remain a
senator was the social rank, the honour and dignity,
with their outward insignia and the deference paid to
them, the front seat, and the reception at court. In
these the wives also shared, and at Rome the influence
of the wife could not be disregarded.

If you met a senator, or a person of senatorial rank,
in the street, you would know him for such by
the broad band of purple which ran down the front,

F

and probably also down the back, of his tunic, and by the silver or ivory crescent which he wore upon his black shoes. His wife, it is perhaps needless to say, made even more show of what is called the "broad stripe." If you met a knight, you would perceive his standing by his two narrow stripes of purple appearing upon the same part of his dress. Each would wear a gold ring, but that in itself would prove nothing, since, despite all attempts at prohibiting the custom, every Roman who could afford a gold ring permitted himself that luxury.

If you entered one of the large semicircular theatres, which are to be described in due course, you would find that the men wearing the broad stripe seated themselves in the chairs which stood upon the level in front of the stage, while those wearing the narrow stripes would occupy the first fourteen tiers of seats rising just behind them. No one else might occupy those places. If some one who had been improperly posing as a knight, or who had been degraded from his rank because he had wasted his credit and his money and no longer possessed either £3200 or a reputation, ventured to seat himself in the fourteen rows in the hope of being unnoticed, he would be speedily called upon by the usher to withdraw. Snobs occasionally made the attempt, and, at a somewhat later date, we have an amusing epigram of Martial concerning one who repeatedly but unsuccessfully dodged the usher and who was at last compelled to kneel in the gangway opposite the end of the fourteenth row, where it might look

to those behind as if he were sitting among the
knights, while technically he could claim that he was
not sitting at all.

Elsewhere also, as for instance at the chariot-races
in the Circus, and at the gladiatorial shows in the
amphitheatre, there were special places set apart for
the two orders.

Below the senators and the knights came the
"people," — the "commons," or "third estate" —
with all its usual grades and its usual variety of
occupation or no occupation, of manners and character
or absence of both. With the life of these, as with
the life of a noble, we shall deal at the proper time.

So much for the Roman citizen proper. Other
elements of the population were the foreigners. At
Rome these were exceedingly numerous, and the city
may in this respect be called — as indeed it was
called — a microcosm, a small copy or epitome of the
Roman world. Gauls, Africans, Greeks, Jews, Syrians,
and Egyptians were perhaps the most commonly to be
seen, but particularly prominent were the Greeks and
the Jews. The Greeks were recognised above all as
the clever men, the artists, the social entertainers,
and the literary guides. The Jews, who formed a
sort of colony in what is now known as Trastevere —
the low-lying quarter across the Tiber — were not yet
the princes of high finance. As yet they were chiefly
the hucksters and petty traders, notorious for their
strange habits and for the fanaticism of their religion,

which nevertheless exercised a strange potency and
made many proselytes even in high places, especially
among the women. Poppaea, the wife of Nero himself, is commonly considered to have been such a
proselyte, although the strange notion that she herself
was a Jewess is without any sort of foundation. It
is a common error to suppose that the Jews came to
Rome only after the destruction of Jerusalem. The
dispersion had occurred long before Rome had anything to do with Judaea, and naturally the enterprising
Jew was to be found in all profitable places, whether
in Alexandria, Antioch, Smyrna, Corinth, Rome, or
farther afield.

In the political sense all these foreigners belonged
to their own provinces and communities. They
might be citizens there, but they were not citizens at
Rome. At Rome they had no public claims and no
official career, unless — as not seldom happened —
they received, for some service or some distinction, the
gift of the Roman citizenship. Sometimes the citizenship was given wholesale to a town, or even to a
province. How the Hebrew father or grandfather of
St. Paul became a Roman citizen, we do not know.
Their own abilities or the emperor's favour might
carry such citizens, or their children, up all the steps
which were open to the ordinary Roman.

After the foreigners come the slaves. At Rome
itself they formed about one-third of the population.
This is not the moment for any detailed account of
their employment, their treatment, or their liberation.

Suffice it for the present that the slave possessed no rights at all. He was the chattel of his master, who possessed over him the full power of life and death, limited only by public opinion and prudential considerations. A Roman might have at his disposal one slave or ten thousand slaves. He could use them as he liked, kill them if he chose, and, subject to certain limitations, set them free if he willed, provided that he did not set too many free at once. The last restriction was especially necessary, inasmuch as a slave who was manumitted by his master with the proper ceremonies became *ipso facto* a Roman citizen, but was still bound by certain ties of loyalty to his former master. For a Roman to possess too large an attachment of "freedmen," as they were called, might prove dangerous. The "freedman," though a citizen, could not himself enter upon a public career; neither, in ordinary circumstances, could his children; but in the third generation the family stood on an entire equality with any other Roman family in that respect.

For the present it may be added that our conception of the meaning of the word "slave" must not be that attached to its modern use. Many such slaves were men of great special or general ability, or men of high culture, especially if Greeks, Syrians, Jews, or Egyptians. They were frequently superior to their masters, and subsequently, as free citizens, added much to either the refinement or the over-refinement of Roman life. Perhaps it is as well, in passing, to point out that the later Roman people was in no small degree descended from all this aggregation of foreigners and emancipated slaves, and that we must speak with the greatest reservation when we describe the modern Roman as a direct descendant of the ancient stock who fought with Hannibal and subjugated the world.

CHAPTER V

ROUGHLY then this is the situation at the centre of government. Sumptuously housed on the Palatine Hill — the origin of our word "palace" — is His Highness Claudius Nero, Head of the State, Commander-in-Chief of the Forces, Empowered to act as Tribune of the People, and Head of the State Religion : in modern times commonly called "the Emperor." Every day and night his palace is surrounded by a regiment of the Imperial Guards, and attached to his person is a special corps for bodyguard, and orderlies. In practice, whatever be the theory, he possesses the control of legislation and appointments; upon him practically depends all recognised distinction of social rank. Down below, to the side of the Forum, is the Senate-House, in which there gathers, twice each month, and oftener if summoned, the great deliberative body which, in spite of all disturbances, civil wars, and limitations or broadenings of its power, is the continuation of the assembly of grave Roman fathers who first met some eight hundred years before. These men, who are men of birth and wealth and commonly of sound public training, are the nominal upholders and directors of the commonwealth, still left to perform many functions and to administer the more peaceful provinces in their own way — especially if they relieve the emperor of trouble — but in practice controlled by His Highness whenever and however it suits his purpose. They and the emperor form a partnership in authority, but the Senate is very distinctly the junior partner. They lend him advice or sanction when he seeks it, and they sometimes act as a break on his impetuosity. It is not well to alienate them, for they are proud; they are jointly, sometimes individually, powerful; and their moral weight with army and public is not to be despised.

Thus stands the central government, while socially there follows the order of the Knights, depending for their rank upon the emperor, and in many cases serving in his employ. Below these the populace, of whose rights and liberties the emperor is an official champion to whom theoretically any Roman citizen can appeal against a sentence of death or against cruel wrong. It is hard to conceive of a stronger position for one man to hold.

When we survey this vast aggregation of various provinces, with their differences of race, language, religion, and habits; when we remember that it was on the whole strictly, energetically, and legally administered; it is hard — even allowing for a wise Senate and capable ministers — to realise a man competent for the position.

Yet Augustus had been conspicuously successful, and Tiberius not less so; Claudius, despite a certain weakness, cannot by any means be called a failure; after Nero, Vespasian and Titus were capable enough; while Trajan deserves nothing but admiration. On the other hand Caligula, it is true, had had more than a touch of the madman in his composition, and had believed himself to be omnipotent and on a level with Jupiter. Nero had begun well, but had been led by vanity, vice, and extravagance to an astounding pitch of folly and oppression. Nevertheless it must be remarked, and it should be firmly emphasised, that what is called the tyranny of Caligula and Nero is mainly — and in Caligula's case almost solely — a tyranny affecting the Romans themselves, affecting the lives and property of the Roman senators and other prominent persons, and affecting the lives and honour of their wives and daughters. The outcry against these two emperors comes from the Romans, not from the subject peoples. At least in Caligula's case the provinces were as peaceful and prosperous as at other times. It is true that the madman once meant to insist on the Jews putting up his own statue in the temple at Jerusalem, but this was because his vanity was aggrieved by their unwillingness. Under Nero the case is much the same. His tyranny for the most part took the shape of cruelty, insult, and plunder in Rome itself. It was only when he was becoming hopelessly in debt that he began to plunder the provinces as well as Italy by demanding contributions of money, and in particular to seize upon Greek works of art without paying for them. It is a mistake to think of Nero as habitually and without scruple trampling under his blood-stained foot the rights and privileges of the provinces, or grinding from them the last penny, or harrying, slaying, and violating throughout the empire.

There is nothing to show that, during the greater part of his reign, the provinces at large felt any material difference between the rule of Nero and the rule of Claudius, or that they rejoiced particularly in his fall. In many quarters he was a favourite. In the latter half of his reign he made himself a brute beast, and often a fool, in the eyes of respectable Romans. But it was, as still more with Caligula, rather in his immediate environment that his tyranny was felt to be intolerable; that is to say, among the men and women who had the misfortune to come in his way with sufficient attraction of purse or beauty to awaken his cupidity. And these were the Romans themselves, senators and knights, not the populace, and in but a small degree, if at all, the provincials in Spain or Greece or Palestine.

Perhaps this is the time to look for a little while at this Nero, whose name has deservedly passed into a byword for heartless bestiality. In the year 64 he is 27 years of age, and has been seated on the throne for ten years. Four years more are to elapse before he perishes with the cry, "What an artist the world is losing!" In his early years his vicious propensities, inherited from an abominable father, had been kept in check partly by his preceptor, the philosopher Seneca, and by Burrus, the commander of the Imperial Guards, partly by his domineering and furious-tempered mother, Agrippina, who seems to have so closely resembled the mother of Lord Byron. But at this date he had got rid

Fig. 13. — Bust of Seneca.
Archeologische Zeitung.

of both his tutors. Burrus was dead, probably by poison, and Seneca was in forced retirement. The emperor had also caused his own mother to be murdered. Poisoning, strangling, drowning, or a command — explicit or implied — to depart this life, were his ways of shaking off any incubus upon a free indulgence of his will. His follies and vices had revealed themselves from the first, and had gone

to outrageous lengths, but now he is entirely un-
hampered in exhibiting them.

Educated slightly in philosophy, but better in
music and letters, he could speak, like others of his
day, Greek as well as his native Latin. His aim
was to be an "artist," but if the want of balance

Photo — Mansell & Co.

FIG. 14. — BUST OF AGRIPPINA, MOTHER OF NERO.

which too often goes with what is called the
"artistic temperament" ever manifested itself in
its worst form, it was in Nero. Apart from his
passion for music and verse, he developed an early
mania for horse-racing, and when he was caught
talking in school — where such conversation was
forbidden — about a charioteer who had fallen out
of his chariot and been dragged along the ground,

he explained that he was discussing the passage
in Homer where Achilles drags the body of Hector
round the walls of Troy. In after life he carried both
forms of mania to amazing lengths. The highest
form of music was then represented by singing to
the harp. Nero's ambition was no less than to
compete with the champion minstrels of the world.
As he remarked, "music is not music unless it is
heard," and he decided to make public appearances
upon the stage like any professional. Whenever
he did so, a number of energetic youths, salaried
for the purpose, were distributed among the audience
as *claqueurs* — the words actually used for them being
perhaps translatable as "boomers" or "rattlers." He
acted parts in plays — a proceeding which would
correspond to an appearance in opera — and made
a peregrination through Greece and back by way
of Naples as an exponent of the art of singing to
the harp. While upon this tour, whenever he was
performing in the theatre, the doors were shut, and
no one might leave the building for any reason whatever. "Many," says the memoir-writer, "got so
tired of listening and praising that they jumped
down from the wall, or pretended to be dead, so
as to get carried out." Naturally he always won
the prize, and, on his side, it should be remarked that
he honestly believed he had earned it. He practised
assiduously, took hard physical training, regulated his
diet for the cultivation of his voice, which was not
naturally of the best, and probably became not at
all a bad amateur. His monstrous self-conceit did

the rest. Besides singing to the harp, he was prepared to perform upon the flute and the bagpipes, and to give a dance afterwards. All this, of course, was undignified and ridiculous, but it was scarcely tyranny. Doubtless there was sufficient suffering among the audience, but that cruelty was hardly deliberate. In the Roman noble, whose ideal of behaviour included dignity and gravity, these public appearances perhaps often aroused more indignation and scorn than did his sensual vices. The same contempt was often evoked by other proceedings of a similar nature. His insatiable fondness for horse-racing, or rather chariot-racing, induced him to appear also as a charioteer. First he practised in his extensive private park or gardens, which were situated across the Tiber on the ground now approximately occupied by St. Peter's and the Vatican. When he appeared at the Olympic games driving a team of ten horses, he was thrown out of the car, and had to be lifted into it again. Though he was eventually compelled to abandon the race, he was, of course, crowned victor all the same. He dabbled also in painting and modelling.

We must not dwell too long upon his eccentricities. One might describe how in his earlier years he often put on mufti and roamed the streets at night with a few choice Mohawks, broke into shops, and insulted respectable citizens, throwing them into the drains if they resisted; how, being unrecognized, he once received a sound thrashing from a person of the senatorial order, and was thereafter attended on such occasions by police following at a distance. One might describe his dicing at £3 or £4 a pip, or his banquets, at one of which he paid as much as £30,000 for roses from Alexandria. After the great conflagration which swept over a large part of Rome in this very year 64 he began to build his enormous Golden House, in which stood a colossal effigy of himself 120 feet high, and in which the circuit of the colonnade made three Roman miles. Whether he deliberately set fire to the city in order to make room for this stupendous palace is open to doubt. It was naturally believed at the time, and, in order to divert suspicion from himself, he turned it upon those persons for whom the Roman populace had at that moment the greatest contempt, because, as the historian puts it, of their pestilent superstition and of a profound suspicion that they harboured a "hatred of the human race." These were the new sect of the Christians, and with burning Christians did Nero proceed to light up his gardens on one famous night, as a means of placating the populace whom he had offended, but who for the most part loved him for his misplaced generosity in the matter of "bread and sports." The tolerant attitude of the Romans towards foreign religions will be discussed in its own place ; but the cruelty of a Nero in the year 64 can hardly be put down as properly a religious persecution in any way typical of the Roman government.

The sensual vices of Nero are indescribable, and that word must suffice. His extravagances, whether in lavish presents or in personal expenditure, soon rendered him bankrupt. He had no means of paying the soldiers or meeting his own appetites. Then began, or increased, his attacks on wealthy persons, his executions and banishments of senators and other wealthy men, and his flimsy pretexts for all manner of confiscation. The Senate he hated and the Senate hated him. Nevertheless, so far as the empire itself was concerned, no systematic or widespread oppression can have been perceptible. His officers and the officers of the Senate were apparently all the time governing and administering the law and the taxation throughout the empire in as sound and steady a way as if an Augustus sat upon the throne.

If we wish to picture Nero to ourselves, here is his description : "He was of a fairly good height; his skin was blotched, and his odour unpleasant; his hair was inclined to be yellow; his face was more handsome than attractive; his eyes were grayish-blue and short-sighted; his neck was fat; he was protuberant below the waist; his legs were very slender; his health was good."

Such was the man to whom St. Paul elected to have his case referred, when at Caesarea he exercised his privilege as a Roman citizen and appealed to the titular protector of the commons. "Thou hast appealed unto Caesar, and unto Caesar shalt thou go." There is indeed no great probability that the apostle was ever brought directly before this precious emperor. We may perhaps draw from our inner

consciousness elaborate and interesting pictures of
the two men confronting each other, but we must
not forget that they will be pure imagination. The
appeal of a citizen did not imply such right to
an interview, for the Caesar in such minor cases

FIG. 15.—BUST OF NERO.

commonly delegated his powers to other judicial
authorities at Rome. Paul's object was gained if
his case was safely removed from the local influences
of Judaea and the weaker policy of its governor,
the "agent of Caesar," to the capital with its broader-
minded men and its superiority to small bribes and
local interference.

CHAPTER VI

ADMINISTRATION AND TAXATION OF THE EMPIRE

WE are now brought to the consideration of the methods by which this huge empire was organised and governed.

And first let us observe that the Romans — strict disciplinarians and great lawyers as they were — never sought to impose upon the subject provinces any uniformity. They never sought, any more than Great Britain has sought, to erect one code of law, one form of administration, one standard of rights, one rate of taxation, one religion, and to make it equally applicable to Spain and Britain, Greece and Africa, Gaul and Asia Minor. There were, of course, common to all the empire certain rules essential to civilisation, certain natural laws and laws of all nations. Murder, violence, robbery, deliberate sacrilege, and so forth were punishable everywhere, though not necessarily by the same authority nor in the same manner. Necessarily it was held everywhere that contracts must be fulfilled and debts paid. Beyond the fact that Rome demanded peace and order and the essentials of civilised life, and provided machinery to secure those ends, she troubled little about differ-

ences of local procedure and varieties of local law,
so long as the Roman rule was duly recognised and
the Roman taxes duly paid. As with Great Britain,
her care was for results, not for machinery, or, as
the great Roman historian puts it, she "valued the
reality of the empire, not the show."

Outside Italy there spread the provinces. These
had been conquered or peacefully annexed at various
times. A number of small states had come in by
perpetual alliance. Some provinces, such as Gaul,
had formerly been divided among tribes and tribal
chiefs. Some, such as Greece, had consisted of highly
civilised city-communities with small territories and
managing their own affairs, although they might all
alike be acknowledging the suzerainty of some
powerful prince. Some, such as Cappadocia, Syria,
and Egypt, had been under their native kings.
Judaea was a peculiar example of a small theo-
cratic state, in which the chief power lay with the
priests.

Rome was too wise to meddle more than she need
with existing conditions. She preferred as far as
possible to accept the existing machinery and to use
it, with only necessary modifications, as her instrument of administration. To the Sanhedrin at
Jerusalem, for example, she conceded a large criminal
jurisdiction over ecclesiastical offenders, so long as
that jurisdiction did not limit the universal rights
of a "Roman citizen."

When a province was conquered, all its territory

became technically the property of the Roman state. Some of it was kept as such, and mines of gold, silver, lead, iron, and salt, or quarries of marble, granite, and gravel, were commonly annexed as state property. If it was expedient to allot some portion of the conquered land to a Roman settlement — commonly a settlement of veteran soldiers called a "colony" — that was done. Such a settlement meant the founding of a town, to which was granted a certain environment of land. Those who took part in its formation were "Roman citizens" and forfeited no rights as such. As the native people came in from the surrounding districts to reside in it, they also, it appears, somewhat easily acquired similar privileges. Here the Roman law existed in its entirety. A colony was almost exactly a little Rome in respect of its system of officers and its legal procedure. Sometimes a town which had not originally been so founded might be made a "colony" by receiving a draft of Romans, and sometimes it was made such in sheer compliment. In the Eastern half of the empire such settlements were comparatively rare; they were but dots upon the map, as at Corinth, Philippi, Antioch in Pisidia, or Caesarea. In the West they were much more numerous. The south of France contained many; a number also existed in southern Spain. So many indeed were planted in these parts that they became, as has been already remarked, completely romanized. Farther north Cologne still perpetuates its Roman name of Colonia. Nevertheless in the West the bulk of the

land of the provinces is far from being taken up, in
the year 64, by colonies.

Apart from the lands thus appropriated, what
happens to the rest of the conquered territory which
is theoretically Roman property? Generally it is
handed back to its original inhabitants, on condition
that they pay rent for it, whether in money or in
kind, or partly in each. Egypt pays in kind when it
sends to Rome the corn in the great merchantmen;
Africa pays in kind when it does the same; the
Frisians of Holland pay in kind when they supply
a certain quantity of hides. Before the days of the
Emperor Augustus there had existed for the empire
in general the abominable system of tithes, which
were farmed by companies. But after him, and at
our date, for the most part the payment is by a
fixed sum of money, which has been calculated upon
the basis of those tithes. In the imperial Record
Office there is a register of the area of land in a given
province, and an assessment of its producing value.
The amount of the land-tax to be paid into the
Roman treasury is therefore fixed. Those who read
in the New Testament that Augustus Caesar sent
forth an order that "all the world — that is, the
Roman world — should be taxed" need find no difficulty in understanding what it means. "Taxed"
is Old English for assessed, as when we speak of
"taxing a bill of costs." The Greek word means
simply that a register should be made. The order of
Augustus was that a census should be taken throughout the provinces; that a return should be made of

population, property, trades, and all that a reasonable
government requires to know; and that payments
should be determined thereby. All the world had
been "taxed" in the modern sense long before
Augustus, and it has been taxed, unfortunately
without much promise of respite, ever since.

The chief revenues of Rome were derived from
this land-tax; but, when combined with other taxes,
a large proportion of it was spent in the administration
of the province from which it was obtained. No
error could be greater than to suppose that Roman
officers simply came and carried off all this money as
booty to Rome for the pampering of its emperor and
populace. Naturally the balance which accrued for
the feeding of Rome, for Roman enjoyment and
Roman buildings was very large; and doubtless this
fact was bad for the *morale* of Rome itself and
requires considerable casuistry to defend it. But it
would be a monstrous misconception to imagine that
all the "tribute paid to Caesar" was absolutely
drained, by an act of sheer oppression, clean out of
the province year by year. No country can be
protected, policed, and have its justice administered
without taxes, and the provincials were not paying
more, and were often paying much less, as well as
paying it in a more just and rational way, than when
they were being taxed by their own kings, their own
oligarchies, or their own socialistic democracies. The
Roman settlements — the colonies — unless specially
exempted, had to pay the land-tax as much as any
other community. The only land which was exempt

from it was Italy, and Italy paid sundry other taxes
to make up for it, at least in part.   But though Italy
was first and foremost in the imperial regard, the
emperor was by no means indifferent to the welfare
of the provinces.   If an earthquake, a fire, or other
great calamity befell a town, it was by no means rare
for the emperor to send a large sum of money in
relief.

Besides the land-tax there was also a tax on
persons and personal property.   The tax on persons
was not precisely a poll-tax, except in places like
Britain and Egypt, where it was difficult to make
proper estimates otherwise, but a tax on occupations
and trades.   This, if we choose, may be put down as
a crude form of income-tax, although it was not
actually assessed on income.   In another sense it
may be regarded as a tax on a license, assuming
that we demand a license for every kind of occupation.
Italy again was exempt from this taxation also.
Obviously a census, and a regularly revised census,
was necessary to carry out this system; and Rome
required a whole army of agents, just as a modern
state would require one, for assessing and collecting
these dues.

The land-tax and the person-tax were the two
chief sources of Roman revenue.   These were regular
and direct.   There were others, subject, like our own
taxes, to increase or decrease according to circumstances, but for the most part kept at very much the
same standards under several consecutive emperors.
For instance there were customs duties, paid on the

frontiers of the empire and also on those of provinces or natural groups of provinces, not as part of any protective system, since the empire is all one, but as a means of raising money from commodities. In Italy there was a duty of $2\frac{1}{2}$ per cent. Luxuries from India and Arabia *via* Red Sea ports were specially taxed at 25 per cent. If you sold a slave, you would pay from 2 to 4 per cent on the purchase-money. Occasionally there was a tax on bachelors. In Italy, but not elsewhere, 5 per cent legacy duty was paid when the recipient was not a near relative, and when the legacy was not under £1000.

Add to these revenues the rents of state pastures, state forests, and state mines. Into the treasury came also unclaimed property and the property of certain classes of condemned criminals.

So much for the nature of the taxation. In point of government, the Romans were singularly liberal. When a province was conquered or annexed, the Senate sent out a commission of ten persons, who carefully considered the existing state of things, the laws and forms of administration actually in vogue, and drew up a constitution for the province, embodying as much of these as was possible or at all commendable; as much, in fact, as was compatible with the Roman connection. This constitution, when sanctioned by the Senate, was binding, whatever governor might be appointed by Rome to the province. Such a governor might interpret the law; he could not alter it.

But though a province was a unit in so far as it was under one governor, the Romans were firm believers in strictly local administration. Their policy in this, as in conquest, was "divide and rule." It did not suit their ends to make any large part of the empire conscious of a corporate existence. The unit of administration was, therefore, a town and its district — a "community." In Gaul there were about sixty such divisions, each roughly corresponding in size to a modern French "department." Such a community had its own local council and officials, who were ultimately responsible to the governor. So long as they performed their municipal or communal functions correctly and honestly they were not interfered with. The chief principle upon which Rome insisted was that their local government should be aristocratic, or rather that office should be based on wealth. The governor, of course, stepped in when he felt it to be his duty. He was required to suppress all secret societies or political unions. A strike of the bakers in one city of Asia Minor was promptly put down by the governor as interfering with social order and social needs.

The communities made their own by-laws, they collected the land-tax of their own district and handed it over to the financial representative of the Roman government. This was done by men of their own people, often of a low class, known in the Gospels as the "publicans," who were so commonly associated with sinners. St. Matthew had been one of the minor agents for such collection in Galilee. Other taxes — those which were indirect — might be collected by the great tax-farming companies of Roman "knights," who offered a lump sum for them to the government, and made what they could out of the bargain.

One incidental consequence of this systematic division into communes was that there spread throughout the empire a strong municipal patriotism, especially in the Greek world. This was followed by liberal local expenditure on the part of rich provincials in beautifying their centres with public buildings and works of art, chiefly, no doubt, given for the sake of the local honours with which they were repaid, but given nevertheless.

Most of the towns or communities throughout the empire were in the position described. Some communities, however, such as Thessalonica, though situated inside a province, were for some special service in the past exempted from the interference of the governor, and were allowed to exercise their own laws to the full, even upon Roman citizens who might happen to reside there. These were called "free" towns. In other cases the community, having come into voluntary alliance with Rome at an early date and before conquest, was still treated as an "allied" state, and was exempted from either interference or taxation, so long as it supplied its quota of soldiers when called upon. Such cities, however, were distinctly the exception, and most of them in the end preferred to come directly within the Roman sphere of administration. They often found their

burdens smaller and less capricious than when they
taxed themselves through their own authorities.

The function of the governor was to see that
the various local bodies did their work, kept within
their rights, and paid their taxes. He also, either
in person or by his deputies, administered justice
wherever the Roman laws were concerned. Where
they were not concerned, he necessarily acted as
Gallio did with the Jewish charges against Paul at
Corinth; he dismissed the case as not demanding his
jurisdiction. Said Gallio: "If it were a question of
a misdemeanour or a crime, I should be called upon
to bear with you; but if they are questions of (mere)
words and names and of your (Jewish) law, you must
see to it yourselves." When the Greeks who were
standing by proceeded to beat the chief of Paul's
Jewish accusers, the governor shut his eyes to the
matter. This may have been a laxity, but it would
almost appear as if Gallio liked their behaviour.

For the purposes of justice a province was divided
into "Assize Districts," and the governor or his
deputies went on circuit. In the court he sat upon
a platform in his official chair and with his lictors
in attendance. The official language of the court
and of its records was of course Latin, but in the
Eastern half of the empire the bench cannot always
have pretended not to understand Greek. Since
it would not, however, understand Hebrew, the
Jews would need to speak through a representative who knew Latin, and this is apparently the

reason for the appearance of Tertullus against St. Paul at Caesarea. A Roman citizen — that is, a person possessed of full Roman rights — if he either denied the jurisdiction or was in danger of being condemned to capital punishment, might, unless he had been caught red-handed in certain heinous crimes, appeal to Caesar and claim to be sent to Rome. Unless the governor had been expressly entrusted with exceptional powers, or unless the case was so self-evident that he had nothing to fear from refusing, he had no alternative but to send the appellant on to the metropolis. Arrived there, the prisoner was taken to the guardrooms or cells in the barracks of a special prefect who had charge of such arrivals from abroad, and his case would in due course be taken either by the emperor himself, if it was sufficiently important, or by magistrates to whom the emperor delegated his powers for the purpose.

Meanwhile, provincials other than full Roman citizens enjoyed no such privilege. They could make no appeal. The governor was supreme judge, and his verdict or sentence was carried out. In matters of doubt, whether administrative or judicial, the governor might refer to the emperor for direction or advice, and we have at a somewhat later date a considerable collection of letters and their replies which passed in this manner between Pliny and the Emperor Trajan.

A glance at the map will show some provinces named in heavy type and some in *italics*. Those in

italics are the provinces to which the Senate has
the right to appoint the governors, in this case called
"proconsuls." Of course His Highness the Head of
the State is graciously pleased to approve the choice
of the Senate; which means that the Senate will not
attempt any appointment which the emperor would
dislike. The revenues of these provinces go into a
treasury controlled by the Senate. Of those named
in heavy type the emperor is himself the governor
or proconsul. Theoretically he is made governor of
all these simply because they contain, or may need,
armies, and he is the commander-in-chief of those
armies. But since he is at Rome, and in any case
cannot be everywhere at once, he governs all such
provinces by means of his deputies, whom he
appoints for himself. They are his lieutenants, and
are so called — to wit, "lieutenants of Caesar" and
"deputies of the commander." The revenues of
these imperial provinces are collected by an "agent"
or "factor" of Caesar, and go into a treasury controlled by the emperor. In any one of his provinces
the emperor would be its governor, and would exercise
the usual military and civil powers of a governor.
His lieutenant to each province simply acts in his
place, receives the same powers, and is the governor
of that province exactly as the proconsul sent by
the Senate is governor in his. But whereas the
governors in the senatorial provinces wear the garb
of peace, and are appointed, like other civil officers,
for one year only, the "deputies of Caesar," the
commander-in-chief, wear the military garb, and are

kept in office just so long as their superior thinks
fit. It is as if in modern times the governor of the
one kind of province made his public appearances in
civilian dress, and the governor of the other kind in
uniform.

The actual outcome of this system was that the
provinces of the emperor were on the whole better
administered than those of the Senate.. In the latter,
changes were too frequent, and a governor might
sometimes strain a point to enrich himself quickly.
But it must on no account be imagined that at this
date a governor could with impunity be extortionate
or oppress the provincials, as he too often did in the
good old days of the republic. He was paid his
salary, which might be anything up to £10,000;
his allowances and power of making requisitions,
such as of salt, wood, and hay when travelling, were
strictly defined by law; any pronounced extortion,
oppression, or dishonesty laid him open to impeach-
ment; and such a charge was tolerably certain to
be brought. Among so many governors it was
inevitable that a number should have been im-
peached. We know of twenty-seven instances,
resulting in twenty condemnations and only seven
acquittals. The emperors at least looked sharply to
their own provinces; nor would they readily tolerate
any gross irregularity in those other provinces which
were nominally controlled by the Senate. On leaving
his province every governor must make out duplicate
copies of his accounts, one to be left in the province,
one to be forwarded to Rome.

In the *Acts of the Apostles* we have mention of
two governors of senatorial provinces — in other
words, two "proconsuls" — Gallio in Achaia (or
Greece), and Sergius Paulus in Cyprus. It is instructive to compare the lenient and common sense
attitude of these trained Roman aristocrats with that
of the turbulent local mobs who dealt with St. Paul
in Asia Minor, Judaea, or Greece. Of the minor
governors of smaller provinces — styled "agents" or
"factors" of Caesar — we meet with Pontius Pilate,
Felix, and Festus.

It remains only to remark that, while the Senate's
treasury, which received the revenues from the senatorial provinces, paid the expenses of their management and also of the administration of Italy, the
emperor's treasury, which received the revenues
from the other provinces, provided for their administration, for the pay of the army, for the corn
and water of Rome, for public buildings, for the
great military roads, and for the imperial post.
Nevertheless the emperor could handle all this latter
money exactly as he chose, and it is upon this
chest that Nero was drawing for all his lavish prodi-
galities and his undeserved and wasteful bounties.
Yet even Nero was scarcely so bad as Caligula, who
managed to spend £22,000,000 in less than one year.

CHAPTER VII

In the year 64 the capital of the Roman Empire was,
it is true, a large and splendid city and an "epitome
of the world," but it had not yet reached either its
zenith of splendour or its maximum of size. Many
of the largest and most sumptuous structures of
which we possess the records, and in most cases the
ruins, were not yet built or even contemplated.
There was no Colosseum; there were no Baths of
Trajan, Caracalla, or Diocletian. The Column of
Trajan, still soaring in the Foro Traiano, and of
Marcus Aurelius, now so conspicuous in the Piazza
Colonna, are of a later date. So also are the three
great triumphal arches which are still standing —
those of Titus, Severus, and Constantine. The
Mausoleum of Hadrian, now stripped of its outward
magnificence of marble and sculpture, and known as
the Castle of Sant' Angelo, was not built for two
generations. On the Palatine Hill the palaces of the
Caesars were wide and lofty, but not more than half
so spacious and imposing as they became by the end
of the following century.

Down in the Forum there stood no Basilica of

Constantine; the place of several later temples and shrines was occupied by edifices of less dignity; many columns and statues, and much ornament of gilt or marble, were still to come. Beside and beyond the two embellished public places which had been added to the public comfort and convenience by Julius Caesar and Augustus, and which were known respectively as the Julian and the Augustan Forum, lay only the houses of citizens or streets of shops. Up from the Forum towards the later Arch of Titus and the Colosseum, the "Upper Sacred Way" ran as but a narrow road between buildings for the most part of ordinary character, principally shops catering for luxury. It was later by two centuries and a half that this street was converted into a broad avenue forming a worthy approach to the "hub of the universe."

In the ruins which lie on the Palatine Hill, or along the valley of the Forum below, or up the Sacred Slope towards the Colosseum, or across where the streets wind round from the "Roman" Forum through the Forum of Trajan to the Corso, the modern visitor to the Eternal City does not behold simply the remnants of the temples, halls, squares, and arches which actually existed in the days of Nero. We must not say of these places that St. Paul trod the very paving-stones or gazed on the very walls which we now find in their worn and broken state. In a few cases it may be so; in most it is certainly otherwise. Either the building was not there, or what we now behold is part of a recon-

H

struction or an enlargement. Fire, flood, earthquake, and the wear and tear of time called for many a rebuilding or restoration. In the very year upon which we have fixed, there swept over all this part of the city perhaps the most disastrous fire that it ever experienced. Another only a little less destructive occurred in A.D. 283, and when we say that the remains of the glory of ancient Rome are still visible in the excavated Forum, we must recognise that the glory which they represent is the glory of the place as restored after that year.

This does not mean that the general plan and appearance were markedly different under Nero, nor that there was any lack of magnificence; it is only meant by way of caution against a frequent misconception.

If there was no Arch of Severus in the Forum, there was an Arch of Augustus, near the Temple of Castor, surmounted by his statue in the four-horsed chariot of the conqueror, and there was an Arch of Tiberius near the temple of Saturn. If to the north there was as yet no bridge or "castle" of Sant' Angelo to celebrate the dead Hadrian, there was, on the near side of the Tiber, not far from the modern Piazza del Popolo, a splendid Mausoleum of the deified Augustus and his family. In the chief Forum the Temples of Vesta, of Julius Caesar, of Castor, Saturn, and Concord existed under Nero in the same spots and in much the same style as they did through all the remainder of Roman history. Above them towered the Capitoline Hill, with its resplendent

VATICAN HILL

Circus of Nero

VILLAS AND GARDENS

PINCIAN HILL

Flaminian Way

Mausoleum of Augustus

CAMPUS

MARTIUS

River Tiber

JANICULAN HILL

VILLAS AND GARDENS

Portico

Baths of Nero

Pantheon

Portico

Portico

Baths of Agrippa

Arch of Claudius

(Aqua Virgo)

Aqueduct

Old Wall

QUIRINAL HILL

VIMINAL HILL

ESQUILINE HILL

Camp of Imperial Guards

of Servius

Rampart

To Tibur (Tivoli)

Old

Subura

Carinae

Circus Flaminius

Theatre of Pompey

Theatre of Balbus

Portico

13 12
15
14 FORUM
16

4
5 6
11
7 Sacred Way
10 8
9

VELABRUM

Transtiberine Region

PALATINE HILL

1
2 3

Circus Maximus

Temple of Claudius

CAELIAN HILL

Aqueduct

(Aqua Claudia)

AVENTINE HILL

Temple of Diana

Capena Gate

Appian Way

To Ostia

To Puteoli

Wharves and Stores

1. Palaces of Tiberius and Caligula.
2. Palace of Augustus.
3. Temple of Apollo.
4. Forum of Augustus.
5. Forum of Julius.
6. Senate House.
7. Basilica Aemilia.
8. Temple of Vesta.
9. House of Vestals.
10. Temple of Castor.
11. Temple of Saturn.
12. Temple of Concord.
13. Record Office.
14. Temple of Jupiter.
15. Temple of Juno.
16. Theatre of Marcellus.
17. Basilica Julia.

ROME: CHIEF TOPOGRAPHICAL FEATURES IN A.D. 64.

R. & R. Clark, Ltd. Printers, Edinr.

Temple of Jupiter on the one summit and its great shrine of Juno on the other. Beyond, in the "Field of Mars" — the site of the densest part of modern Rome — was an almost continuous cluster of public buildings and resorts, of theatres, temples — including the first form of that incomparable edifice, the Pantheon, the only building of ancient Rome which

FIG. 16. — SOME REMAINS OF THE CLAUDIAN AQUEDUCT.

still remains practically whole — of baths, porticoes, and enclosed promenades.

Away in the opposite direction stretched the Appian Way, and in the year 64 the beautiful tomb of Caecilia Metella, which is so familiar in picture, stood as perhaps the noblest among the multitude of patrician tombs. The Apostle Paul certainly passed close by it on his way from Puteoli. The aqueduct,

of which so many arches still meet the eye as you
cross the Campagna, was the work of Nero's predecessor, Claudius, and it still bears his name — the
Aqua Claudia. Where now you go out of the gate
to St. Paul's Outside-the-Walls there stood — more
free and visible than now — that pyramid of Cestius,
close to whose shadow lie the graves of the English
Shelley and Keats. There was no gate at this spot
in the days of Nero, for the great wall, of which so
many portions — more or less restored — are still conspicuous, had no existence till a much later date.
when the empire was already tottering to its fall, and
when Aurelian was driven to recognise that the
heart of the empire, after remaining secure for
centuries, must at last look to be assailed. There
was, it is true, an inner wall of ancient date (to be
seen upon the plan) which had enclosed the "Seven
Hills" before Rome was mistress of more than her
own small environment. But the city had long ago
overflowed this boundary, and the newer quarters
lay as open to the country as do our own modern
cities.

How far the suburbs stretched, or precisely how
far Rome proper extended, in the days of Nero, is no
easy matter to decide. We shall in all probability
be near the mark if we accept the line of the later
wall of Aurelian as practically the limit of what
might be included in the "Metropolitan Area." The
total circumference of the whole city would be about
twelve English miles, a circuit which fell somewhat

short of that of Alexandria and probably of Antioch, although in actual importance these cities took but the second and third rank respectively.

Some parts within this line were thickly inhabited, in some the houses must have been but sparse. Particularly along the upper slopes of the hills — of the Pincian, Quirinal, Esquiline, Caelian, and Aventine — were the spacious houses and gardens of the wealthy. The Palatine was almost, though not completely, monopolised by the emperors' palaces and sundry temples. The Campus Martius was mostly a region of public buildings and grounds for promenade and exercise, although some of the finest shops stood very close to where they stand to-day, in that Flaminian Way which is now called the Corso of Humbert. On one side below the Palatine Hill, space was taken up by the vast Circus or racing-ground; on the other lay the public places known as the Fora. It was left for the poorer inhabitants to crowd themselves into the valleys of the town, either between the Forum and the spurs of the several hills which trend towards the centre — up under Quirinal, Viminal, Esquiline, or Caelian — to the left behind the buildings as you now go from the bottom of the Forum to the Colosseum; or between the Forum and the Tiber in the low-lying ground called the Velabrum and there-abouts; or else across the river in that "Transtiberine" region which still bears the name of Trastevere.

If, therefore, it is asked what may have been the population of Neronian Rome, it need cause no surprise if the number should appear comparatively small to

one who is accustomed to our huge modern towns.
Rome had never been a seat of manufactures. Its
wealth and luxury came almost wholly from its empire,
and it was emphatically a city for the rich and ruling
classes. In Nero's day it was still growing, and even
in its fullest times it is doubtful if the population
ever exceeded or even reached a million and a quarter.
Perhaps for the year 64 we may most safely put it
down at about 750,000.

Now suppose yourself to be standing at F in the
recognised centre of Roman life, the "Roman Forum."
Here, before we begin our rapid exploration of the
city, it is well to clear our minds of one false notion
which too commonly prevails. Think of any modern
town you please, and remember that, whatever may
be the accumulation of architectural magnificence
around any given spot, the people of that town treat
it all with familiarity and without any waste of sentiment. They will set up their shops or stalls wherever
they are allowed; they will carry on their traffic and
their amusements; they will saunter and sit on steps
and misbehave without feeling oppressed by any
appreciable awe of their surroundings. So was it,
and even more so, in ancient Rome. The fact that
there were shrines or public buildings on all sides did
not prevent the Romans from loitering and loafing in
the Forum, from sitting on the steps of a temple or a
basilica, or leaning against its columns or statues, or
playing at a sort of draughts or of backgammon on
its marble platforms — the lines to put the "men"

FORUM
OF
AUGUSTUS

1. Golden Milestone.
2. Arch of Tiberius.
3. Arch of Augustus.

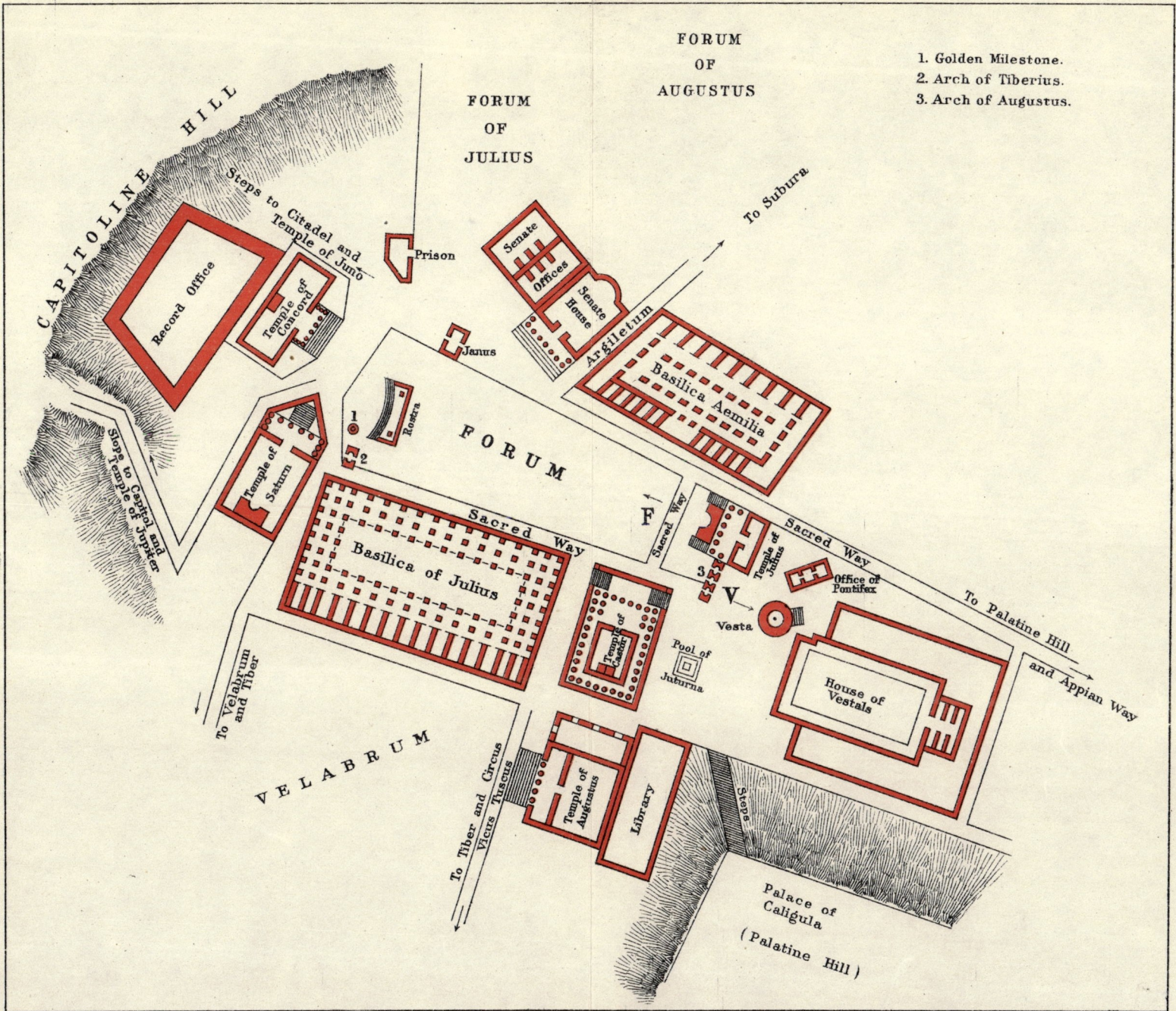

FORUM
OF
JULIUS

CAPITOLINE HILL

Steps to Citadel and Temple of Juno

Record Office

Temple of Concord

Prison

Senate Offices

Senate House

To Subura

Argiletum

Janus

Basilica Aemilia

Steps to Capitol and Temple of Jupiter

Temple of Saturn

1

2

Rostra

FORUM

F

Sacred Way

Basilica of Julius

Sacred Way

Sacred Way

3

Temple of Janus

Office of Pontifex

To Palatine Hill

V

Vesta

and Appian Way

To Velabrum and Tiber

Temple of Castor

Pool of Juturna

House of Vestals

VELABRUM

To Tiber and Circus
Vicus Tuscus

Temple of Augustus

Library

Steps

Palace of Caligula

(Palatine Hill)

R. & R. Clark, Ltd. Printers, Edinburgh.

PLAN OF THE FORUM A.D. 64.

upon are here and there still visible upon the pavements — or even scratching a name or a drawing on a
pillar. In certain parts the Forum was alive with
the bustle of financial business and, doubtless under
certain limitations, with the traffic of the pedlar.
Curiosities were exhibited, the crier shouted his
advertisements, and, in short, the place was almost as
freely used for the vulgar purposes of ordinary life
as for the dignified gatherings and ceremonies which
to our minds appear so much more appropriate to it.
Though we are not yet dealing with the social life of
Rome, whether indoor or outdoor, it seems advisable
to make this observation before proceeding.

Let us now stand at F and look about us toward
the Capitol, noting only the chief features of the scene.
The reader would do well to consider the plan along
with the frontispiece to this book. We are upon an
open space paved with marble slabs, round which
stand sundry honorary statues and various minor
monuments into which we need not now enquire.
Facing us, toward the far end, is a platform about 80
feet long and 11 feet in height, with marble facing.
A trellis-work rail, or pierced screen, runs along it at
either side, and also extends along the front for one-
third of the distance from either end. The one-third
in the middle of the front is open. This platform is
approached by a flight of steps at the back, while in
the sheer face are set as ornaments rows of bronze
"beaks" or "rams" cut from ships captured in war.
From these "beaks" the platform obtains its name —

the Rostra. It is the platform for harangues delivered
to the Roman people — the Roman citizens who are
politely assumed to be the body politic — and the open
space on the front is the position for the orator. It
is from this stand that important announcements are
made to the people at large. An emperor or his
nominee may speak from it; a magistrate may deliver
some pronouncement; a political exhortation may be

FIG. 17. — THE ROSTRA: BACK VIEW. (Probable restoration for A.D. 64.)

uttered; in the case of a public funeral, or even of
the private obsequies in some eminent family, an
oration over the deceased may be spoken with that
finished and animated elocution which the Romans so
zealously cultivated, and which the Italians still affect
with no little success. It is not indeed the same
platform as was used by Cicero and the orators of
the republic: this stood elsewhere, and doubtless the
substance of public speaking had declined deplorably
since that day. Nevertheless many a torrent of

rich and sonorous Latin must have streamed over
the Forum from that noble standing-place, and it
must still have been worth while for a Roman to
develop both his speaking voice and his oratorical art.

Still further back, to the right behind the Rostra,
there stands the Temple of Concord, where the Senate
in older times gathered on more than one occasion to
listen to Cicero, and where the emperors have formed
practically a gallery of works of art ; to the left is the
Temple of Saturn, long used as the Roman Treasury,
of which eight pillars still remain as perhaps the
most conspicuous feature among the existing ruins.
Another object in the background to the left, at the
rear of the Rostra, will be a stone pillar coated with
gilded bronze, upon which the first emperor, Augustus,
inscribed the names of the great roads leading out from
Rome into the length and breadth of the empire, with
a list of the chief towns to which those roads would take
you, and their distances.   The name of this pillar is the
"Golden Milestone."   Behind these objects, running
along the high face of the Capitoline Hill, are visible
the arcades of the Record Office, of which the greater
portion still exists, though stripped of its architectural
graces and built over and about in more modern times,
in the state represented in Fig. 18.   Still higher on the
summit to the left, with its gilded tiles glistening in
the sun — at least they were gilded within the next
few years — rises the most sacred structure of all, the
building most closely identified in the Roman mind
with the eternity of the empire.   This is the splendid
temple of Jove, Supreme and Most Benign.   Of

this edifice nothing considerable except its platform now remains, its site being occupied by an object of which the existence would have been inconceivable to the ancient Roman — to wit, the German Embassy. On the other summit, a fortified citadel to your right, stands the temple of the consort of Jupiter. In this shrine she was known as Juno Moneta, and since, attached to her temple in this citadel, was the office of the Roman coinage, her name Moneta has become familiar to modern mouths in the form of "the Mint." If you seek the place of this temple now, you must look for it under the Church of Santa Maria in Ara Coeli.

Next, instead of looking up at the hill, glance to your left, and you will see running along that side of the Forum, beside the Sacred Way, a spacious public building known as the Basilica of Julius, that is to say, of Julius Caesar. It is an edifice of a type familiar in cities of the Roman world. You mount the steps from the Sacred Way and find yourself under an outer two-storied arcade suitable for lounging or promenading while discussing business or gossip with your friends. Passing from this inwards you are in a building which consists of a covered colonnade, or nave, about 270 feet in length, with a row of pillars on either hand. On each side is a gallery, or upper floor, from which spectators may look down upon the interior, or, from the outer side, upon the open Forum. At the far end is a recess with a raised tribunal, shut off, if necessary, by railings. In other basilicas there may be an apse at this point, similarly

FIG. 18. — RUINS OF FORUM. (Record Office in background with modern building above.)

107

enclosed. This serves as a court of justice, round which the curious may stand, or upon which listening spectators may gaze from the ends of the galleries above. Meanwhile up and down the open space of the nave all kinds of verbal business may be transacted by appointment, exactly as such business used to be carried on in old St. Paul's Cathedral in London or in churches elsewhere. In what may be called the inner side-aisle are situated offices of various kinds, including those of sundry public corporations, boards, or commissions. The whole of this great hall is paved with coloured marbles; its pillars are coated with marble; its ceiling is adorned with painting and gilt; it is embellished with statues; and it is lighted from above by a clerestory. Though the question has been debated, it is almost certain that it was mainly from buildings like this, or from rooms similarly constructed in palatial houses, that the early Church developed its basilicas — with their nave, aisles, and clerestory, and with their railed apse at the end, where was placed the chair of the bishop on its dais. Across the Forum on the opposite side, to your right, lies another structure of the same kind, in artistic respects more excellent. In this, the Basilica Aemilia, the chief business was that of the bankers and money-changers, although it served various other purposes according to convenience.

If you could see round the farther end of this basilica to the right, you would perceive the beginning of one of the busiest streets in Rome — the Argiletum — chiefly known to fame as a favourite

quarter of the booksellers, who fasten on their doorposts, or on the pillars which support a balcony or
upper floor, the lists of the newest or most popular
publications to be bought within. And where that
street enters the Forum, though standing back a
little from your line of vision — perhaps you can

FIG. 19. — N.E. OF FORUM, A.D. 64. (Complementary to frontispiece.)

From left: in background, Record Office, with Temple of Concord and Rostra below ; on
   summit, Temple of Juno and Citadel ; below, Prison, with shrine of Janus in front.
   To right : Basilica Aemilia, with gable of Senate-House beyond. (Largely after
   Tognetti.

catch sight of the top of it over the corner of the
Basilica — is the temple-like Senate-House with its
offices. Here is the meeting-place of the six hundred
who nominally govern jointly with the emperor. If
you visit Rome to-day you will find the greater part
of the actual chamber, though miserably despoiled,
bearing the name of the church of S. Adriano.

The little building, half arch, half shrine, which you observe standing free where the roads converge upon the Forum, is the famous sanctuary of Janus, of which the doors are never shut unless there is complete peace throughout the Roman world. So long as Rome is anywhere engaged in a great or little war, the open doors of Janus tell the fact to a people which might otherwise be unconscious of so slight or remote a circumstance.

We need not describe in detail the temple of Castor, or rather of the "Twin Brethren," which stands immediately to your left, or that of the deified Julius Caesar, which is just behind you, on the spot where the body of the great dictator was burned. It is perhaps more interesting to note the ordinary — though not by any means the only — form of the Roman temple in general. Those who have seen the so-called Maison Carrée at Nîmes will possess a fair notion of the commonest or most typical shape and arrangement. For the most part we have a rather lofty platform, mounted from one end by steps, which are flanked by walls or balustrades, often bearing at their extremities equestrian statues or other appropriate figures. Upon the platform stands the temple proper, consisting of a chamber containing the statue of the god. Where more than one deity are combined in the same temple — as in that of Jupiter on the Capitoline Hill, where the supreme deity has Juno and Minerva to left and right of him — there may either be as many separate chambers or

as many chapel-like bays as there are deities. The
altar for sacrifice stands outside opposite the entrance,
being placed either upon the top of the main platform or more commonly on a minor platform of
its own in the middle of the steps. In most cases
the chamber stands back behind a row, in some
instances two rows, of columns, which support the

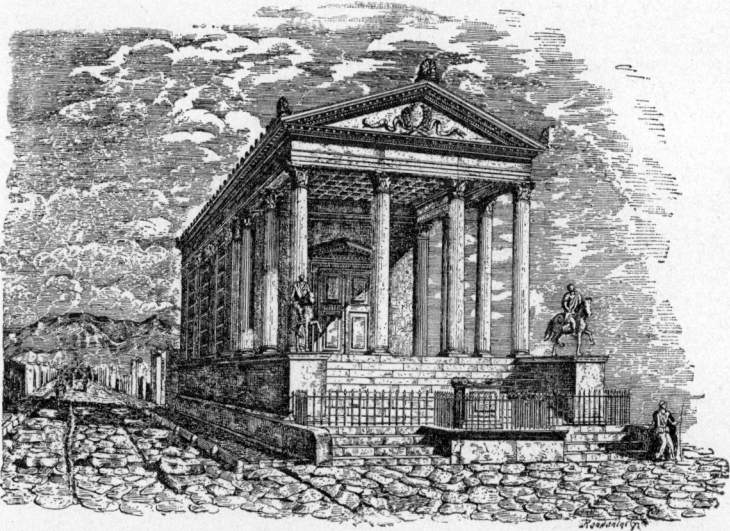

FIG. 20. — TEMPLE OF FORTUNA AUGUSTA. (Pompeii.)

characteristic entablature seen in the illustrations.
In the case of the more grandiose temples a series of
columns may run all round the building, carrying an
extension of the roof, under which is thus formed a
covered colonnade. More commonly the sides and
back of the chamber have only what are known
as "engaged" columns, as it were half-embedded
in the wall. The roof is gabled and tiled, with

ornaments along the eaves. The front has an embellished entablature, with its triangle of masonry
called the "pediment," consisting of a cornice over-
hanging a sunken surface decorated with a sculptured
group. Over each angle, right, left, and summit, is
a base of stone supporting some conspicuous ornament,
such as a statue, an eagle, or a figure in a chariot.
In the middle of the front of the building, behind the
columns of the portico, are double doors, commonly
made of decorated bronze, with an open grating of
the same metal above them. The whole is outwardly
of marble, either all white or with colour in the pillars,
but the core of at least the platform is commonly
made of the immensely strong Roman concrete, or
else of blocks of the less beautiful and costly kinds
of stone.

In point of architectural style the Romans of this
date — who in artistic matters were but imitators of
the Greeks and far less certain in taste than their
masters — affected the Corinthian, as being the most
florid. Even this they could not leave in its native
purity, but for the most part converted it into Graeco-
Roman or composite varieties. A prime fault of the
Roman taste was then, as it has always been, a love
of gorgeousness, of excessive and obtrusive ornament.
In almost any Roman church of to-day we find the
walls and pillars stuck about with figures, slabs, and
so-called decorations to such an extent that the finer
lines and proportions are often ruined. The ancient
Roman likewise was commonly under the impression
that the more decoration you added, the more

magnificent was the building. There were doubtless many buildings in simpler and purer taste, probably executed by Greek artists under the authority of some Roman who happened to possess a finer judg-

FIG. 21.— SO-CALLED TEMPLE OF THE SIBYL AT TIVOLI.

ment or less self-assertiveness. Nevertheless the fault of over-elaboration is distinctly Roman.

We must not omit to say that, besides temples of this typical rectangular form, there were others of a round shape, encircled by columns, like that graceful structure at Tivoli commonly, though mistakenly, known as the temple of the Sibyl, and that

I

small building which still exists in an impoverished
condition near the Tiber, and which used to bear the
erroneous title of the temple of Vesta. Others again
were simply round and domed, like the true temple
of Vesta in the Forum, or the superb and impressive
Pantheon in the Campus Martius. So far as the
bare round was broken in these cases, it was either
by a pillared portico, as with the Pantheon, or by
engaged columns and ornament, as with the true
temple of Vesta.

The mention of the temple of Vesta reminds us
that it is time to face about, and, passing behind the
temple of Julius, to look in the opposite direction,
from V. Before us lies this circular shrine, a
form gradually developed from the primitive round
hut which once served as house to the prehistoric
ancestors of the Roman stock. As it was the duty
of the maiden daughters of that ancient tribe to keep
alight the fire upon the domestic hearth, so through
all the history of Rome it was the duty of certain
chosen virgins to keep perpetually burning the
hearth-fire of the city. The roof of the temple is
open in the middle, and you may perhaps see the
smoke issuing from it. But if you are a male, you
may not enter. No man, except the chief Pontifex,
may set foot inside the shrine of the virgin goddess,
who is attended by virgin priestesses. Close behind
the temple stands the house of these Vestals. They
are in a large measure the ancient prototype of the
modern nun, and their house is the prototype of the

convent. Six nobly-born young women, sworn to
chastity, and dressed in a ritual garb, live in an
edifice of much magnificence under the rule of one
who is the chief Vestal, a sort of Mother Superior.
Many pedestals of the statues of such chief priestesses
still remain, and we can
clearly trace the arrangement of their abode, with
its open court — once
containing a garden and
cool cisterns of pure
water — its separate
room for each Vestal, its
baths, and its resources
of considerable comfort
and even luxury.

Fig. 22. — Vestal Virgin.

If, as you face this
way, you look up to your
right, you will perceive
the Palatine Hill rising steeply above you, with its
summit crowned by the lofty palaces and gardens
constructed by the Caesars. At the side and corner
which look down upon the Forum stands the part
built by Caligula, the epileptic who thought himself no less than a god, and who in consequence
not only turned the temple of Castor into a lower
vestibule to his own house, but also built a bridge
across the valley over the temple of Augustus and
the Basilica of Julius to the Capitoline Hill, so
that he might visit and converse with Jupiter,
his only compeer. From the top of the Basilica he

occasionally threw money into the Forum to be
scrambled for by people who crushed each other to
death in the process. It would require too much
space if we climbed the sloping road which leads
on to the Palatine and examined the various
structures upon that hill. As we now see it in
its ruins it is perhaps the most mysteriously impressive place in the world. But many alterations and
enlargements of the palaces were made after the
date of Nero, and we cannot now be sure of the
precise aspect of the hill-top in his day. Suffice
it that, overlooking the Forum, overlooking the
Velabrum Valley which leads from the Forum to
the Tiber, and overlooking the middle of the valley
where the vast Circus or race-ground separated the
imperial hill from the Aventine, there were portions
of the huge imperial abodes, rising in several stories
gleaming with marble, and enjoying the purest air
and the widest views obtainable within the city.
Nero himself, it is true, was not content with such
mere human housing. After the great fire of this
year 64, he proceeded to make for himself what he
called "a home fit for a man," and so built — though
he never finished — that famous or infamous "Golden
House," which ran from the Palatine all across the
upper Sacred Way and the hollow now occupied by
the Colosseum far on to the opposite hills — a house
of countless chambers, with three miles of colonnade,
enclosed gardens large enough to be called a park,
and a statue of himself 120 feet in height. The
epigram went that the people of Rome must migrate,

inasmuch as what had once been a city was now but a private house. This, however, had not yet occurred, and we have rather to think of palaces and gardens rich indeed, but by no means occupying the whole of the Palatine Hill alone. There were, of course, numerous buildings more or less connected with the imperial establishment, among them being quarters for the officers and soldiers of the guard. There were also a number of temples, one of which, the magnificent shrine of Apollo, the god of light and learning, stood in a court marvellously enriched with sculptured masterpieces, while connected with it were libraries filled with Greek and Latin books and adorned with the busts and medallion-portraits or statues of great authors.

If we proceeded now to walk up the Sacred Way, along the narrow street edged by jewellers' and other shops, we should meet as yet with no Arch of Titus, nor in descending beyond should we see any Colosseum, but only a block of ordinary dwellings, to be swept away later in this year by the fire which made room here for the ornamental waters of Nero's Golden House. Turning to the right along the valley between the Palatine and Caelian Hills, we should not have to pass under any Arch of Constantine; but, after glancing up to the left at the great unfinished temple of Claudius and going under the Claudian aqueduct which carries water to the Palatine, we should proceed between private houses and gardens till we reached a famous gate in the ancient wall and found ourselves on that noted Appian Way, which would take us to Capua and thence over the Apennines to Brindisi and the East. Just outside the gate we should find the livery-stables, with their vehicles and horses or mules waiting to be hired for the stage which would carry us as far as the slope on the southern edge of the Alban Hills.

But we will not proceed in this direction. From our stand at V in front of the temple of Vesta we will turn back, walk over the Forum to the right of the Rostra, between the sanctuary of Janus and the front of the Senate-House. Thence we will cross an enclosed forum, or public place, erected by Julius Caesar, with its temple of "Venus the Mother" in the middle, and so enter the Forum of Augustus. This is worth a pause. As you pass to-day up the narrow Via Bonella and perceive near the Pantani Arch a few imposing columns and a patch of rather depressing bare wall, it requires much effort to realise that here was once a noble space enclosed by marble-covered walls 100 feet in height, and that those walls contained in a series of niches a gallery of statues of all the military heroes and patriots of Roman history from Aeneas downwards. Meanwhile the few columns at your side are the sole survivors of the number which surrounded the splendid temple of Mars the Avenger, the shrine which was identified in imperial times with the military power of Rome, and which received the standards captured from the enemy, just as captured flags are to be seen in many a modern church.

Leaving this Forum, we will not bear to the right
to find ourselves amid the dense population of the
Subura and its neighbourhood,, but we will turn to
the left and pass between the Capitoline and Quirinal
Hills, which then met more steeply and closely than
they did fifty years later, when Trajan had cut away
the rising ground and levelled an open space which

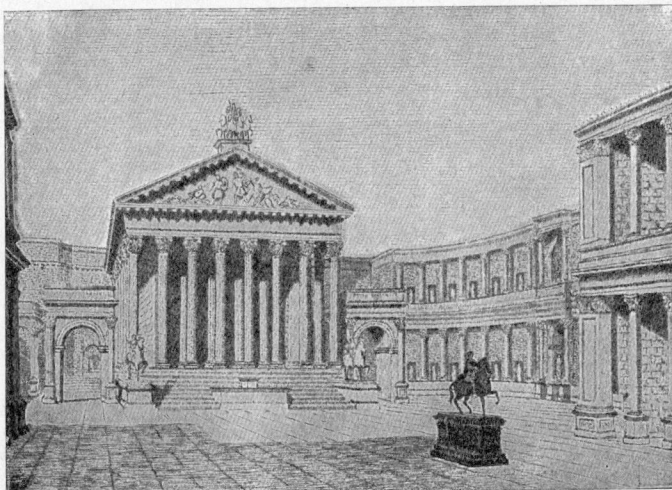

FIG. 23. — TEMPLE OF MARS THE AVENGER IN FORUM OF AUGUSTUS.
(After Ripostelli.)

must have been an incalculable advantage to the
convenience of the city. It is perhaps well to observe
here that the piling up of fallen ruins and the
deliberate levellings and gradings, both in ancient
and modern times, have greatly altered the appearance of the often-mentioned hills of Rome, especially
of the Quirinal, Viminal, and Esquiline.

Emerging from this too narrow passage-way and
proceeding a short distance, we enter that straight

Flaminian Road which has been replaced by the
modern Corso beginning at the Piazza Venezia. For
the first part of its course it was also known as
"Broadway." We are now in that more open part of
Rome which lies outside the ancient wall, and which
is commonly spoken of loosely as the Campus Martius.
Here again, it is impossible to inspect all the various
sights visible in the year 64. A few examples must
suffice. As you walk along this straight thoroughfare — the commencement of the road which would
eventually carry you to the North of Italy — you will
find but few buildings of any note on your right.
Lying to your left is a long and wide cloistered space
which contains not only certain public offices and a
pillared promenade, but also the richest shops in
Rome, where are sold gold and silver work, objects of
art, tapestries, and fine fabrics from Alexandria, Syria,
and farther East. The place is, in fact, mainly a huge
bazaar. Up the Flaminian Way beyond this enclosure
we go under a triumphal arch erected by the late
Emperor Claudius to record his conquest of Britain,
where he subdued "eleven kings" without Roman loss.
Keeping straight on we pass, this time on our right,
another large enclosure surrounded by arcades, where
is now the east side of the Piazza Colonna. In and
about this locality are carried on not only promenades
and saunterings but also various athletic exercises,
including feats of horsemanship. Farther on still,
and you will see to your left the Mausoleum of
Augustus, rising some 220 feet into the air. Its base,
coated with sculptured marble, contains one grand

sepulchral chamber for Augustus himself, and fourteen
smaller chambers for members of his family. Above
this base towers a conical mound of earth planted
with evergreen trees, and on the summit is a colossal
statue of the first emperor. Close by is a paved
space, where the bodies of the Caesars are cremated
before their ashes are placed in the Mausoleum.
From this spot a ready faith saw their immortal
part carried up to heaven by the eagle, messenger
of Jove.

Turning back and passing across the Campus we
arrive at the public baths erected by Nero, and then
at the Pantheon. This building, though shorn of many
of its decorative splendours both within and without, still stands structurally intact, at least as it was
restored and enlarged two generations later than our
date. It is scarcely possible to say how far its shape
was altered at its restoration under Hadrian, but we
may provisionally treat the edifice as already belonging to our period. It is still, after all these centuries,
an entirely noble pile, and forms a fit receptacle for
the tomb, not only of Victor Emanuel, but of Raphael.
Its form is that of a rotunda, with walls of concrete
20 feet in thickness and with a dome of concrete cast
in a solid mass. The middle of the dome is open to
the sky, and by that means the building is lighted in
a manner most perfectly suited to it. Could we
behold it fully restored and at its best, we should see
above its portico, which is supported by huge marble
pillars each made of a single stone, large bronze reliefs
of gods and giants. To one side of the doors would be

a colossal statue of Augustus; on the other a colossal
statue of the builder Agrippa, the son-in-law of that
emperor. Inside there is a series of niches for colossal
effigies of Mars, Venus, and other deities connected
with the Julian family. The marble pillars dividing
the niches have capitals of fine bronze, and the
coffered ceiling of the dome, now bare and colourless,
shines with gilt on blue, like the sky lit up with stars.
The doors, which have mysteriously remained entire,
are also of noble bronze; the roof consists of tiles
of bronze thinly plated with gold. The gold has
naturally vanished, after passing into Saracen hands;
of the bronze nearly half a million pounds weight has
been stripped from the building, some to make cannon
for the defence of the Castle of St. Angelo, some to
form the twisted columns which now support the
giant baldacchino under St. Peter's dome.

At a short distance behind this magnificent temple
Agrippa — who was in charge of the aqueducts and
water-supply — had also built the first great public
baths. It would probably be incorrect to found any
detailed description of them upon what we know of
the stupendous structures of Caracalla and Diocletian,
which were perhaps the most amazing exhibitions of
public luxury ever seen in the world. Of these we
know how huge and splendid were the halls, with their
coloured marbles, their mosaic floors, their colossal
masterpieces of statuary, their elaborate arrangements
of baths — cold, tepid, hot and dry-sweating — their
conversation-rooms and reading-rooms. But we cannot pretend to say how far the Agrippan and

Neronian baths of the year 64 corresponded in magnificence to these. We shall be safer in simply assuming that, since the baths of Pompeii were in full swing in the year in question, Rome must have possessed establishments of a similar kind but on a larger and more sumptuous scale.

Leaving without further mention the various temples of Minerva, Isis, Serapis, and other deities which might be found about the Campus Martius, we note an undistinguished stone amphitheatre, the only resort of the kind as yet possessed by the metropolis. In this were exhibited the sanguinary combats of gladiators with each other, and the fights with wild beasts performed by trained professionals or by criminals selling their lives as dearly as possible. Of these "sports" we have to treat in a later chapter. Coming nearer to the Tiber, while returning towards the city proper, we pass in succession the three great theatres, lofty semicircular constructions of stone and concrete faced with marble, one computed to hold 40,000 spectators, but probably accommodating not more than 25,000, and the others some 20,000 and 12,000 respectively. In these matters we must allow both for Roman exaggeration and Roman close-packing. The theatres rise in three stories, of which the outward sides consist of open arcades adorned with pillars in varied styles, while round their bases are shops for the sale of sweetmeats, beverages, perfumes, and other articles which the theatre-goer or the loitering public may require. What a theatrical performance was like is a matter belonging to the

question of spectacles and amusements.   At the back
of the largest theatre — that of Pompey — lies a large
square surrounded by colonnades of a hundred pillars,

FIG. 24. — EXTERIOR OF THEATRE OF MARCELLUS.   (Present state.)

where sycamores form avenues and fountains play,
while statues of finished workmanship stand where
they produce the best effect.   Particularly grateful to
the Roman lounger were the seats in the large semi-

circular bays, so placed as to offer full protection from
too hot a sun or too cold a wind.

FIG. 25. — THEATRE OF MARCELLUS. (Restored.)

By the time that we have passed the last theatre
of the three we have arrived at the river end of
the low valley leading into the Forum between the
Capitoline Hill and the Palatine, a place which had
once been a cattle-market but had now become an

open place surrounded by dwellings of the humbler sort. It still, however, bore the name of "Cattle-Market." If from this point we followed the river bank, we should come to the wharves, to which the

FIG. 26.—A GREEK EXEDRA. (Baumeister.)

smaller ships bring up the Tiber the freights of grain transhipped from the larger vessels from Alexandria or Carthage, or of marble from the quarries of Numidia, Greece, and Phrygia, or of granite and porphyry from Upper Egypt. All along this bank are the offices and storehouses of such cargoes, and

Fig. 27.—Circus Maximus (restored) ; Imperial Palaces on Palatine to left.

here too is performed much of the shaping of those blocks which Rome is using in such astonishing profusion. Along the river by the stone embankment the ships are moored, with their cables passed through huge stone corbels or sculptured lions' mouths. No busier part of Rome could be found than this, but we have no time to proceed further in this direction.

In front of us rises the Aventine Hill, another quarter of the wealthy, but otherwise chiefly distinguished by its temples of Juno the Queen and of Diana. Turning our eyes from the Aventine to the left we see lying in the valley between Aventine and Palatine — where now are the Jewish Cemetery and the grimy Gasworks — the vast Circus Maximus or Hippodrome. This structure, devoted chiefly to chariot-racing, is some 700 yards in length and 135 in width, and will at a pinch hold nearly a quarter of a million spectators. In all probability it would seat 150,000. It consists, as the illustration will show, of long tiers of seats sweeping down the sides and round the curved end of an oblong space. As with the theatres, its outside view presents three tiers of marble arches, and through the lowest tier are numerous staircases leading to the various sections of the seats within. Those seats themselves are laid upon large vaults of concrete; the lower rows are of marble, the upper ones are as yet of wood. How the chariot-races were run, and what is meant by the "sports of the circus," will naturally require a separate narration.

Coming back from the entrance of this mammoth

place of amusement and turning up the Velabrum Valley, we pass by a temple of Augustus, to which is attached a public library, and issue by the temple of Castor into the Forum to our first standing-point at F.

K

CHAPTER VIII

STREETS, WATER-SUPPLY, AND BUILDING MATERIAL

AFTER this rapid walk through the more interesting parts of the capital, we may consider one or two connected topics of natural interest.

Amid all this splendour and spaciousness of public buildings, what is the aspect of the ordinary streets? In this respect Rome was by no means fortunate. As in Old London, Old Paris, or Old New York, the streets had for the most part grown up as chance circumstances would have it. There were very few thoroughfares laid out straight from the first like the Flaminian or "Broad" Road. Alexandria and Antioch were the creations of monarchs who began with a clear field and a consistent scheme. Their straight, broad streets might well be the envy of the capital. The Romans, then as now, possessed the engineering genius, but they could not well undo the work of a struggling past, which had necessitated the crowding of population within the defences of a wall. They knew how to supply the city abundantly with water, and how to drain it with sewers of great capacity and strength. The chief of such sewers — the Cloaca Maxima —

which passed underneath the Forum to the Tiber
and was laid down more than twenty-five centuries
ago, is still in working order. But no republican
or imperial government ever took it in hand to
Hausmannise the city, even after one of those dev-
astating conflagrations which might seem to have
cleared the way. It is true that all traffic of vehicles,
except for special processions, for Vestal Virgins,
and a few other cases — was forbidden for ten hours
in the day. All through the morning and afternoon
there were no wheels in the Roman streets, unless
some public building imperatively demanded its load
of stones or timber, or unless the few privileged
persons were proceeding in their carriages to some
festival. Neverthelesss the rich men and women in
their litters or sedan-chairs, attended by their servants or their clients; the porters carrying their heavy
loads; the itinerant hucksters; and the ordinary
man on errand or other business bent, made up
crowds which were often difficult to pass through.

Another consequence of the old compression within
narrow walls was that, as population increased, the
houses grew more lofty. How high the Romans built,
or were allowed to build, in republican times we
cannot tell. The tendency was certainly to build
higher and higher, and sky-scrapers would perhaps
have become the rule if the ancient Roman had understood the use of materials both sufficiently light
and sufficiently strong, or if he had been forced to
establish his work on secure foundations. In point
of fact there had been, and there continued to

be, too much of jerry-building. Houses sometimes collapsed, and many were unsubstantially shored up. A flood or an earthquake was apt to find them out, and there was frequent peril in the streets. The majority of the abodes of people of humble means were not like those in smaller towns, such as Pompeii, still less like those in the country. They were "tenement houses," large blocks let out in rooms and flats, and it was natural that landlords should make haste to run them up and to increase the number of their stories. When Augustus became emperor he enacted what may be called a Metropolitan Building Act, which insisted on firmer foundations and limited the height to 70 feet. That act was apparently still in force in the age of Nero, and we may take it that along the more frequented streets the houses commonly ran to a height of four or five stories. They looked the taller because of the narrowness of the street itself. While it is perhaps, though not necessarily, an exaggeration for the epigrammatist —who lived "up three pair of stairs, and high ones" — to say that he could touch his opposite neighbour with his hand, it is at least an indication of the truth. Some of the narrower lanes between blocks cannot have been more than a few feet across.

Nor does it appear that the occupants of rooms opening on the streets were very particular as to what they threw out in the way of rubbish or dirty water. It is true that there were aediles, or officers to look after the order of the streets and public places,

but their efforts seem to have been mainly directed
to preventing conspicuous obstruction. Practices
which we should regard as heinous were treated
lightly or disregarded. To make matters worse, the
shopkeepers, who occupied the lower fronts of most
of such houses, took the greatest liberties in en-
croaching upon the roadway when exhibiting their
wares, and it was not till twenty years later than
our date that the Emperor Domitian ordered them
to keep within their own thresholds.

Apart from the question of the freedom of traffic,
it can be readily imagined that, with all the wooden
counters, doors, and shutters down below, and with
the disproportionate quantity of woodwork in the
beams, floors, and even walls above, fires were of the
commonest occurrence, and, with streets so high and
narrow, the conflagration of a whole quarter of the
town was speedy and complete. Augustus had
divided the metropolitan area into fourteen regions,
and had distributed over these a force of 7000 watchmen to keep the peace and to deal with fires at
night; but it was not to be expected, if a fire
occurred in a lofty block, that this body, assisted or
hampered by the neighbours, could do much with
the buckets, siphons, and wet blankets which formed
the extinguishing apparatus of the time.

Another serious danger, or, when not danger,
at least discomfort, came from the trick which the
Tiber has always had of flooding the lower parts of
the city. Somewhat later than our date the river
was restrained by strong stone embankments, which

one had to descend by steps in order to reach the river at the ferries or other boats; but this must have been but inadequately achieved in the early period of the empire, and a severe flood might bring the houses in the Velabrum, for example, tumbling about the ears of their inhabitants.

On the whole the streets of Neronian Rome were neither very comfortable nor very safe to walk in. At night there was no lighting, except when, at some great festival, illuminations might be made by order of the emperor for a whole night or perhaps a series of nights. In ordinary times torches and lanterns must be provided by yourself, and even the 7000 watchmen scarcely gave you a full feeling of security. The precise arrangements made for scavenging are unknown, but presumably it was done by the public slaves under the supervision of the aediles. It is, however, easy to discover from contemporary complaints that the streets were often annoyingly wet and slimy.

One thing the ordinary Roman appears never to have minded, any more than it is minded at the present day. This was noise. There are studious men enough in ancient literature who complain that sleep or study is impossible in Rome. They exclaim upon the bawling of the hawkers, the canting songs of the beggars, the banging of hammers, the sing-song of schoolboys learning to read in the open-air verandahs or balconies which often served as schools, and the shouting in the baths. All night long there was the rattle of carts and the creaking of heavy waggons. But the average Roman cared, and still cares, very little for quiet or sleep, and no emperor attempted to check the annoyance. Perhaps he could devise no check. Perhaps he himself, being on the Palatine, and his counsellors, being in their own comparatively secluded houses on the hills, scarcely realised the full enormity of the nocturnal roar of Rome. In any case the fact of the noise is unquestionable. It was then very much as it is now if one tries to sleep in rooms in the Corso or the Via Babuino. The saying that "God made the country and man made the town" is met with in a Roman writer of the age of Augustus, and the noise is one factor in the difference.

The ancient Romans, we have said, were masters of practical engineering, and a chief glory of the city was its abundant supply of water. Apart from the Tiber and the natural springs, there were in the year 64 at least eight aqueducts bringing drinkable water into the city. It was the emperor's concern to see to this matter, as he did to the corn-supply, but in practice he appointed what he might call his Minister of Water-supply, and gave him liberal means to provide a large staff of engineers, surveyors, masons, pipe-layers, inspectors, and custodians. It is a common error to imagine that the Romans were ignorant of the simple hydraulic law that water will find its own level, and to suppose that their aqueducts were built in consequence of that ignorance. In point of fact they knew the law as well as we do. Their earlier aqueducts were conduits almost wholly underground; their later were all on arches. When they wished to carry water to a height within the city, up a water-tower to a distributing cistern, or to the top storey of a building, they did so by pipes, just as we should; but when they brought water from forty miles away they preferred to bring it in channels lined with impermeable cement and carried upon arches, which wound across the country according to the levels in order to avoid the excessive pressure of too steep a gradient. The reasons for their choice are simple enough. Their chief difficulty was in making pipes of iron of sufficient capacity. On the other hand, it was easy to construct a cemented channel in masonry of any size you desired. In the next place the water about Rome rapidly lays a calcareous deposit, and it is much easier to clear this from a readily accessible channel than from pipes buried in the ground. The pipes which the Romans commonly made were of lead, bronze, or wood. None of these could be made and cleared cheaply enough to serve for the volume of water required for household use, the baths, and the public fountains of Rome. Meanwhile slave labour was inexpensive, and the cost of building an aqueduct of any length was of little account to the Roman.

When the water reached the city it was conducted into settling and distributing reservoirs and its flow regulated. Thence it was carried by pipes, mostly of lead, wherever it was required. When Agrippa was minister of water-supply he constructed in the city 700 public pools or basins and 500 fountains, drawing their supply from 130 collecting heads or reservoirs. And it is to the credit of Agrippa and of Rome that all these pools, fountains, and reservoirs were made pleasant to the eye with suitable adornment. There is mention of 400 marble columns and 300 statues, but these are to be regarded as only chief among the embellishments.

The streets of Rome were commonly paved with blocks of lava quarried in the neighbourhood from the abundant deposits which had formed in a not very remote volcanic period.

The materials employed for substantial building were various; in the older days red and black tufa — a stone so soft as to require protection by a layer of stucco; later the dark-brown peperino, the golden-creamy travertine, marble white and coloured, and concrete. The modern visitor to Rome who regards the ruins but superficially would naturally imagine that many of the edifices were mainly constructed of brick. In reality there was no building so composed. The flat triangular bricks, or rather tiles, which are so much in evidence, are but inserted in the face of concrete to cover the nakedness of that material. Concrete alone might serve for cores and substructures, but those parts of the building which showed were required to present a more pleasing surface. At the date of Nero this might be achieved by a fronting of marble slabs and blocks, but more commonly it was obtained by means of the triangular red or yellow tiles above mentioned. In buildings of slightly earlier date the exterior often presented a "diamond pattern" or network arrangement of square pieces of stone inserted in the concrete while it was still soft. The huge vaults and arches affected by the Romans made concrete a particularly convenient material, and nothing could better illustrate its strength than the tenacity with which it has endured the strain in the unsupported portions of the vaults of the Basilica of Constantine. Any of the more imposing buildings which were not mainly of concrete were composed of blocks of stone, held to each other by clamps soldered in with lead. Few, if any, such buildings were made entirely of marble. In the case of those composed of the other varieties of stone already named, the surface was commonly coated either with stucco or with marble facings attached by hook-like clamps fixed into the main structure. Externally the appearance of Rome — so far as its public buildings are concerned — was that of a city of marble. The present appearance of the ruins is due to the marble facings having been for centuries torn away, either to be used elsewhere, or more often to be burned down for lime.

FIG. 28. — BUILDING MATERIALS.
(From Middleton.)

CHAPTER IX

THE ROMAN TOWN HOUSE

WE have taken a general survey of the city of Rome, its open places, streets, and public buildings. We may now look at the houses in which the Romans lived, and at the furniture to be expected inside them.

Mention has already been made of ·the large and lofty tenement houses or blocks, often mere human rookeries, which were let out in lodgings to those who did not possess sufficient means to occupy a separate domicile of their own. These buildings, which were naturally to be found in the busier streets and more thickly inhabited quarters, were not, however, the habitations most typical of the romanized world. They were created by the special circumstances of the city, and might recur in other towns wherever the conditions were similar. The cramped island part of Tyre, for example, possessed houses even loftier than those of Rome. Where there was sufficient room — that is to say, where there was no large population crowded into a space limited by nature or by walls of defence — the ordinary house was of a very different character. It was built on a different plan and

seldom ran to more than two stories, if so high. We
shall shortly proceed to describe such a house; but
it is first desirable to say something more of the
tenement "block" in the metropolis. It is to be
regretted that no such building has actually come
down to us; we are therefore compelled to form our
notions of one from the scattered references and hints
of literature. Nevertheless if these are read in the
light of customs still observable in Rome itself and
in other parts of Italy, the picture becomes fairly
definite.

A block — or "island," as it was called — might be
a building of four or five stories, surrounded by four
of the narrow streets, lanes, or alleys which formed a
network in the city. Whether managed by the landlord, by his agent, or by a tenant who sub-let at a
profit, it was divided into lodgings, which might
consist either of a single room or of a suite. Some
such rooms and flats were "ordinary," others were
described (as they are still in the advertisements of
modern Rome) as "suitable for a gentleman," or, to
use the exact language of the day, "suitable for a
knight." Access to the respective quarters of the
house was to be gained, not solely through a main
door, but by separate stairs leading up directly from
the streets and lanes. It would appear that each
tenant had his own key, corresponding, though hardly
in convenience of size, to our latch-key. Whereas it
will be found that the ordinary private house of one
storey was for the most part lighted by openings in
the roof and by wide courts, this arrangement could

manifestly be applied only partially to the tall tenement buildings. There might, it is true, exist in the middle interior of such a block an open space or "well," with galleries running round it at each floor, so that the inner rooms could obtain light from that quarter. It is also to be assumed that stairs ran up to these galleries, so that the inward rooms or flats were made accessible in this way. Mainly, however, the light came from windows opening on the street. If we glanced up at these from below we should find them narrower than ours at the present day — since we have discovered how to produce large and entirely diaphanous sheets of glass — but probably not narrower than those of a century ago. They were either mere openings with shutters, or, in the better houses, were glazed with transparent material. In the brighter part of the year they contained their boxes of flowering or other plants, and were often provided with a shade-awning not unlike those so familiar in Paris.

The roof of such a building was either gabled and covered with tiles or, though perhaps less often, it was flat. The flat roof sometimes formed a terrace, on which the plants of a "roof-garden" might be found growing either in earthenware tubs or in earth spread over a layer of impermeable cement. The lowest floor, level with the street, commonly consisted of shops, which were open at full length in the day, but were shuttered and barred at night. As with the shops which are now built into the sides of large hotels and the like, they had no communication with the interior of the building. Regularly, however, they possessed a short staircase at the back or side leading to an upper room or *entresol*, where, in the poorer instances, the shopkeeper might actually reside. To the aristocratic Roman, with his contempt of petty trade, "born in the shop-loft" was a contemptuous phrase for a "son of nobody."

Meanwhile the more representative houses of the strictly Roman part of the Roman world — that is to say, the dwellings of Romans or of imitators of Romans, wherever they might be settled, as distinct from the Greek and Oriental houses or from the various kinds of primitive huts to be found among the Western provincials — were of three chief kinds. These were the town house, the country seat, and the country homestead. There was, of course, nothing to prevent a wealthy Roman from building his town house exactly like a country seat, or *vice versa*, if he had so chosen, but from considerations of purpose, apart from those of local space and view, it would have been altogether irrational to take either course. The conditions of his life in town and country differed even more widely than they do with us. The average Roman, moreover, was a lover of variety in respect of his habitation. We find in a somewhat later epigrammatist that one grandee keeps up four town houses in Rome itself, and moves capriciously from one to the other, so that you never know where you will find him. At different seasons or in different moods he might prefer this or that situation or aspect. As for country seats of various degrees of

magnificence, a man might — like many modern nobles
or royalties — possess three, four, a dozen, or twenty.
He might, for example, own one or more on the
Italian Lakes, one in Tuscany, one on the Sabine or
Alban Hills, one on the coast within a half-day's run
of Rome, one on the Bay of Naples, one down in the
heel of Italy, and so on. Pliny the Younger, who was
born in the reign of Nero, was not a particularly rich
man, yet he owned several country seats on Lake
Como alone, besides others nearer to Rome on north
and south, at the seaside, or on the hills.

We may begin with a town house, and our simplest
procedure is to take a plan exhibiting those parts
which were most usual for an establishment of even
moderate pretensions. Let it be understood that
it is but the symmetrical outline of a general
scheme which was in practice submitted to indefinite
enlargement or modification. In the house of Livia,
the mother of Augustus, on the Palatine Hill at
Rome, and in various houses at Pompeii — such as
those of the Vettii, of "Sallust," of the "Faun,"
or of "The Tragic Poet" — there will be found
much diversity in the number and arrangement of
the rooms, halls, and courts. Nevertheless the main
principle of division, the general conception of the
portions requisite for their several purposes, was
practically the same. Some of the differences and
enlargements may be illustrated after we have considered our first simple outline. Before we undertake
this, however, it may be well to warn any one who

may have visited or be about to visit Pompeii, that
he must exclude from his thoughts all those small
premises of a room or two which face so many of the
streets. These were mostly shops, with which we
are not now dealing. He must also exclude all the
public edifices. This done, he must remember that
we now possess only portions of the walls without the
roofs, and that in such circumstances apartments
always appear to be much smaller than they are by
actual measurement, or than they appear when they
contain their furniture and appointments properly
disposed. Finally, he must not take a Pompeian
house, even the most spacious, as a fair example of
either the size or splendour of the great houses in the
metropolis. Pompeii was but a small place, with a
population of no great wealth or standing, and its
houses would have cut but a provincial figure among
those of the same date on the Aventine, Caelian,
Esquiline, or Quirinal Hills. Nevertheless they are
extremely useful to us in reconstructing the type. It
is that type and not the exception which we now
consider.

A town house might either be detached or it
might stand in a street, like one of the tenement-
blocks, with shops let into the less important parts
of the outer wall of the ground floor. Much would
naturally depend upon the means and dignity of the
owner. In any case the interior portions would
belong to the private residence. As a rule the
exterior of the ordinary house was little regarded.
No architecture was wasted upon it; decoration and

other magnificence belonged to the interior. Provided
a house possessed a more or less imposing doorway
its exterior walls might be left either to shops or to
a dull monochrome of stucco, pierced here and there,
if necessary, at 9 or 10 feet from the ground by
barred slits, which cannot be called windows, for the
admittance of light. The general principle of a
Roman house, as of a Greek, was that of rooms
surrounding spaces lighted from within. Privacy

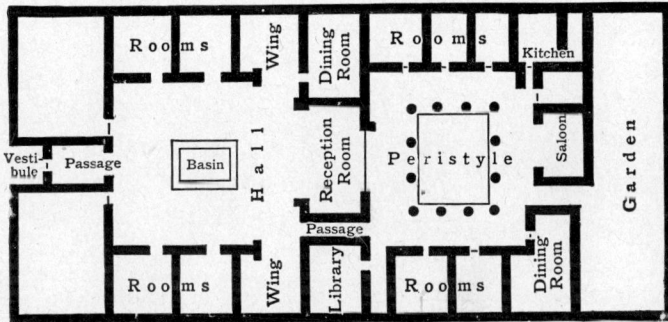

FIG. 29.—TYPICAL SCHEME OF ROMAN HOUSE.

from the outer world was not indeed so scrupulously
sought by the Romans as by the Athenians —
principally because of the more free position occupied
by the Roman women — nevertheless it was secured by
the absence of ground-floor windows opening on any
thoroughfare.

Before the actual door there was commonly an
open recess or space a little backward from the
street, in which callers could wait until the door was
opened. This was the "vestibule," and in the case of
the larger houses of the nobles it was often adorned

L

with honorary statues, on horseback or otherwise, while above the door might be seen the insignia of triumphs won by the family, a decoration in some measure corresponding to the modern hatchment, except that it was permanently fixed. This regularly remained as a mark of the house even when it changed owners. It was in such a vestibule of his Golden House that Nero erected his own colossal statue, destined afterwards to give its name to the Colosseum. Over the larger vestibules there might be a partial roof, but generally, and perhaps always at this date, they were without cover.

Facing you in the middle of the vestibule are double or folding doors, more or less ornate with bronze, ivory, and other work, and generally bearing a large ring or handle to serve either as a knocker or to pull the door to. Above them is a bronze grating or fretwork for further adornment and to admit light and air. Some householders, more superstitious or conventional than the rest, affected an inscription, such as "Let no evil enter here," and over some humbler entrance you might find a cage containing a parrot or magpie, which had been trained to say "Good luck to you" in Greek. At either side of the door, or of the actual entrance to the vestibule, is a column or pilaster, either made of timber and cased with other woods of a more beautiful and costly kind, or consisting of coloured marble with an ornate capital. These "doorposts" were wreathed with laurel or other foliage on festal occasions, such as when the occupant had won some distinguished honour in the field, in the courts, or at the elections, or when a marriage took place from within. At funerals small cypress trees or branches would be placed in and about the vestibule. At one side of it

FIG. 30.—ENTRANCE TO HOUSE OF PANSA. (Pompeii.)

you might sometimes find a smaller door, to be used for the ordinary going in and out when it was unnecessary or inconvenient for the larger doors to be opened.

The doors themselves turn, not upon hinges of the

modern kind, but upon pivots, which move, often too noisily, in sockets let into the threshold and lintel. The fastenings consisted of locks — often highly ingenious — of a bar laid across from wall to wall, of bolts shot across or upward and downward, and sometimes of a prop leaning against the inside of the door and entering a cavity in the floor of the passage. The floor of the entrance passage itself might be paved with marble tiles, or made simply of a polished cement with or without patterns worked in it; or it might consist of small cubes of stone, white and black or more variously coloured, frequently worked into figures, and now and then accompanied by an inscription just within the threshold, such as "Greeting" or "Beware the Dog." In one Pompeian house the floor bears the well-known mosaic likeness of a dog held upon its chain. At the side of the passage there is often a smaller room for the janitor. When there is none, he must be supposed to have used a movable seat.

Passing through the passage, you find yourself in a rectangular hall, upon which was lavished the chief display in the way of loftiness and decoration. In the middle of the ceiling is an open space, square or oblong, to which the tiles of the gabled roof converge from above, and in the middle of the floor beneath is a corresponding basin, edged and paved with coloured or plain marble. The basin is of no great depth, and contains the water which has been poured into it from the ornamental pipe-mouths of bronze or terra-cotta pro-

jecting, like gargoyles, from the edge of the opening
above. Sometimes the basin contained a fountain.
There is of course an outlet pipe for the surplus
water, but some of that overflow often ran into a
covered cistern, over which you would find a small
circular well-mouth, ornamented with sculptured
reliefs. The opening in the ceiling may be formed
simply by the space between the four cross-beams, or
it may be supported by a pillar — of marble or of brick
cased with marble — at each corner, or it may rest upon
a greater number of such pillars. It is this opening
which lets in the light and air to the hall, and it
should always be remembered that the Italian house
had more occasion to seek coolness and freshness
than warmth. On a day of glaring sunshine and
heat it was always possible to spread under the
opening an awning or curtain of purple or other
colour, of which the reflected hues meanwhile lent a
richness to the space below. If we take one of the
finer houses, we shall see, in glancing at the ceiling
which covers the rest of the hall, that it is divided
into sunken panels or coffers, which are adorned with
reliefs in stucco and are painted, or else are decorated
with copper, gold or ivory. The height may be
whatever the owner wishes, but perhaps 25 feet would
be a modest average estimate. The floor in such a
house will generally consist of slabs of marble or of
marble tiles arranged in patterns. In houses of less
show it may be made of the same materials as those
described for the entrance passage. To right and left
are various chambers, shut off by lofty doors or by

portières or both. To these light is admitted from
their doors and the gratings over them, from the high
window-slits already mentioned in the outer wall, or
sometimes, when there is no upper storey, from sky-
lights. And here let it be observed that the notion
that the Romans of this date used very little glass
is altogether erroneous, as the discoveries at Pompeii
and elsewhere sufficiently prove.

The walls of the hall are in the better instances
either coated with panels of tinted marble, or parcelled
out in bright bands or oblongs of paint, or decorated
with pictures of mythological, architectural, and
other subjects worked in bright colours upon darkened
stucco. To our own taste these colours — red, yellow,
bluish-green, and others — as seen at Pompeii, are
often excessively crude and badly harmonised. But
while it is true that the ancients appear to have been
actually somewhat deficient in colour-sense, it must
be borne in mind that many of the Pompeian houses
were decorated by journeymen rather than by artists,
and, above all, full allowance must be made for the
comparatively subdued light in which most of the
paintings would be seen. The hall might also contain
statuary placed against the walls or against the
supporting pillars, where these existed. At the
farther end from the entrance you will perceive to
right and left two large recesses or bays, generally
with pilasters on either side. These "wings" were
utilised for a variety of purposes. One of them
might occasionally serve for a smaller dining-room,
or it might hold presses and cupboards. In noble

Fig. 31.—Interior of Roman House. (Looking from Reception-hall to Peristyle.)

houses one of them would contain certain family
possessions of which the occupants were especially
proud. These were the effigies of distinguished ancestors, which served as a family-tree represented in
a highly objective form. At our chosen date there
would be a series of portrait busts or else of portrait
medallions, in relief or painted, while in special
receptacles, labelled underneath with name and rank,
were kept life-like wax masks of the line of distinguished persons, which could be brought out and
carried in procession at the funeral of a member of
the family. Though there was no "College of Heralds"
in antiquity, it was commonly quite possible for a
wealthy *parvenu* to get a pedigree invented for him.
It is true that by use and wont the "right of effigies"
was confined to those families which had held the
higher offices of state, but there was no specific law
on the subject, and the Roman *nouveau riche* could
act exactly like his modern representative in securing
his "portraits of ancestors."

Having thus glanced to right and left, to the ceiling and the floor, we now look at the end of the
hall facing us. The middle section of this is open,
and is framed by a couple of high pillars or pilasters
and a cornice, which together formed perhaps the
most distinguishing feature of this part of the house.
Between the pillars is an apartment which may or
may not be raised a step or two above the level of
the hall. This, unlike the hall itself, is of the nature
of a sitting-room, reception-room, or "parlour" (in
the old sense of that word), and contains appropriate

furniture. In it the master receives a guest, inter-
views his clients, makes up his accounts, and transacts
such other private business as may fall to his lot. At
the back it may be entirely closed, or it may contain
a large window, through which we can catch a vista
of the colonnaded and planted court beyond. The

FIG. 32.—HOUSE OF CORNELIUS RUFUS. (Pompeii.)

floor may here consist of a large carpet-like mosaic,
such as that famous piece, taken from the House of
the Faun at Pompeii and now in the Naples Museum,
which represents a battle between Alexander and the
Persians. To one side of the entrance to this
"parlour" there will often stand on a pedestal the
bust of the owner, as "Genius of the home." On the

other side there is a passage serving as the means of
access to the second or inner division of the house.

On making our way through this passage we find
ourselves in a space still more open than the hall.   It

FIG. 33.—PERISTYLE WITH GARDEN AND AL FRESCO DINING-TABLE.

is commonly an unroofed, quadrangular court surrounded by a roofed colonnade, and thence known as
the "peristyle." Or the colonnade may extend only
round three sides, the back being free to the garden.
In the uncovered space lying between the rows of
pillars there are ornamental shrubs and flowers,

marble tables, a cistern of water containing goldfish, a fountain, and marble basins into which fresh water is spouted from bronze or marble statuettes, from figures of animals, or from masks. Under the colonnade are marble floors or other more or less rich pavements,

FIG. 34. — PERISTYLE IN HOUSE OF THE VETTII. (Present state.)

decorated walls, and such works of art as the owner most affects.

When it seems desirable for shade and coolness, coloured curtains or awnings may be suspended between the columns, so that one can sit or walk with comfort under the cloistered portion. At the sides are apartments for different purposes. At the far end, or elsewhere, there is regularly the largest dining-room, often with mosaic floor and generally with pictured walls. Whereabouts in the house the family or an

invited party should dine would depend partly on the
number to be present, partly on the season of the
year, and partly on some passing inclination. A
house of any pretensions would possess several rooms
used, or capable of being used, for this purpose.
Some dining-rooms had what we should call French
windows on three sides, permitting the diners to
enjoy the view of the garden or the shrubbery outside.

Other large and airy apartments or saloons off
the peristyle were used for social conversation, or
as drawing-rooms. Farther back still, approached
by another passage or door, there was often to be
found a garden, containing an arbour or a terrace
covered with a trailing vine, of the kind known in
modern Italy as a *pergola*. In suitable weather *al
fresco* meals were often taken here, and occasionally
there were fixed couches and tables of masonry always
ready for that purpose.

Coming back from the garden into the court, we
might explore other passages, leading to the kitchen or
to the bathrooms of hot, warm, and cold water. These
offices would be respectively situated wherever circumstances made them most convenient. In the kitchen
the part corresponding to our "range" consisted of a
flat structure of masonry, on which the fire was lighted.
The cooking pots were placed either upon ridges of
masonry running across the fire or upon three legged
stands of iron. The accompanying illustrations will
sufficiently show what is meant. The bedrooms, little
better than cells, of the slaves, and also the store-

rooms, were variously distributed. Underground cellars were apparently exceptional, although examples may be seen at Pompeii.

Somewhere in one of the bays of the hall, at the

Fig. 35.—Kitchen Hearth in the House of the Vettii.

back of the peristyle court, or elsewhere, would be found a small shrine for the worship of the domestic gods. This was variously constructed. Sometimes it was a niche or recess containing paintings or little effigies and with an altar or altar-shelf beneath, sometimes a miniature temple erected against the wall. There was apparently no special place to which,

Fig. 36.—Kitchen Hearths (Drawing).

rather than any other, it was to be assigned. To the nature and meaning of the household gods we may refer again when dealing with the general subject of religion.

In the homes of persons of culture there would also be included a library and, perhaps less regularly, a picture-gallery. The library, which sometimes comprised thousands of rolls, would be a room not only

FIG. 37.— SHRINE (IN BACKGROUND) IN HOUSE OF THE TRAGIC POET.

surrounded by large pigeon-holes or open cupboards containing the round boxes for the parchment rolls, but also traversed by lower partitions provided on either side with similar shelves. About the room, over or by the shelves, stand portrait busts or medallions of great authors, both Greek and Roman, the "blind" Homer being represented in traditional

form, but the majority, from Aeschylus and Thucydides down to Virgil and Livy, being authentic
and excellent likenesses. In the picture-gallery would
be found paintings either done upon the stucco walls
in a frame-like setting or upon panels of wood attached

FIG. 38. — HOUSEHOLD SHRINE.

to the walls, very much as we hang our modern
pictures.

It was scarcely ever the case that a second storey
— where one existed at all — extended over the whole
house. If upper rooms were used, they were placed
over those parts where they would interfere least

with the light, the comfort, and the appearance of the ground-floor arrangements. The stairs leading to them were variously disposed and as little as possible in evidence. In such upper apartments there was naturally not the same risk from the curious or the burglar as in the case of the lower, and windows of perhaps 4 by 2½ feet were therefore freely employed. In some instances, though we cannot tell how frequently, the second storey projected on strong beams over the street, as in the example at Pompeii known as the "House of the Hanging Balcony."

It remains to make brief observations upon one or two matters interesting to any practical householder. These are the questions of water-supply, drainage, warming, and roofing.

In respect of water there was no difficulty. It was brought in the ordinary way, from those reservoirs which formed the ends of the aqueducts or conduits, by means of pipes, mostly made of lead, though sometimes of bronze. These were conducted to the points where they were required, and there the flow was manipulated by means of taps and plugs. In order to make a water-pipe, a sheet of lead or bronze was rolled into a cylinder, the joining of the two edges taking the shape of a raised ridge, which was soldered. One end of a section was squeezed or narrowed so that it might be inserted into the widened end of the next. Lead pipes of no inconsiderable size, stamped with the name of the owner, are to be seen preserved in the Palatine House of Livia, and a number of

smaller ones remain at Pompeii. For drainage there
were the sewers, and also pipes to carry the less

FIG. 38 A.—LEADEN PIPES IN HOUSE OF LIVIA. (Palatine.)

offensive overflow of water into the street channels,
which in their turn led into underground drains.

FIG. 39.—PORTABLE BRAZIERS.

For the warming of a house the Romans not only
employed portable braziers with charcoal for fuel, but

M

in the larger establishments there existed a system of
"central" heating, by which hot air was conducted
from a furnace in the basement through flues running
beneath the floor and up through the walls, where its
effect might be regulated by adjustable openings or
registers. The only fixed fire-place in a town house
was in the kitchen. From this the smoke was carried
off by a flue, constituting to all intents and purposes a

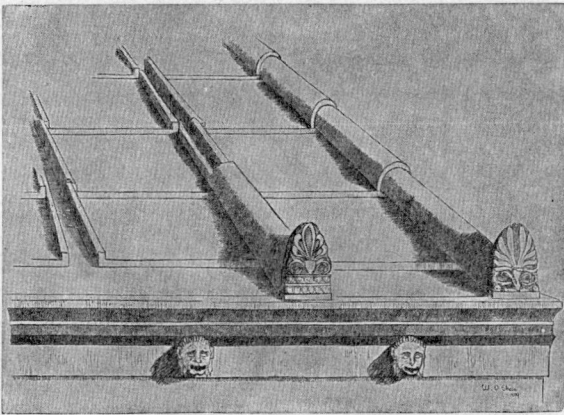

FIG. 40. — MANNER OF ROOFING WITH TILES.

chimney. The belief that the Romans were un-
acquainted with such things as chimneys has been
proved to be untrue.

The roofing, when constructed, as it most frequently
was, in a gabled form, consisted of terra-cotta tiles
arranged on a regular system. First came the flat
layers, each higher row overlapping the lower. The
descending edges of a row of these flat plates, as they
lay side by side, were turned up into a kind of flange
of about $2\frac{1}{4}$ inches in height, so that at the points of

contact a ridge was formed down the roof. Over this line was laid a series of other tiles shaped into a half-cylinder, the lower end of each tile overlapping the next. By this means the rain was prevented from penetrating the crevice between the flanges. At the bottom, above the eaves, the line of semicircular tiles ended in a flower-like or mask-like ornament, which broke the monotony of the horizontal edge of the roof.

After this description of what may be considered a representative Roman house, it is necessary to repeat that it is but typical. Many were considerably smaller, containing, for example, no peristyle. Many on the contrary were far more spacious and sumptuous, possessing more than one hall and more than one peristyle, and varying the nature as well as the number and position of those portions of the house. In exceptional cases the hall had no opening in the ceiling and therefore no basin below, but was covered with a simple gabled roof which shed the rain-water into the street. In exceptional cases also there was no "parlour" of the kind described a little while ago. The situation of the house, enlargements made after the main part was built, the joining of two houses into one, or other causes, often modified the rectangular and symmetrical appearance presented in the plan hitherto given. Such modifications are, however, better illustrated by a comparison of the plans of two well-known Pompeian houses than by any amount of verbal description. The first is that

of Pansa, which forms the main portion of a whole
block, smaller dwellings and shops unconnected with
the Pansa establishment being built round and into
it at various points. The arrangements of this house
closely approach the normal or simple type described
in this chapter. The second is the famous house of

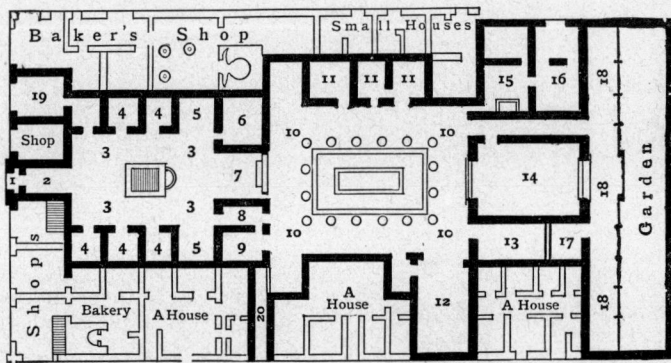

FIG. 41.—HOUSE OF PANSA AT POMPEII.

The parts within the dark lines belong to the one house; the rest are
other houses and shops built into the block.

1. Vestibule.	6. Dining-Room.	11. Rooms.	16. Carriage Room.
2. Passage.	7. Parlour.	12. Dining-Room.	17. Boudoir.
3. Hall.	8. Passage.	13. Winter Dining-Room.	18. Portico.
4. Rooms.	9. Library ?	14. Saloon (Drawing-Room).	19. Saleroom.
5. Wings.	10. Peristyle.	15. Kitchen.	20. Passage to Side Door.

the Vettii, which departs somewhat freely from the
customary disposition of apartments.

It would be tempting to indulge in rhetoric and
to dwell upon the magnificence of some of the more
luxurious houses of the wealthy Romans; to describe
their ostentation of rich marbles in pillar, wall, or
floor — the white marbles of Carrara, Paros, and
Hymettus; the Phrygian marble or "pavonazzetto"

with its streakings of crimson or violet; the orange-golden glow of the Numidian stone of "giallo antico"; the Carystian marble or "cipollino" with its onion-like layers of white and pale-green; the serpentine variety from Laconia, and the porphyry from Egypt. We might descant upon the lavish wall-paintings, representing landscapes real and imaginary, scenes

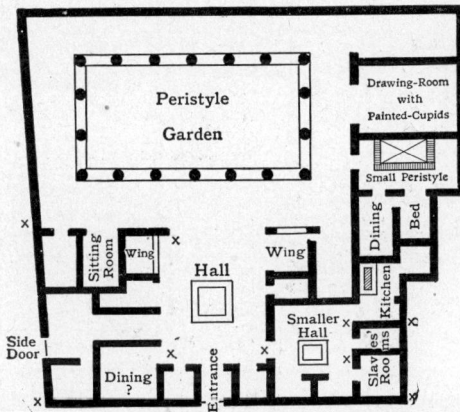

FIG. 42.—HOUSE OF THE VETTII AT POMPEII.

A second storey extended over the corners and front parts included under the nine small crosses.

from mythology and semi-history, floating figures, genre pictures, and pictures of still life; or upon the mosaics in floor and wall depicting similar subjects and often serving to the occupants not so much in the place of pictorial art as in the place of wall-papers and of Brussels or Kidderminster carpets. We might speak of the profuse collections of statuary, of the gilding on ceiling and cornices, of the colours shed by the rich curtains and awnings

of purple and crimson, of the grateful sound of water
plashing in the fountains and basins or babbling

FIG. 43.—SPECIMEN OF PAINTED ROOM.

over a series of steps like a broken cascade in
miniature. But perhaps too much of such description
might only encourage still further the erroneous

notion that the Roman houses were all of this
nature, and that even the average Roman lived in
the midst of an abundance of such domestic luxury
and art. It requires but a little sober thought to
realise that such homes were, as they have always
been, the exception. It would be as reasonable to
judge of an average London house by the most
opulent specimens in Park Lane, or of an American
house by the richest at Newport, as to judge of
the abodes of Romans in the time of Nero by the
examples which appeal so strongly to the novelist
or the romancing historian. Suffice it that beside
the modest and frugal homes, the tenement flat, and
the hovel, there were houses distinguished by immense
luxury; and, since Romans have at all times sought
the ostentatious and grandiose, perhaps such dwellings were larger and more pretentious in proportion
to wealth than they are in most civilised countries
at the present day. Seneca, who made himself
extremely comfortable in the days of Nero, exclaims
upon the rage for costly decoration. Says he of the
bathing of the plutocrat: "He seems to himself poor
and mean, unless the walls shine with great costly
slabs, unless marbles of Alexandria are picked out
with reliefs of Numidian stone, unless the whole
ceiling is elaborately worked with all the variety
of a painting, unless Thasian stone encloses the
swimming baths, unless the water is poured out
from silver taps." These, indeed, are comparatively
humble. "What of the baths of the freedmen?
What a mass of statues! What a multitude of

pillars supporting nothing, but put there only for ornament ! What an amount of water running over steps with a purling noise — and all for show !"

FIG. 44.—SPECIMEN OF WALL-PAINTING.   (Pompeii.)

CHAPTER X

THROUGHOUT the romanized parts of the empire —
in other words, wherever Romans settled, in Italy,
Spain, Gaul, Britain, and also wherever the richer
natives imitated the Roman fashions — the house in
any city or considerable town was built as nearly as
possible after the type described.

In the country the poor naturally had their much
simpler cottages and cabins of a room or two,
commonly thatched or shingled, knowing nothing
of hall and court and all these arrangements of art
and luxury. In the case of the more well-to-do
country people of Italy — the larger farmers, wine-
growers, olive-growers, and the like — the homestead
was of a kind which made for simplicity and comfort.
It was in such homes that one would find the most
wholesome life and the soundest moral fibre of the
time.

Normally the homestead would be a large, and
often a rambling, building of one storey, except
where a tower served as a store-room for the mellowing wine or a loft for the mellowing fruit. When

we read in Horace about the liberal stack of wood
to be kept in readiness near the hearth, and about
the wine-jar drinking in the smoke in the store-room,
we must think of his country homestead on the
Sabine Hills, not of a house in Rome, for at Rome
there was no blazing hearth to sit round and no
smoky tower-loft for the ripening of the Caecuban.

You enter an open court or yard, round the sides
of which may run the stalls of the horses and oxen
of the farm, the tool-rooms, the lofts of hay and
corn, the quarters of the labourers—herdsmen, ploughmen, vine-dressers — and the great farm-kitchen. It
is in this kitchen that you will find the bright hearth
in winter-time, where all the members of the homestead gather round the fire. It is here that they
then all eat, and in it the women of the establishment
perform their work, spinning and weaving and mend-
ing. Off from the court will be situated the wine-
press, or the olive-press, the granaries, the fruit
mellowing on mats, and the various rooms or bins
where wine is fermented and stored, or where the
olive-oil is treated and stocked. Commonly a more
retired court will contain the private rooms of the
owner, and somewhere in the homestead will be
found the fowl-yard, with its hens, ducks, geese, and
guinea-fowl, the sties, and the preserves for various
toothsome animals, including perhaps dormice and
snails.

Frequently a Roman of the city affected a country
house of this character, to which he would flee during
the tyrannous reign of the Dogstar or the Lion — in

other words, during that hot season of the year which
requires no description for those who have been so

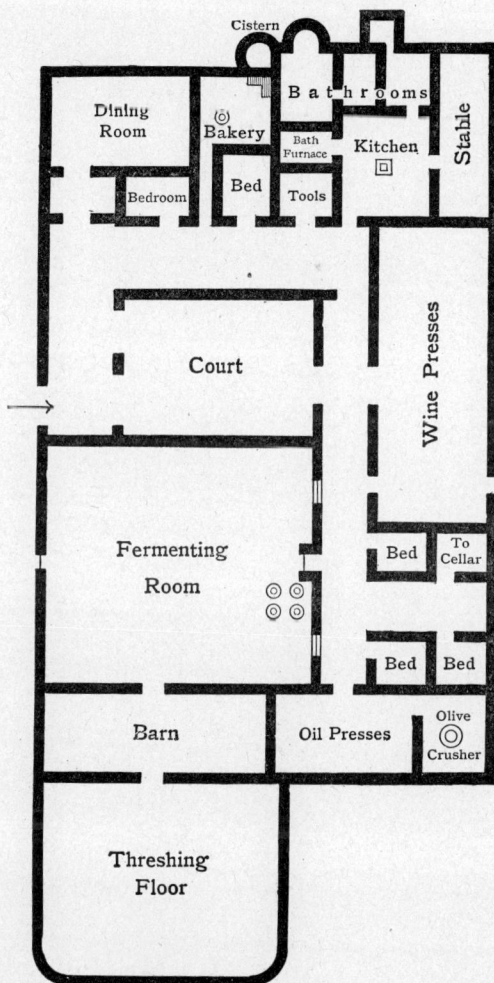

FIG. 45. — PLAN OF HOMESTEAD AT BOSCOREALE.

ill-advised as to sojourn in Rome in July, August,
and early September. Many of his town slaves he

would take with him, and what was a holiday for
him was also a holiday for them. His rural homestead would possess great charm for the quieter type
of man who had no real love for the pomps and shows,
the rattle and tumult, of the city. The vision of
wholesome country-produce — of fresh milk and eggs
and vegetables, and of tender poultry — is one which
still attracts our city-folk. But the vision, then as
now, was often subject to disillusion. Complaints
are many that you had to feed the homestead
in place of it feeding you, and when Martial has
given a pleasant picture of a family reaching the
gate of Rome with a coachful of the typical produce
of the country, he ends by suddenly letting you
know that they are not coming in from their country
house but are going out to it. The complaint of
the English seaside town that there will be no fish
"till the train comes in from London," is thus a
sufficiently old one. Yet the same Martial supplies
another picture, painted with such zest of frank
enjoyment that we are at once convinced of its
truth. Some portions of it perhaps admit of translation in the following terms : —

> Our friend Fundanus' Baian seat,
> My Bassus, is no pleasance neat,
> Where myrtles trim in idle lines,
> Clipped box, and planes unwed to vines
> Rob of right use the acres wide :
> 'Tis farm-life true and countryfied.
> In every corner grain is stacked,
> Old wines in fragrant jars are packed :
> About the farmyard gabbling gander
> And spangled peacock freely wander :

With pheasant and flamingo prowl
Partridge and speckled guinea-fowl:
Pigeon and waxen turtle-dove
Rustle their wings in cotes above.
The farm-wife's apron draws a rout
Of greedy porkers round about;
And eagerly the tender lamb
Waits the filled udder of its dam.
With plenteous logs the hearth is bright,
The household Gods glow in the light,
And baby slaves are sprawling round.
No town-bred idlers here are found:
No cellarer grows pale with sloth,
No trainer wastes his oil, but both
Go forth afield and subtly plan
To snare the greedy ortolan.
Meanwhile the garden rings with mirth,
While townfolk dig the yielding earth:
No need for the page-master's voice;
The saucy long-haired boys rejoice
To do the manager's commands.
At morn 'tis not with empty hands
The country pays its call, but some
Bring honey in its native comb,
Or cones of cheese; some think as good
A sleepy dormouse from the wood;
And honest tenants' big girls bring
Baskets with "mother's offering."

The visit to the country in the season of the "mad star" and the scirocco was as necessary to the ancient Roman as is his *villeggiatura* to the modern. But there were other seasons when he fled from town. If in the heat of summer he sought the hills, in the colder months he might seek the south of Italy, and in the spring or autumn the seaside at various points from the mouth of the Tiber to southward of Salerno. He might run away from inconvenient business or

ceremonies, or through a mere desire to get rest or
sleep or change. He might wish, as Cicero and Pliny
did, to get away from the "games" and to study and
write in quiet. He might fancy that his health called
for baths in the hot springs on the Bay of Naples,
or for sea-bathing somewhere on the Latian or
Campanian coasts. To put it briefly, he was very
much like our worried, bilious, or exhausted selves.
His life of ceremony was a hard one, and often he
ate and drank too much. But whereas nowadays
we can make free choice of any agreeable spot, since
every such spot possesses its "Grand Hotel" or
"Hôtel Superbe," where we can always find the
crowd and discomfort which we pretend to be escaping,
the Roman idea was different. It corresponded more
to that of our English nobles, who, in Elizabethan or
Queen Anne days or later, built themselves country
seats, one, two, or more, indulging in architectural
fancies and surrounding all with spacious gardens,
ponds, and rockeries. The Roman man of wealth
created no hotels. He dotted his country seats about
in places where the air was warm for winter and
spring, or cool for summer and autumn, by the sea-
shore, on the lower hills, or high on the mountain
side. You would find them on the Italian lakes or
elsewhere toward the north. In greater numbers
would you find them on the hills near Rome, at the
modern Tivoli or Palestrina, on the Alban heights
near what are now Frascati, Albano, or Genzano,
along the shore at Antium, Terracina, Baiae, Naples,
Herculaneum, Pompeii, Castellamare, and Sorrento.

Perhaps it is not too much to say that more than
a hundred and twenty miles of this coast were
practically a chain of country houses. The shore
of the Bay of Naples has been compared to a collar
of pearls strung round the blue. Wherever there
was a wide and varied landscape or seascape, there
arose a Roman country house. We are too prone to
assume that the ancients felt but little love or even
appreciation of scenery, and to fancy that the feeling
came as a revelation to a Rousseau, a Wordsworth,
or a nineteenth-century painter. That Roman literature does not gush about the matter has been
absurdly taken for proof that the Roman writer did
not copiously enjoy the glories presented to his eyes.
But, though Roman literature does not gush, it often
exhibits the same feelings towards scenery which at
least a Thomson or a Cowper exhibits. Perhaps it
was so accustomed to scenic beauties that it took
for granted much that an English or German writer
cannot. At any rate we are sure that the Roman
chose for his country seat a site commanding the
widest and most beautiful outlook, and that he
even built towers upon his house to command the
view the better. In this respect he was like the
mediaeval monks, when they chose the sites of
monasteries at San Martino or Amalfi, and his love
of a belvedere was probably quite as great as theirs.

The country seat differed widely from the town
house. We must forget the plan which has been given
above, with its hall and court lighted from within,

and made private from the passing crowds in the street. In the country there is no need of such an arrangement. Moreover there are no formal receptions to necessitate the hall, and there are ample gardens to make the peristyle superfluous. Here the walls of the house may break forth into large and open windows, while all around may run pillared verandahs. Built in any variety of shape, according to the situation and the fancy, it may contain an immense variety of sitting-rooms, dining-rooms, bed-rooms, facing in every direction to catch the sun, the shade, the breeze, or the prospect, as the case may be. Not that magnificence is any more neglected than in the great English country seats. The pillars and pavements are as rich as means allow, and works of painting and statuary are perhaps even finer and more numerous than in town; there is more time to look at them, and there are better facilities for showing them off. Many of the best works of ancient sculpture now extant in the museums have come from such country seats. There were of course vulgar houses in bad taste, where the owner's notions of magnificence consisted in ostentatious extravagance and a desire to outdo his neighbour. As now, every-thing depended either on the culture of the man or on the amount of his good sense in leaving such matters to his artistic adviser.

Outside the house lie the gardens and grounds. For the most part these are laid out in the formal style adopted so often in more modern Italy and favoured so greatly in England in the early eighteenth

century. Perhaps the Villa d' Este at Tivoli, though
of course not ancient, may convey some approximate
idea of the prevailing principle. Along one side of
the Roman house we should find a smooth terrace
ornamented with statues and vases, to be used as a
promenade. There are straight walks and avenues
between hedges and trees and shrubs — cyprus, laurel,
box, and other manageable plants — cut to the shape
of beasts and birds and inanimate objects. There are
flower-beds — of the rose, the crocus, the wallflower, the
narcissus, the violet, but not, for example, the tulip —
laid out in geometrical patterns. There are trellis-
work arbours and walks covered with leafy vines or
other trailing plants. There are clumps of bay-trees,
plane trees, or myrtles, with marble seats beneath.
There is either an avenue or a covered colonnade,
where the ground is made of soft earth or sand, and
where the family may take exercise by being carried in
a litter up and down in the open or under the shade.
There are greenhouses and forcing-houses, where
flowers are grown under glass. There are fish-ponds,
fountains, and water-channels, with artificial cascades
and a general suggestion of babbling streams. Out
beyond lie the orchards and the vegetable gardens,
where are grown most of the modern fruits, including
peaches, apricots, and almonds, but not yet including
either the orange or the lemon.

The country immediately round the mansion of
the wealthy man was commonly his own estate. A
portion of this was frequently woodland, affording
opportunities for hunting deer, wild boar, and other

N

game. For the boar the weapon was a stout spear,
and the general practice of the sportsman was to
wait at a certain spot until the beast was driven
towards it by a ring of beaters. Deer were caught
in nets or transfixed with javelins while running.
In more open places the hunter, accompanied by
hounds, rode after a hare. But though far too much
of Italy was taken up by preserves of this un-
productive kind, the large estates were mostly turned
to agricultural purposes. Different owners, different
practices; but the possessor of a number of country
seats would in some cases work the land for himself by
means of slaves — often in disgrace and labouring in
chains — under the direction of a manager or bailiff,
while in others he would parcel out his land on
various terms among free tenants. It is gratifying
to discover that in bad seasons a generous landlord
would sometimes remit a portion of his dues, and
that he recognised various obligations of a *grand
seigneur* to his district. Among them was the
keeping up and beautifying of the local shrines and
contributing to buildings and works for the public
comfort.

Such would be the country seat when established
landward. By the seaside, especially in a much-
frequented resort like Baiae, the room was more
limited and the equipment modified. The extensive
garden would be absent, and the height of the building
increased by a second or even a third storey. It
was no uncommon thing for such a "villa," as it was
called, to stand out on a promontory, where it could

be greeted by the sea on either side. In many cases it was actually built out into the sea on piles or on a basis of concrete, and the occupant made a special delight of fishing from his window, and of letting the true sea-water flow into his swimming bath.

CHAPTER XI

On the customary furniture of a Roman house we need not spend many words. For one thing, it was simple and scanty as compared with the furnishing and upholstering of to-day. For another, its nature presents little that would be strange to us or that would require explanation.

Among the most conspicuous differences between Roman and modern furnishing must be reckoned the absence of carpets, the comparatively small use of tables and chairs, the absence of upholstery from such chairs as were used, and the greater part played by couches. In place of carpets there were the ornamental floors, whether in geometrical pattern-work, arrangements of veined marbles, or mosaic pictures composed of small blocks of coloured stone or glass. The making of carpets was well understood in the East, and Rome would have found no difficulty in obtaining as many as it chose, but so far as it employed tapestries they were for portières and curtains, for the coverings of dining-couches and beds, or for throwing across a chair-back. The Roman kept his floors, walls, pillars, and ceilings carefully cleared of dust and stains by means of brushes of feathers or light hair, brooms of palm or other leaves, and sponges. He thus saved himself both the labour and the unwholesomeness of carpets.

We need not enter into dry details concerning such articles as were similar to our own. Of the Roman seats it is enough to say that they were either square stools without back or arms, or folding-stools, or they were true chairs either with straight arms and backs (the origin of the modern throne) to be used by the owner when receiving clients or visitors on business, or with a long sloping back and without arms, as used particularly by women. A movable cushion consti-

FIG. 46. — ROMAN FOLDING CHAIR. (Schreiber.)

tuted all the upholstery. But the Roman man seldom took his ease in a chair: even his reading and writing were commonly performed while reclining upon a couch. When writing, he doubled the right leg and rested

FIG. 47. — BRONZE SEAT. (Overbeck.)

his tablets on his knee, and it may be presumed that habit made the practice easy and natural. The couch is, indeed, perhaps the chief article of Roman furniture. So regular was it to recline that, where

we should speak of a sitting-room, the Romans spoke
of a "reclining-room." At business they sat; but
they reclined in social conversation — unless it was
brief — when reading, when taking the siesta, and
when dining. Their beds in the proper sense were
similar to our own, though less heavy than those of
our older fashion. To mount them it was often

FIG. 48. — FRAMEWORK OF ROMAN COUCH.

necessary to use steps or an elongated footstool. A
slave in close attendance upon a master or mistress
sometimes slept upon a low truckle-bed, which, in the
daytime, could be pushed under the other. The
couches for day use were lower and of lighter and
narrower build, with a movable rest at the head and
with or without a back.

Upon the frame of such couches a good deal of
decoration was lavished in the way of veneerings of

ornamental wood, or thin plates of ivory or tortoise-
shell, or reliefs in bronze or even in gold or silver.
The feet might also, in the richer houses, consist of
silver or of ivory. For
the dining-rooms of
people of wealth a
special feature was
made of such work
upon the conspicuous
parts of the frames,
while the cushions and
coverings were of costly
fabrics, richly dyed
and embroidered or
damasked. The method

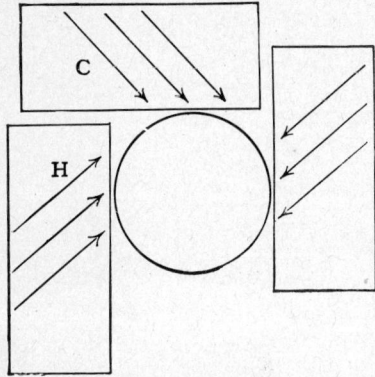

FIG. 49. — PLAN OF DINING-TABLE WITH
THREE COUCHES.

of serving and eating a dinner is a subject which belongs to our later treatment of a social day, and it

FIG. 50. — SIGMA.

must here suffice to picture the ordinary arrangement
of a dinner party.

In the middle is the table, either square or, if
round, made if possible of a single piece of costly

wood richly grained by nature in a wavy or peacock
pattern and obtained by sawing through the lower
part of the trunk of a Moorish tree. The price
depended on the size. Of one such circular slab we
learn that it cost £4000. It may be needless to
remark that many tables were only "imitation."
When not in use, and sometimes even then, such
tables were protected by coloured linen cloths.
By preference this ancient equivalent of "the best
mahogany" was supported on a single leg, consisting of elephants' tusks or of sculptured marble.
On three sides are placed the couches, covered with
mattresses stuffed with flock or feathers, and provided
with soft cushions for the left arm to rest upon.
Sometimes, instead of the three separate couches, there
was but one large couch shaped like a crescent, either
extending round half the large circular table, or having
more than one smaller table placed before it. Tables
in other rooms were scarcely to be found, since, as
has already been remarked, they were not required
for reading or writing or for holding the various
articles which we moderns place upon them. Besides
the dining tables we should generally find only a
sideboard placed in the dining-room for the display of
articles of plate. This was either of ornamental wood
or of marble with a sculptured stand, and was
distinctly meant for show. In place of tables for
supporting necessary objects we find tripods, either of
bronze or marble, with a flat top and sometimes with
a rim.

Other articles of household furniture were chests

and presses or wardrobes. It was almost a rule that
in the hall, at the side or end, should stand a low heavy
chest — occasionally   more   than   one — sometimes
made of iron, sometimes of wood bound with bronze

FIG. 51. — TRIPOD FROM HERCULANEUM.

and decorated with metal-work in relief. In this were
contained supplies of money and other articles of value,
and for this reason it was strongly locked and often
fastened to the ground by a vertical rod of iron.
Such a chest is still to be seen in its place in the

House of the Vettii at Pompeii. Of portières, curtains, and awnings enough has been said, except that they were also used for draping the less ornamental walls. Mirrors were apparently plentiful. No mention is

FIG. 52. — CHEST (STRONG-BOX).

made of such articles in glass, probably because the ancients had not yet learned to make that material sufficiently pure and true or to provide it with the proper foil or background. For the most part they were made of highly polished copper, bronze, or silver. The smaller ones were held in the hand, the handle and back parts being richly and often tastefully ornamented. There is an epigram extant which tells of a vindictive Roman dame who struck her maid to the ground with her mirror, because she detected a curl wrongly placed. Other mirrors were made so as to stand upon a support, and there is mention of some sufficiently large to show the full length of the body.

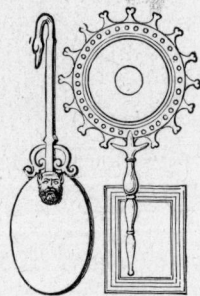

FIG. 53. — MIRRORS.

In the absence of gas or electricity or even kerosene, there was no better means of lighting a house than by oil-lamps. Even those were provided with no chimney. Naturally every effort would be made to obtain such oil as would produce the least smoke or smell, but doubtless the difficulty was never completely overcome. It is therefore natural to hear of the oil being mixed with perfume. In the less well-to-do houses there might be wax candles, in still poorer houses candles of tallow or even rush-lights, formed by long strips of rush or other fibrous plant thinly dipped in tallow. Generally speaking, however, the Roman house was lit by lamps filled with olive-oil.

FIG. 54. — LAMPS.

The commonest were made of terra-cotta, the better sorts of bronze or silver, often richly ornamented and sometimes very graceful. As typical specimens we may take those here illustrated.

The little figure standing on the one lamp is holding a chain, to which is attached the probe for forcing up the wick or for clearing away the "mushrooms" that might form upon it. Lamps are made in all manner of fantastic shapes — ships, shoes, and other objects — and may burn either one wick or a considerable number, projecting from different nozzles. For the purpose of lighting a room they may either

be placed upon the top of upright standards, four or
five feet high and sometimes with shafts which could
be adjusted in height like the modern reading-stand;
or they may be hung from the ceiling by chains, after
the manner of a chandelier, or held by a statue, or
suspended from a stand shaped like a pillar or a tree,
from whose branches they hang like fruit.   For use

in the street there were
torches and also lanterns,
which had a metal frame
and were "glazed" with
sheets of transparent horn,
with bladder in the cheaper
instances, or with trans-
parent talc in the more
costly.

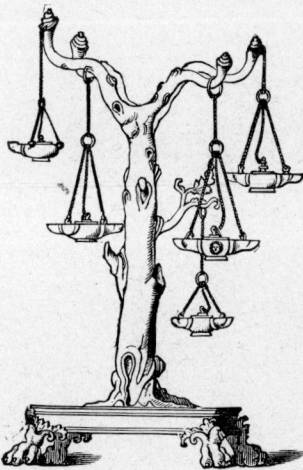

FIG. 55.—LAMPHOLDER AS TREE.

As with the Greeks, a
Roman house was lavish in
the use and display of cups
and plate in great diversity
of shape and material.   Glass vessels were numerous
and, except for a perfectly pure white variety, were
produced both at Rome and Alexandria with the
most ingenious finish.   A kind of porcelain was also
known, but was very rare and highly valued.   For
the most part the poor used earthenware cups and
plates or wooden trenchers.   The rich sought after
a lavish profusion of silver goblets studded with jewels
and sometimes ventured on a cup of gold, although
the use of a full gold service was by imperial ordinance

restricted to the palace.   There were drinking vessels,
broad and shallow with richly embossed or *repoussé*
work, or deep with double handles and a foot, or
otherwise diversified.   There were all manner of
plates and dishes of silver or of silver-gilt.   There
were graceful jugs and ladles and mixing-bowls.
What we regard as most essential articles, but
missing from a Roman table, are knives and forks.

Fig. 56.— Cup from Herculaneum.

Table-forks, indeed, were unknown till a very modern
date, but even knives were scarcely in use at Rome
except by the professional carver at his stand.   There
were also heaters, in which water could be kept hot
at table and drawn off by a small tap.

If now we stepped into the kitchen we should find
there practically every kind of utensil likely to be of
use even for the modern cuisine.   There is no need

LIFE IN THE ROMAN WORLD

here to catalogue the kettles and pots and pans, the strainers and shapes and moulds, employed by Roman cooks. Perhaps it will suffice to present a number of them to the eye. In general, however, it deserves to be remarked that such a thing as a pail, a pitcher,

FIG. 57.—KITCHEN UTENSILS.

a pair of scales, or a steelyard was not regarded in the Roman household as necessarily to be left a bare and unsightly thing because it was useful. The triumph of tin and ugliness was not yet. Such vessels as waterpots are still to be seen made of copper in graceful shapes, if one will notice the

women fetching water on the Alban Hills. How
far the domestic utensils resembled or differed from
those still in use may be judged from the specimens
illustrated.

FIG. 58.—PAIL FROM HERCULANEUM.

There existed no clocks of the modern kind, but
the Romans do not appear to have suffered much
practical inconvenience in respect of telling the time
and meeting engagements. Sundials, both public

and private, were numerous, but these were obviously
of no use on gloomy days or at night. The instrument
on which the Romans mainly relied was therefore the
"water-clock," which, though by no means capable
of our modern precision of minutes and even seconds,
could record time down to small fractions of the hour.
The principle was that of the hour-glass, water taking
the place of sand. From an upper vessel water slowly
trickled through an orifice into a lower receptacle,
which at this date was transparent and was marked
with sections for the hour and its convenient fractions.
In this way the time would be told by the mark to
which the water had risen in the lower portion. The
Romans were not unaware of the difference between
the conditions of summer and winter flow of water,
but it would appear that they had attained to proper
methods of "regulating" their rather awkward time-
pieces. It is as well to add that in the wealthier
houses a slave was told off to watch the clock and
to report the passing of the hours, as well as to
summon any member of the family at the time
arranged for an appointment.

CHAPTER XII

WE have seen in what sort of a home a Roman dwelt in town or country. Meanwhile it goes without saying that the non-Roman or non-romanized populations of the empire were living in houses and amid furniture of their own special type — Greek, Syrian, Egyptian, or as the case might be. They were also living their lives after their own fashion in respect of dress, meals, occupations, and amusements.

We may now look at the manner in which a typical Roman might spend an ordinary day in the metropolis, and endeavour to form some clear idea of the outward aspects of such a life. In the first instance our Roman shall be a man of the senatorial aristocracy, blessed with both high position and ample means, but one who, for the time being, holds no public office, whether as a governor, a military commander, a Minister of Roads or Water-Supply, an officer of the Exchequer, or of Justice. Instead of referring to him awkwardly as "our citizen," we will call him Silius. The same name may be borne by a large number of other persons, for it is the name of an early Roman

family which in course of time may have divided into
several branches or "houses," answering to each other
very much as the "Worcestershire" So-and-Sos may
answer to the "Hampshire" So-and-Sos, except that
the distinction in the Roman case is not territorial.
Our Silius will therefore naturally bear further names
to distinguish him. One will be the special appellation of his own "house" or branch, derived in all
probability from its first distinguishing member. Let
us assume, for instance, that he is a Silius Bassus.
As, again, there are probably a number of other persons
belonging to the same branch and entitled to the
same two designations, he will possess a "front name,"
answering to our "Christian" name, and he shall be
called for our purposes Quintus Silius Bassus. It is
the middle name of the three which is regarded as
the name, but when there is no danger of mistake
our friend may be addressed or written of as either
Silius or Bassus. In private life among his intimates
he prefers to be called Quintus. The individual
name, family name, and branch name were frequently
followed by others, but at least these three are
regularly owned by any Roman with claims to old
descent. To us, however, he will be Silius.

He lives, let us say, in one of the larger town-houses
on the Caelian Hill, looking across the narrow valley
towards the Palatine, somewhere near the modern
church of SS. Giovanni e Paolo. It is before daybreak that the loud bell has awakened the household
slaves and set them to their work. In the road below
and away in the city the carts, which are forbidden

during the full daytime, are still rumbling with their
loads of produce or building-material. All night long
the less happily housed inhabitants have tolerated
this noise, together with the droning and grating of
the mills grinding the corn in the bakers' shops. It
is, however, now approaching dawn, and imperial
Rome, which goes to sleep late, wakes early. No few
Romans, even of the highest classes, have already been
up for an hour or two, reading by lamplight, writing
letters or dictating them to an amanuensis, who takes
them down rapidly in a form of shorthand. Out in
the streets the boys are on their way to school, the
poorer ones carrying their own lanterns — at least if it
is the time of year when the days are short — their
writing-tablets and their reading-books, probably
Virgil and Horace, who were standard authors serving
in the Roman schools as Shakespeare and Pope do in
our own. Boys of well-to-do parents are accompanied
by an elderly slave of stern demeanour. In the distance
are heard the sounds of the first hammers and the
cries of the venders of early breakfasts.

Silius rises, and with the help of a valet, who is of
course a slave, dresses himself. His household barber
— another slave — shaves him, trims his hair in the
approved style and cleans his nails. At this date
clean shaving was the rule. Every emperor from
Augustus to Hadrian, fifty years later than Nero, was
clean shaven, and the fashion set by emperors was
followed as closely by the contemporary Roman as
"imperials" and "ram's-horn" moustaches have been
imitated in later times. The hair was kept carefully

neither too long nor too short. Only in time of mourning was it permitted to grow to a negligent length. By preference it should be somewhat wavy, but there was no parting. Dandies had their hair curled with the tongs and perfumed, so at to smell "all over the theatre." If they were bald, they wore a wig; sometimes they actually had imitation hair painted across the bare part of the scalp. If nature had given them the wrong colour, they corrected it with dye. If the exposed parts of the body were hairy, they plucked out the growth with tweezers or used depilatories. But these were the dandies, and we need not assume Silius to have been one of them.

It is to be a day of some formality, and Silius will therefore attire himself accordingly. In other words, he will put on the typical Roman garb. Of whatever else this may consist, it will comprise a band round the middle, a woolen — less often a linen — tunic with or without sleeves, and over this the voluminous woollen toga; on the feet will be shoes. Of further underwear a Roman used as much or as little as he chose. If, like the Emperor Augustus, he felt the cold, he might indulge in several shirts and also short hose. Such practices, however, were commonly regarded as coddling. Breeches were worn at this date only by soldiers serving in northern countries, where they had picked up the custom from the "barbarians." Mufflers were used by persons with a tender throat.

Inasmuch as Silius is of senatorial rank, his tunic, which will show through the open front of his toga, bears the broad inwoven stripe of purple running

down the middle, and his shoes — which otherwise
might be of various colours, such as yellow with red
laces — are black, fastened by cross straps running
somewhat high up the leg and bearing a crescent of
silver or ivory upon the instep. The stripe, the shoes,
and the crescent mark his senatorial standing. That
which marks him as a citizen at all is the toga — an
article of dress forbidden to any inhabitant of the
empire who could not call himself in the full sense
"*Civis Romanus.*" It was a cumbrous and heavy

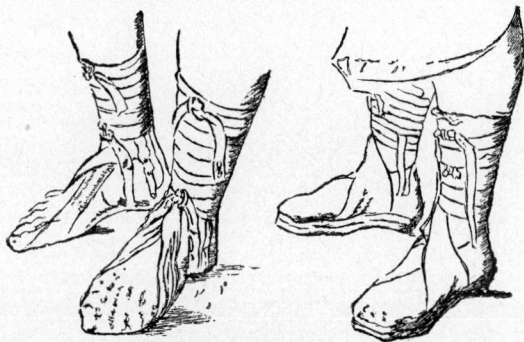

FIG. 59. — PATRICIAN SHOES.

garment (when spread out it formed an oval of about
15 feet by 12), with which no man who wanted to
work or travel or simply to be comfortable would
hamper himself. St. Paul was a Roman citizen, but,
if he ever wore a toga at all, it would only be when
he desired to bring his citizenship home to a Roman
court, and we should probably be quite mistaken in
imagining that he travelled about with a toga in his
baggage, or, as the Authorised Version calls it, his
"carriage." When out of town, in his country-seat

or when amusing himself at home in the city, especially in the warmer weather, the Roman cast off his toga with a sigh of relief. In the provincial towns of Italy, though theoretically as much in demand, this blanket-like covering was little used by any man except on the most formal public and religious occasions, and, as a poet says, "when dead," for then the toga was indispensable. Nevertheless at Rome it was the necessary dress for all men of position when appearing in any sort of public life. The Roman emperors insisted upon its use in all places of public amusement — the theatre, circus, or amphitheatre. In a court of justice the president certainly could not "see" a pleader unless he wore it. You cannot be present at a formal social ceremony — a wedding, a betrothal, a coming of age, a levée — without this outward and visible mark of respect. Nor was it sufficient that you should wear it. It must be properly draped and must fall to the right point, which, in front, was aslant over the lower part of the shin, while behind it fell to the heel. Your wardrobe slave must see that it has been kept properly folded and pressed. If you claimed to be a gentleman, and were not in mourning and not an official, it must be simply and scrupulously white. Poorer people might wear a toga of a duller or dark-grey wool, which would better conceal a stain and require to go less frequently to the fuller. The same dull hue was also worn in time of mourning, or as an ostentatious token of a gloomy spirit, as for example, when one of your friends was in peril of condemnation in the law-courts, or when you fancied that

some serious injustice was being done or threatened
to your social order. The only person privileged to

FIG. 60. — ROMAN IN THE TOGA.

wear a toga of true purple was the emperor. On the
whole the Roman dress was very simple; far more so
than in mediaeval times or the days of Elizabeth or

Charles II. Velvet and satin were not yet known, furs hardly so, and there were very few changes of fashion.

Silius will also wear at least one large signet-ring as well as his plain ring of gold, but he will leave it to the dandies to load their fingers with half-a-dozen and to keep separate sets for winter and summer. When Quintilian, in his *Training of the Orator*, touches upon the subject of rings, he recommends as requisite for good form that "the hand should not be covered with rings, and especially should they not come below the middle joint." A handkerchief will be carried, but only to wipe away perspiration.

Having finished his dressing, he may choose this time for taking his morning "snack," corresponding to the coffee and roll or tea and bread-and-butter of modern times. It is but a light repast of wine or milk, with bread and honey, or a taste of olives or cheese or possibly an egg. Schoolboys seem to have often eaten a sort of suet dumpling. In the strength of this meat our friend will go till mid-day.

As he has no very early call to the imperial court upon the Palatine, he will now proceed to hold his own reception of morning callers. For this purpose he will come out to the spacious hall, which has been already described as the most essential part of a Roman house, and will there establish himself in the opening of the recess or bay which has also been described as a kind of reception-room or parlour. Before he arrives, the hall has been swept and polished

by the brooms and sponges of the slaves, under the
direction of a foreman. The number of Silius' household slaves is very great. Very many Romans of
course owned no slave at all; many had but one or
two; but it was considered that a person of anything
like respectable means could hardly do with less than
ten. Silius will probably employ several times that
number. We have mentioned the valet, the barber,
the wardrobe-keeper, and the amanuensis. We must
add to these the cooks, the pastry-makers, the waiters,
the room-servants, the doorkeeper, the footmen,
messengers, litter-carriers, the butler and pantrymen.
Some of the superior slaves have drudges of their
own. The librarian, accountant, and steward are all
slaves. Even the family physician or architect may
be a slave. Many of these men may be persons of
education and talent. Their one deficiency is that
they are not free. Many of them are in colour and
feature indistinguishable from the people outside;
most, however, show their origin in their foreign
physique. They are Phrygians, Cappadocians, Syrians,
Jews, Egyptians, Ethiopians, Numidians, Spaniards,
Gauls, Germans, Thracians, and Greeks. Their master
either inherited them from his father or friends, or
he bought them in the slave-market. For whatever
reason they became slaves — whether as prisoners of
war, by birth, through debt, through condemnation
for some offence, by kidnapping like that practised
by the Corsairs or the modern Arabs, or through
being sold by their own parents — they had become
the property of slave-dealers, who picked them up in

the depots on the Black Sea or at Delos or Alexandria, and brought them to Rome. There they were stripped and exposed for sale, the choicer specimens in a select part of a fashionable shop, the more ordinary types in the auction mart, where they were placed upon a stand or stone bench, were labelled with their age, nationality, defects, and accomplishments, and were sold either under a guarantee or without one. For an ordinary room-slave Silius, or his agent for him, has paid perhaps £20; for a servant of more special skill, such as a particularly soft-handed barber, perhaps £50; the price of a muleteer who was "too deaf to overhear private conversation in a carriage" might thereby be enhanced to £150; for a slave with educational or artistic accomplishments — a good reader, reciter, secretary, musician, or actor — he may have paid some hundreds. If he is a man of morbid tastes, and affects a particular kind of dainty favourite, he may go as far as a thousand. Curly-haired pages and amusing dwarfs are generally dear. It is the business of the house-steward to see that each slave receives his daily or monthly rations of corn, a trifling sum of money for other needs, and perhaps an allowance of thin wine. Many a slave also received a considerable number of "tips" from guests, as well as perquisites and presents from his master. With economy he was thus enabled to purchase his own freedom. The master might also in some cases provide the slave with the essentials of his dress, to wit, a coarse tunic, a rough cloak, and a pair of shoes or sabots.

Over all these persons, so long as they are slaves, the owner possesses absolute power. He can box their ears, or condemn them to hard labour — making them, for instance, work in chains upon his lands in the country or in a sort of prison-factory — or he may punish them with blows of the rod, the lash, or the knout; he can brand them upon the forehead if they are thieves or runaways, or in the end, if they prove irreclaimable, he can crucify them. Branded slaves who afterwards became free and rich sought to conceal the marks by wearing patches. There were inevitably some instances in which masters proved so intolerably cruel that their slaves were driven to murder them. To prevent any

Fig. 61. — Slave in Fetters.

conspiracy of the kind the law ordained that, when a master was so killed, the slaves should one and all be put to death. It is gratifying to learn that in the reign of Nero the whole populace sided with a body of slaves in this predicament and prevented the law from being carried out.

But, being a typical Roman, Silius has a strong sense of justice; moreover he values public opinion as well as his own. Also, being a typical Roman, he behaves with strictness and for the most part with a distinct haughtiness of manner, graduated, no doubt, according to the standing of the individual. When, as was often the case, he did not even know the name of a slave whom he came across in hall or peristyle, he frequently addressed him as "Sirrah" or "Sir" or " You, Sir." To the waiter at table and for ordinary commands, where the master affects no ceremony, the commonest term is "boy," precisely as that word is used in the East or *garçon* in French. If Silius knew the actual appellation assigned to the slave when bought and was disposed to be kindly, he accosted him by it, calling him "Syrian," or "Thracian," or "Croesus," or by his proper Greek or Egyptian name. The slave, unlike the Roman citizen, owned but one name, and the shorter the better.

We meet, as is only natural, with many examples of great trust and confidence between master and slave, and, in the case of the superior types, no few instances of great kindness and consideration. Pliny speaks of his "long friendship" for a cultivated slave named Zosimus, whom he set free, and whom, because he was liable to consumption, he sent to Egypt and the Riviera for the good of his health. A faithful or very useful slave could make tolerably sure of being some day emancipated with all due form and ceremony, either during the master's lifetime or by his last will and testament. In such a case he became a Roman citizen of the rank known as "freedman," and after the second generation there was nothing to prevent his descendants from aspiring to any position open to any other Roman. Sometimes even his son attained to public office. On

attaining his citizenship the freedman became entitled
to "the three names," and it was the rule that he
should adopt the family name of his master. A
freedman of Silius is himself a Silius. Also by preference he will be a Quintus Silius; but he will not
be a Bassus. The third name will still, for his own
lifetime, be such as to mark him for what he is.
Moreover, though free, he is himself still bound to
pay a dutiful respect to his former master's family,
but beyond this he is at his own disposal and in
possession of every right in regard to person and
property. Many such men were extremely skilful
in trade and made themselves rich enough to vie
with the Roman aristocracy in outward show. The
freedmen of the Emperor, who occupied positions of
influence at court as chamberlains, stewards, private
secretaries and the like, and were the powers behind the throne, became enormously wealthy. Their
houses were adorned with the finest marble columns,
the most richly gilded ceilings, and the most costly
works of art; the choicest fruits ripened under glass
in their forcing-houses, and, when they died, their
monuments were among the most sumptuous by the
side of the great highways. "Freedmen's wealth"
became a proverb. They were occasionally even
appointed to those minor governorships held by
"agents" of Caesar, and the Felix of the New
Testament was himself a freedman of Nero's predecessor and brother to one of the richest and most
influential of the class. In the provincial cities of
Italy freedmen, though they were not themselves

eligible for the ordinary offices, might in return for acts of munificence be admitted to what may be called an inferior grade of knighthood — a sort of C.M.G. — styled the "Order of Augustus." They thus became notables of their own town in a way of which they were sufficiently proud, as the Pompeian inscriptions show. It was part of the shrewdness of Augustus to kill two birds with one stone, by erecting a provincial order directly attached to the cult of the Emperor, and by encouraging the local self-made man to spend money liberally upon the embellishment and comfort of his own municipality.

Well, Silius, meeting with or escorted by various slave attendants, passes from the inner rooms through the passage into the hall and finds waiting for him a throng of visitors known as his "clients" or dependants. The position of these persons is somewhat remarkable. They are commonly free Roman citizens of the "genteel" middle class, who openly admit that they depend for the bulk of their living upon the patronage of the noble or the rich. The custom arose from a very old condition of things, under which certain classes of citizens, not being entitled to appear in the law-courts or in public business on their own behalf, put themselves under the protection of a person so entitled, who, in return for certain acts of support and deference, appeared as their advocate and champion. At a later time, even though their rights had become complete, men might still seek counsel, legal advice, and advocacy from a person of influence

and eloquence. In return they paid him the honour
of escort in the streets, supported him in his
candidature for public office, applauded his speeches,
and exercised on his behalf such influence as they
possessed. The standing of a prominent Roman was
apt to be measured by the number and quality of the
persons thus attaching themselves to him. If next it
is remembered that very few money-making occupations were looked upon with favour by the Romans,
and that the higher orders were for the most part
very rich, it will be obvious that there would grow
up the custom of the patron making liberal presents
to his dependants — money gifts, or gifts of small
properties and of useful articles — as well as of inviting
them to his table. The clients themselves brought little
presents on the patron's birthday or some other special
occasion, but these were merely the sprats to catch
the whale. It gradually resulted that the patronage
extended by the aristocrat or plutocrat was mainly
one of a direct pecuniary nature. As in other cases
where a dubious custom develops gradually, there
ceased to be any shame in this relation. Many
members of the middle class, impoverished and earning
practically no other income, lived the life of genteel
paupers. They would attend the morning reception
of a grandee, either bringing with them, or causing
a slave to bring, a small basket, or even a portable
cooking-stove, in which they carried off doles of food
distributed through his servants. The scene must
have borne no slight resemblance to that of the charity
"soup-kitchen." In process of time, however, this

practice became inconvenient for all parties, and most
of the patrons compounded for such doles by making
a fixed payment, still called the "little basket,"
amounting perhaps to a shilling in modern weight of
money for each day of polite attention on the part of
a recognised "client." If a client was acknowledged
by more than one patron, so much the better for the
amount of his "little baskets." In some cases the dole
was paid to each visitor at the morning call; in others
only after the work of the patron's day was done and
when he had gone to the elaborate bath which
preceded his dinner in the later part of the afternoon.
By this means the complimentary escort duty was
secured until that time.

Among the dependants were nearly all the genteel
unemployed of Rome, including the Grub-Street men
of letters, who in those days could make little, if
anything, by their books, and who therefore sought
the same kind of assistance as did our own literary
rank and file in the early eighteenth century. When
we read the authors of the period we are inevitably re-
minded of Samuel Johnson waiting in the ante-chamber
of Lord Chesterfield, and of the flattering dedications
of books which were so liberally or illiberally paid for
by the recipients of such compliments. From his
little flat, often a single room and practically an attic,
in the tenement-house, the client would emerge before
daylight, dressed *de rigueur* in his toga, which was
often sadly worn and thin. He would make his way
for a mile or more through the carts, the cattle, and
the schoolboys, sometimes in fine weather, sometimes

through the rain and cold, when the streets were muddy and slippery, and would climb the hill to his patron's door, joined perhaps on the way by other citizens bent on the same errand. Gathering in that open space or vestibule which has already been described, they waited for the janitor to open the door. If the doorkeeper of Silius was like the generality of his kind, he would take a flunkey's pleasure in keeping them waiting, and also, except in the case of those who had been wise enough to ease his manners with a "tip," or who were known to be in special favour, a flunkey's pleasure in exhibiting his contempt. Brought into the hall, they stood or sat about and conversed until Silius appeared. Then, according to an established order of precedence — which apparently depended on seniority of acquaintance, while again it might be affected by a *douceur* — they were presented one by one to the patron.

One must not expect a Roman noble to deign always to remember the names of humble persons — sometimes he actually did not — and therefore a slave, known as the "name-caller," announces each client in turn. The client says, "Good morning, Sir," and Silius replies, "Good morning, So-and-So," or "Good morning, Sir," or simply "Good morning." There is a shaking of hands, or, if the patron is a gracious gentleman and the client is of old standing, Silius may kiss him on the cheek and offer some polite inquiry or remark. A very haughty person might merely offer his hand to be kissed and perhaps not open his mouth at all, even if he condescended to

P

look at you. But these habits were hardly so characteristic of our times as of a somewhat later date.

The reception over, the client obtains information as to the movements of his patron during the day. On the present occasion it appears that Silius himself is to proceed at once to pay his own morning homage to a still higher patron, His Highness Nero, who is at home on the Palatine Hill, and whose levée calls imperatively for the attendance of certain members of the aristocracy. At the palace there exists a roll of persons known as the "friends of Caesar" — a roll which depends solely on the favour of the emperor. Naturally it contains the names of a number of the highest senators and of the chief officers of the state, but a place in it is not gained simply by such positions, nor is it restricted to them. There may be a few knights and others on the list. To be removed from the roll is to be socially a marked man and a person to be avoided. Silius is, at least for the time being, one of the "friends." Nero is not yet in sufficient financial straits to require that Silius should be squeezed or sacrificed, nor has he chosen to take offence at something which a spy or informer has reported of him. Our friend therefore enjoys the entrée to the palace, and to the palace he goes.

It is a clear fine morning, and he has plenty of time. He therefore perhaps elects to go on foot. Learning this, a number of his clients form a procession. Some are honoured by walking at his side, a

few go in advance and so clear a way through the
crowd — which is already moving at the top of the
Sacred Way — to the point where you turn off on the
left and ascend to the entrance to the Palatine Hill.
Some of the clients will walk behind, where also
will be a lackey or two in waiting. On the way
Silius may perhaps meet with Manlius, another
noble, whom he probably greets with "Good morning,
brother," and a kiss upon the cheek. This kissing,
it may be remarked, ultimately became an intolerable
nuisance, particularly among the middle classes, and
the epigrammatist, after complaining of the cold noses
and wet osculations of the winter-time, pleads to
have the business at least put off till the month of
April.

When it is a bad or sloppy day, Silius will decide
to go in his litter, or Roman form of the palanquin.
Being a senator he may use this conveyance, otherwise at this date he could not. There are also sedan
chairs, but as yet there exists a prejudice against these
as being somewhat effeminate. At this decision four,
six, or eight tall fellows, slaves from Cappadocia or
Germany by preference, clad in crimson liveries,
thrust two long poles through the rings or the
coloured leather straps which are to be found on
the sides of the litter, and place these poles upon
their shoulders. To all intents and purposes the
litter is a couch with an arched roof above it, of the
shape here indicated, but covered with cushions, which
are often stuffed with down. Its woodwork is decorated
with silver and ivory. The litter may either be carried

open on all sides, or with curtains of coloured stuffs
partially drawn, or it may be enclosed by windows
of talc or glass. In the days when litters were in
promiscuous use, persons who did not possess one, or
perhaps the slaves to bear it, might hire such a vehicle
from the "rank," after the modern manner of hiring

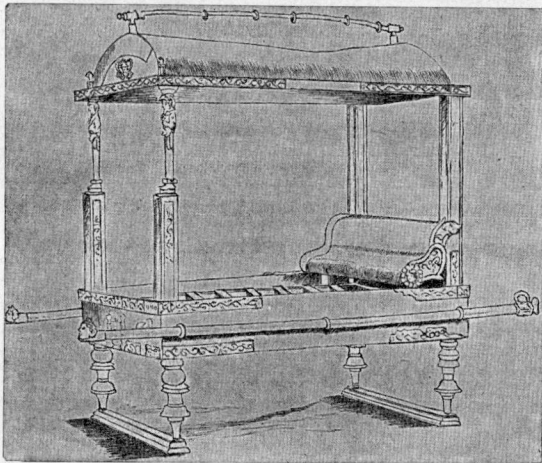

FIG. 62.—LITTER.

a cab. In this receptacle Silius is carried amid the
same procession as before.

He will wear nothing on his head. On a journey,
or when the sun was particularly strong in the roofless
theatre or circus, he might put on a broad-brimmed
hat, very much like that of the modern Italian priest.
Instead of the hat it was common, when the weather
so required, either to draw a fold of the toga over the
head or to wear a hood closely resembling the monkish
cowl. This might be either attached to a cloak or
made separately for the purpose. The hood was also

employed when, particularly in the evening, the
wearer had either public or private reasons for con-
cealing his identity as he moved abroad, commonly
issuing in such cases from his side door. But on
an ordinary day, and when attending a ceremony,
the Roman head is bare. So also are the hands, for
gloves are not yet in use.

On arriving at the palace — outside which there
is generally standing a crowd of the curious or the
snobs — Silius passes through the guards, Roman or
German, at the doors, is taken in hand by the court
slave or freedman who acts as usher, and himself goes
through a process similar to that which his own clients
have undergone. There are times, and just now they
may be frequent, at which he will have to submit to
a search, for fear he may be carrying a concealed
weapon. If he is high in favour or position, he
belongs to the batch of "first admittance," or first
entrée. If not, he must be contented with "second."
He will find that His Highness Nero, exacting as he
may be concerning the costume of his callers, will not
trouble to put on his own toga, as a more respectable
emperor would have done, but will appear in anything
he pleases, frequently a tunic or a wrapper of silk,
relieved only by a handkerchief round the neck.
Nor will his High Mightiness always condescend to
lace his shoes. If he is in a good humour, he may
bestow the kiss, remember your name, and call you
"my very dear Silius." If he has been accustomed
to do so, but omits the warmer greeting on this

occasion, it may be taken as boding you no good. It is, however, very probable that in this year 64 he will refuse the kiss to almost every one of the senators, for he has already come openly to detest them. It will suffice if he so much as offers his hand to be saluted. Caligula, being a "god," had sometimes offered his foot, but only that crack-brained emperor had so far attempted this enormity.

The day happens to be one on which the emperor has nothing further to say and requires no advice. Silius is therefore free to go his ways. There is also no meeting of the Senate, no festival, chariot-race, or show of gladiators. He has therefore only the ordinary day before him, and he proceeds, as practically every other caller does, towards the Forum and its neighbourhood. If on his way he meets with a great public official — a consul or a praetor — proceeding on duty, he politely makes way, and, if his head chances to be covered, he uncovers it. He loyally recognises the claims of that toga edged with purple, and of those lictors walking in front with the symbolic bundles of rods containing the symbolic axe. Whatever he may think of the men, he pays all respect to their office. The Forum is now full, the banking and money-changing are all aglow in the Basilica Aemilia, the loungers are playing their games of 'three men in a row," or perhaps their backgammon, on the pavement of the outer colonnade of the Basilica of Julius. Groups are reading and discussing the columns of the "Daily News," which are either posted

up or have been purchased from the professional
copiers. This is an official, and therefore a censored,
publication in clear manuscript, containing proclama-
tions, resolutions of the senate, bulletins of the court,
results of trials, the births and deaths registered

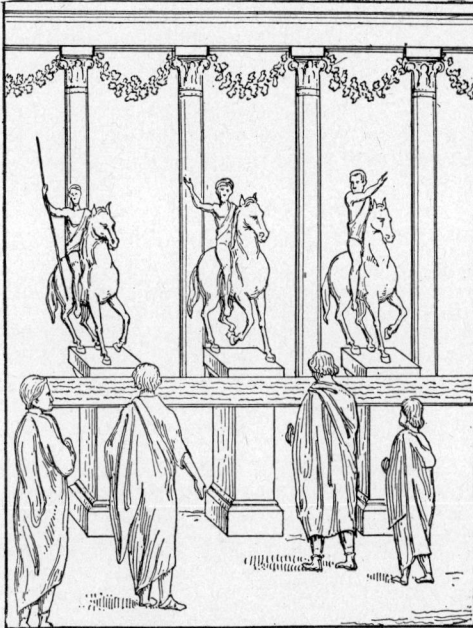

FIG. 63. — READING A PROCLAMATION. (Pompeii.)

The writing is upon a long board in front of equestrian statues.

in the city, announcements of public shows and
sports, striking events, such as fires, earthquakes,
and portents, and occasional advertisements. Silius
may perhaps stop and read; more probably his slaves
regularly purchase a copy for his private use. Criers
are meanwhile bawling to you to come and see
the Asiatic giant, or the mermen, or the two-headed

baby. The old sailor who has been wrecked, or pretends to have been, is walking about with a harrowing picture of the scene painted on a board and is soliciting alms. The busybody is gossiping among little knots of people and telling, manufacturing, or magnifying the latest scandal, or the latest news from the frontier, from Antioch, from the racing-stables, the law-courts, or the palace. Perhaps Silius has a little banking business to do, and he enters the Basilica to give instructions as to sending a draft to Athens or Alexandria in favour of some friend or relative there who is in want of money, or whom he has instructed to make artistic or other purchases. In about seven days his correspondent will obtain the cash through a banker at Athens, or in about twelve or fourteen days at Alexandria.

Perhaps, however, one of his clients has asked for his help in a case at law, which is being tried either over the way in the Basilica of Julius, or round the corner to the right in the Forum of Augustus. If a man of study and eloquence, he may have consented to act as pleader — taking no fee, because he is merely performing a patron's duty. *Noblesse oblige.* In the year 64 a pleader who has taken up a cause for some one else than a dependant is allowed by law to charge a fee not exceeding £100, but the law says nothing, or at least can do nothing, as to the liberal presents which are offered him under some other pretext. If he is not to plead, Silius may at any rate have been requested to lend moral support by seating himself beside the favoured party and perhaps appearing as a witness to character. If he pleads in any complicated or technical case, it will generally be after careful consultation with an attorney or professional lawyer. Round the apse or recess in which the court sits there will stand a ring of interested spectators, and among them will be distributed as many as possible of his own dependants, who will religiously applaud his finely-turned periods and his witticisms. There was generally little chance of missing a Roman forensic witticism; its character was for the most part highly elaborate and its edge broad. In a later generation it was not rare for chance bystanders to be hired on the spot as *claqueurs*. The court itself consists of a large body of jurymen of position empanelled, not for the particular case, but for particular kinds of cases and for a period of time, and over these there presides one of the public officials annually elected for the judicial administration of Rome. The president sees that the proceedings are in accordance with the law, but the verdict is given entirely by the jury.

If there is no need for Silius to attend such a court, he may find many other demands upon his time. Among Romans of the higher classes etiquette was extremely exacting. Contemporaries themselves complain that social "duties" or "obligations" frittered away a large proportion of their day, and that they were kept perpetually "busy doing nothing." One man or woman is making a will, and asks you to be one of the witnesses to the signature and sealing;

another is betrothing a son or daughter, and invites
you to be present and attest the ceremony ; another
has a son of fifteen or sixteen concerning whom it is
decided that he has now come of age, must put on
the white toga of a man in the place of the purple-
edged toga of the boy, and be led into the Forum in

FIG. 64. — SEALED RECEIPT OF JUCUNDUS.

Beside each seal is a signature ; the writing in the hollow leaf is a summary
of the receipt, which is itself shut between the two leaves bound with string.

token of his new freedom; you must not omit the
courtesy of attending. Another desires you to go
with him before the magistrate while he emancipates
a slave. Worst of all, perhaps, is the man who has
written a poem or declamation, and who proposes to
read it, or to get a professional elocutionist to read it,
to his acquaintances. He has either hired a hall or

borrowed a convenient room from a friend, and you
are kindly invited to be present. We learn that
these amateur authors did not permit their victims to
forget the engagement, but sent them more than one
reminder. At the reading or recitation it was your
duty to applaud frequently, to throw complimentary
kisses, and to exclaim in Greek, "excellent," "capital,"
"clever," "unapproachable," or "again," very much
as we say "encore" in what we think is French, or
"bravo" in Italian. The native Latin terms most
commonly in use may perhaps be translated as
"well said," "perfect," "good indeed," "divine,"
"a shrewd hit." On one occasion a certain Priscus
was present at the reading of a poem, and it happened
to open with an invocation to a Priscus. No sooner
had the author begun, "Priscus, thou bidst me
tell . . ." than the man of that name called out
"Indeed I don't." This "caused laughter" and
"cast a chill over the proceedings." Pliny apologises
for the man, as being a little light in the head, but he
is manifestly tickled all the same. It is scarcely a
wonder that the Roman was glad to escape from all
these formalities of "toga'd Rome" to his country
seat, or to the freer life of Baiae.

His business in the Forum accomplished, Silius returns to his house on the Caelian. As, on the slope
of the Sacred Way, he passes the rich shops of the
jewellers, florists, and perfumers, he may be tempted
to make some purchase, which the attendant slaves
will carry to the house. Arrived there, he will take
his luncheon, a fairly substantial though by no means

a heavy meal. He may perhaps be a married man. If nothing has yet been said about his wife, it is because in the higher Roman households the husband and wife owned their separate property, lived their own lives, and were almost equally free to spend their time in their own way, since marriage at this date was rather a contract than a union. If, however, he is a benedict, it is probable that at this meal the family will meet, no outside company being present. Silius himself reclines on a couch, the children are seated, and the wife may adopt either attitude. After this our friend will probably take a siesta, precisely as he might take it in Italy to-day. The practice was indeed not universal; nevertheless it was general. He will not go to bed, but will sleep awhile upon a couch in some quiet and darkened room. If he cannot sleep, or when he wakes, he may perhaps read or be read to. Where he will spend the afternoon till the bath and dinner is a matter of his own choice.

CHAPTER XIII

SOCIAL DAY OF A ROMAN ARISTOCRAT *(continued)* —
AFTERNOON AND DINNER

WE will suppose that Silius is specially inclined for
action and society. The afternoon is growing chilly,
and, as he has no further ceremonial to undergo, he
will probably throw over his toga a richly coloured
mantle — violet, amethyst, or scarlet — to be fastened
on the shoulder with a buckle or brooch. In very
cold weather, especially when travelling, Romans of
all classes would wear a thick cloak, somewhat like
the cape worn by a modern policeman or cab-driver,
or perhaps more closely resembling the *poncho* of
Spanish America. This, which consisted of some
strong and as nearly as possible waterproof stuff, had
no opening at the sides, but was put on by passing
the head through a hole. To-day Silius puts on the
coloured mantle, and gets himself carried across the
Forum, through the gap between the Capitoline and
Quirinal Hills, and into the Campus Martius, somewhere about the modern Piazza Venezia and the
entrance to the Corso. Here he may descend from
his litter, and purchase a statuette, or a vessel of
Corinthian bronze or silver, or an attractive table

with the true peacock markings, or a handsome slave. While doing so, he may find amusement in observing a pretender who "shops" but does not buy, wearying the dealers by pricing and disparaging the costliest tables and most artistic vessels, and ending with the purchase of a penny pot which he carries home himself. He may then stroll along under the pictured and statued colonnades, perhaps offering the cold shoulder to various impecunious toadies who are there on the look-out for an invitation to dinner, perhaps succumbing to their blandishments. His lackeys are of course in attendance, and clients are still about him. In passing he is greeted by some person who is hanging officiously round a litter containing an elderly lady or gentleman, and whom he recognises as what was called an "angler" — that is to say, one whose business is to wheedle gifts or a legacy out of childless people of wealth. This was a regular profession and extremely lucrative when well managed.

A little further, and he stops to look at the young men curvetting and wheeling on horseback over the riding-ground. Away in the distance others are swimming backwards and forwards across the Tiber. Or he steps into an enclosure, commonly connected with the baths, where not only young men, but their seniors, even of high rank, are engaged in various exercises. Some of them are stripped and are playing a game with a small hard ball, which is struck or thrown, and smartly caught or struck onward by right or left hand equally, from the three corners of a triangle. Some are playing with a larger and lighter article, something like a football stuffed with feathers, which seems to have been punched about by the fist in a way calling for considerable judgment and practice. Others are jumping with dumb-bells in

FIG. 65. — DISCUS-THROWER.

each hand, or they are running races, or hurling a disk of stone, or wrestling. Yet others are practising all manner of sword strokes with a heavy wooden weapon against a dummy post, merely to exercise themselves and keep down their flesh.

Probably Silius will himself take a hand in the three-cornered game, unless he possesses a private court at home and is intending to take his bath there instead of in one of the larger public or semi-public establishments. Whether he bathes in the baths of Agrippa at the back of the Pantheon, or in those of Nero, or in his own, the process will be much the same. The arrangements are practically uniform, however great may be the differences of sumptuousness and spaciousness. We have not indeed yet reached the times of those huge and amazing constructions of Caracalla and Diocletian, but there is no reason to doubt that the existing public baths were already of much magnificence. Regularly we should first find a dressing-room with painted walls, a mosaic floor, and glass windows, and provided with seats, as well as with niches in the walls to hold the clothes. Adjoining this is a "cold" room, containing a large swimming-bath. Next comes a "warm" chamber, with water heated to a sufficient and reasonable degree, and with the general temperature raised either by braziers or by warm air circulating under the floor or in the walls. After this a "hot" room, with both a hot swimming-bath and a smaller marble bath of the common domestic shape — though of much larger size — provided with a shower, or rather with a cold jet. Lastly there is a domelike sweating-chamber filled with an intense dry heat. The public baths built by Nero were particularly notorious for their high temperature. After the bath the body was rubbed over with perfumed oil, in order to close the

Fig. 66. — Stabian Baths. (Pompeii.)

225

pores against the cold, and then was scraped down
with the hollow sickle-shaped instrument of bronze or
iron depicted in the illustration.   The other articles
there shown are a vessel con-
taining the oil, and a flat dish
into which to pour it for use.
These, together with linen
towels, were brought by your
own slave.

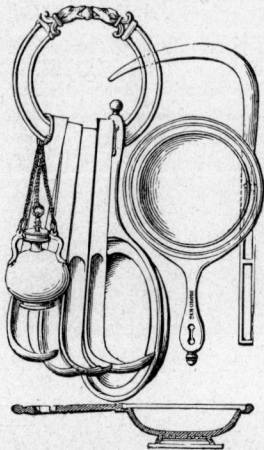

Silius is now carried home,
and as it is approaching four
o'clock, he dresses, or is dressed,
for   dinner.   His   toga   and
senatorial   walking-shoes   are

FIG. 67.—BATHING IMPLEMENTS. thrown off, and he puts on
light   slippers   or   house-shoes,   and   dons   what   is
called a "confection" of light and easy material
— such as a kind of half-silk — and of bright and
festive colours. Some ostentatious diners changed
this dress several times during the course of a protracted banquet, giving the company the benefit of as
great a variety of "confections" as is afforded by a
modern star actress in the theatre. If the days are
long and it is suitable weather, he may perhaps dine
in the garden at the back of the peristyle.   Otherwise
in the dining-room the three couches mentioned in a
previous chapter (Fig. 48) are arranged along three
sides of a rectangle. Their metal and ivory work
gleams brightly, and they are resplendent with their
embroidered cushions.   In the middle of the enclosed

space shines the polished table, whether square or
round. The sideboard is laden with costly plate; the
lamps are, or soon will be, alight upon their tall
shafts or hanging from their chains; the stand for the
carver is awaiting its load. The dining-room steward
and his subordinates are all in readiness.

At the right time the guests arrive, endeavouring
to show neither undue eagerness by being too early
nor rudeness by being too late. Each brings his own
footman to take off his shoes and to stand behind him,
in case he may be needed, though not to wait at table,
for this service belongs to the slaves of the house.
After they have been received by the host, the
"name-caller" leads them to their places, according to such order of precedence as Silius chooses to
pre-arrange. The regular number of guests for the
three couches will be nine — the number of the Muses
— or three to each couch. To squeeze in more was
regarded as bad form. If the crescent couch and the
large round table are to be used the number may be
either six or seven. The position of Silius himself as
host will be regularly that marked H on the plan,
while the position of honour — occupied by a consul if
one be present — will be that marked C.

Each guest throws himself as easily as possible
into a reclining attitude, resting his left elbow on
the cushion provided for the purpose. He has
brought his own napkin, marked with a purple stripe
if he is a senator, and this he tucks, in a manner still
sufficiently familiar on the continent of Europe, into
the upper part of his attire. Bread is cut and ready,

but there are no knives and forks, although there is a spoon of dessert size and also one with a smaller bowl and a point at the other end of the handle for the purpose of picking out the luscious snail or the succulent shell-fish. The dainty use of fingers well inured to heat was necessarily a point of Roman domestic training.

There have been many — perhaps too many — descriptions of a Roman dinner, but the tendency, especially with the novelist, is to exaggerate grossly the average costliness and gluttony of such banquets. Undoubtedly there were such things as "freak" dinners almost as absurd as those of the inferior order of American plutocrat. Undoubtedly also there was often a detestable ostentation of reckless expenditure. But we are endeavouring to obtain a fair view of representative Roman practice, and must put out of our minds all such vagaries as those of the ceiling opening and letting down surprises, or of dishes composed of nightingales' tongues and flamingoes' brains. These were always, as a later writer calls them, "the solecisms of luxury." Nero himself, or rather the ministers of the vulgar pleasures which he regarded as those of artistic genius, devised an abundance of such expensive follies and surprises, but we must not permit the professional satirist or Stoic moralist to delude us into believing them typical of Roman life. Praise of the "simple life" and the simple past is no new thing. It is extremely doubtful whether at an ordinary Roman dinner-party there was any such

lavish luxury as to surpass that of a modern alder-
manic banquet. We can hardly blame the people
who could afford it for obtaining for their tables the
best of everything produced around the Mediterranean
Sea, any more than we blame the modern citizen of
London or New York for obtaining the choicest foods
and dainties from a much wider world. Doubtless
a Roman dinner too often meant over-eating and
over-drinking, and doubtless neither the ordinary
table manners nor the ordinary table conversation
would recommend themselves to us. The same might
be said of our own Elizabethan age. But any one
intimately acquainted with Latin literature as a
whole, and not merely with the more savoury
passages commonly selected, will necessarily incline
to the belief that novelistic historians have too often
been taking what was exceptional, eccentric, and
strongly disapproved by contemporaries, for the
usual and the normal. If we read about Romans
swallowing emetics after gorging themselves, so that
they might begin eating afresh, we may feel both
disgust and pity, but we must not imagine such a
practice to have been a national habit.

The dinner regularly consisted of three divisions:
a preliminary course of *hors d'œuvres*, the dinner
proper, and a sort of enlarged dessert. It might
or might not be accompanied or followed by various
entertainments, and closed by a protracted course
of wine-drinking. All would depend upon the tastes
of the host and the nature of the company. The

meal, it may be mentioned, begins with an invocation corresponding to our grace. The *hors d'œuvres* are taken in the shape of shell-fish, such as oysters and mussels, snails with piquant sauce, lettuce, radishes, and the like, eggs, and a taste of wine tempered with honey.

Next comes the dinner proper, commonly divided into three services, comprising a considerable choice of fish (particularly turbot, flounder, mullet, and lampreys), poultry and game (from chicken, duck, pigeon, and peacock, to partridges, pheasants, ortolans, and fieldfares), hare, joints of the ordinary meats, as well as of wild boar and venison, a kind of haggis, a variety of the vegetables most familiar to modern use, mushrooms, and truffles. There is abundant, and to our taste excessive, use of seasonings, not only of salt, vinegar, and pepper, but of oil, thyme, mint, ginger, and the like. The *pièce de résistance* — a wild boar, or whatever it may be — regularly arrives as the middle of the three services. The substantial meal ends with a small offering to the household deities. After this follows the dessert, consisting of fresh and dried fruits, and of cakes and sweet-meats artistically composed.

During the dinner a special feature is made of the artistic arrangement of the various viands upon the large trays or stands from which the guest makes his choice, for the several dishes belonging to one course were not brought separately to table. In full view of the guests the professional carver exhibits his dexterity with much demonstration of grace and rapidity, and well-dressed and neat-fingered slaves render the necessary service. Of plates and dishes of various shapes and purposes, silver and silver-gilt, there is great profusion.

The conversation meanwhile depends upon the company. Sometimes it turns upon the chariot-races and the chances of the "Red" or "Green"; sometimes it is social gossip and scandal. If the guests are of a graver cast of mind, it may be concerned with questions of art and literature, or even philosophy. The Roman particularly affected encyclopaedic information, and frequently posted himself with such miscellaneous matter derived from a salaried domestic philosopher or *savant* — commonly, of course, a Greek. But upon politics in any real sense conversation will either not turn at all, or else very cautiously, at least until some one has drunk more than is good for him. It is only too easy to drop some remark which may be construed into an offence to the emperor, and there are too many ears among the slaves, and perhaps too many among the guests, to permit of any risk in that direction. In some rather serious companies a professional reader or reciter entertained the diners with interesting passages of poetry or prose; before others there might be a performance of scenes from a comedy. At times vocal and instrumental music was discoursed by the domestic minstrels; or persons, generally women, were hired to play upon the harp, lyre, or double flageolet. Such performances would also be carried on during the carousal which often followed

deep into the night, and to these may be added
posture-dances by girls from Cadiz, juggling and
acrobatic feats, and other forms of "variety" entertainment. Dicing in public, except at the chartered
Saturnalian festival, was illegal — a fact which did
not, of course, prevent it from being practised — but
it was permitted in private gatherings like this,
provided that ostensibly no money was staked. The

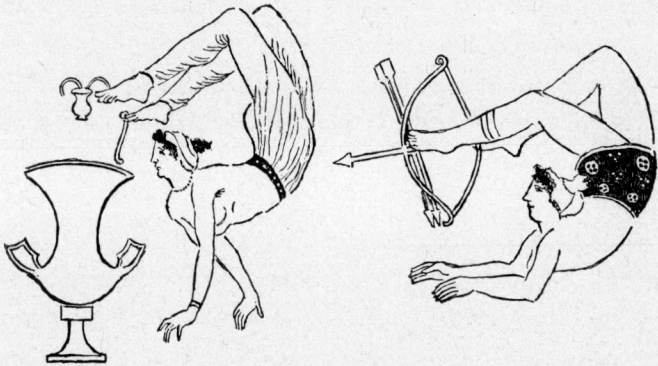

FIG. 68. — ACROBATS.

dice are rattled in a tower-like box and are thrown
upon a special board or tray. You may play "for
love," or, as the Romans called it, "for the best man,"
or you may play for forfeits. Naturally the forfeits
became in practice, in spite of the law, sums of
money. The best possible throw is called "Venus,"
the worst possible "the dog." A sort of draughts
or of backgammon may be preferred at more quiet
times of social intercourse; but a game like "head
or tail," called in Latin "heads or ships," was a game
for the vulgar.

If it was decided to indulge in a prolonged carousal

in form, heads were wreathed with garlands of roses, violets, myrtle, or ivy; lots were cast for an "umpire of the drinking," and he decided both how much wine — Falernian, Setine, or Massic — should be drunk, and in what degree it should be mixed with water. A large and handsome mixing-bowl stands in the dining-hall. From this the wine is drawn by a ladle holding about as much as a sherry-glass, and a certain number of such "glasses" are poured into each cup according to the bidding of the umpire. While being poured into the "mixer" the wine is passed through a strainer and in the hot weather the strainer would be filled with snow brought down from the nearest mountains and artificially preserved. Healths were drunk in as many "glasses" as the name contained letters; absent ladies were toasted in a similar way; and at some hour or other guests asked their footmen for their shoes and cloaks, and departed to their homes under the escort of attendants, who carried the torches or lanterns and were ready to deal with possible foot-pads and garroters, if any were lurking in the unlighted streets for pedestrians less wary or less protected. The "Mohawks" also will let them alone, and perhaps their homeward way may be entertained by the sounds of serenaders at the door of some beautiful Chloe or Lydia on the Upper Sacred Way or near the Subura.

It is not, however, to be supposed that every evening meal, even of a noble, took the form of a dinner-party. It is indeed probable that there were

few occasions upon which, while in town, he was not
either entertaining visitors or being himself entertained.
Occasionally there would be an invitation to dine at
Court, where perhaps eighty or a hundred guests of
both sexes, distributed in different sets of nine or
seven over the wide banquet-hall, would eat off gold
plate, and be entertained from three or four o'clock till
midnight with all the unbridled extravagance that a
Petronius or some other "arbiter of taste" might
devise for the Caesar. The snob of the period set an
enormous value upon this distinction. The emperor
could not always review his list of invitations, nor
could he on every occasion be personally acquainted
with every guest. It was therefore quite possible for
his servants now and then to smuggle in a person ambitious of having dined at the palace. Under Caligula
a rich provincial once paid nearly £2000 for such an
"invitation." When the emperor found it out, he was,
if anything, rather flattered; the next day he caused
some worthless trifle to be sold to the same man for
the same amount, and on the strength of this
acquaintance invited him to dinner, this time pocket-
ing the money for himself.

Yet there must have been no few evenings upon
which Silius preferred the company of an intimate
friend or two, making all together the "number of the
graces," and dined with less form and ceremony.
At such times the meal would be of comparatively
short duration, and there would be deeper and more
intimate matter of conversation. Now and then the
dinner would be purely domestic; and, after it, Silius

would perhaps pass an hour or two in reading, or in listening to the slave who was his professional "reader." If he was himself an author, as an astonishing number of his contemporaries actually were, he might spend the time in preparing a speech, composing some non-committal epic or drama, jotting down memoranda for a history, or concocting an epigram or satire to embody his humorous fancies or to relieve his exasperation. If, as was often the case, he kept in the house a salaried Greek philosopher — in a large measure the ana-logue of the domestic chaplain of the later seven-teenth century — he might enjoy his conversation and pick his brains; or, if a man of real earnestness of purpose, discuss with him the tenets of his particular philosophy, Stoic, Epicurean, or Eclectic. This was the nearest approach which the ancient Roman made to what we should call theological or religious argument.

On other days a patron would naturally entertain a number of his clients at dinner, and on no occasion would he be better able to show how much or how little he was a gentleman in the modern sense of the term. It is not merely from the satirist that we learn how discourteous the Roman grandee might be at his own table if he chose. It was no uncommon thing for a patron to set before these humbler guests dishes or portions of dishes markedly inferior to those which were offered to himself and to any aristocrat whom he had placed near him. In this sense the client was often made to feel very distinctly that he was "sitting below the salt." While the mellowest

Setine or Falernian wine was poured into the patron's own jewelled goblet of gold or silver or crystal, his client might be drinking from thick glass or earthenware the poorer stuff grown on the Sabine Hills. The fish presented to Silius and his "brother" noble might be a choice turbot, and the bird might be pheasant, while Proculus the client must be content with pike from the Tiber and the common barndoor fowl. The later satirist Juvenal presents us with inimitable pictures of the hungry dependants at the table of their "king," waiting "bread in hand" (like the sword drawn for the fray) to see what fortune would send them. On the other hand there were, of course, patrons who made no such distinctions. The younger Pliny, who was himself a gentleman almost in the modern sense — if we overlook a too frequent tendency to contemplate his own undeniable virtues — writes a letter to a young friend in the following terms: "I need not go into details as to how I came to be dining with a person with whom I am by no means intimate. In his own eyes he combined elegance with economy; in mine he combined meanness with extravagance. The dishes set before himself and a few others were of the choicest; those supplied to the rest were poor scraps. There was the same difference in his wine, which was of three kinds. The intention was not to offer a choice, but to prevent the right of refusing. One kind was for himself and us; another for his less important friends (for his friends are graded); another for his and our freedmen. My next neighbour noticed this, and asked me if I approved of it. I said

'No!' 'Well,' said he, 'what is your own practice?' 'I treat every one alike, for I invite people to a dinner, not to an insult, and when they share my table I let them share everything.' 'Your freedmen as well?' 'Yes, at such times I regard them as guests, not as freedmen.' At this he said, 'It costs you a good deal?' 'Not at all.' 'How can that be?' 'Because it is not a case of their drinking the same wine as I do, but of my drinking the same wine as they do.'" The letter is perhaps nearly half a century later than our chosen period, but there is no reason to think that manners had undergone any great change in the interval.

CHAPTER XIV

SILIUS was a noble, with a nobleman's privileges and also his limitations. The class next in rank below his consisted of the "knights," of whom something has already been said. It will be remembered that these men of the "narrow stripe" were the higher middle class, who conducted most of the greater financial enterprises of Rome and the provinces. While the senatorial order could govern the important provinces, command legions, possess large estates, and derive revenues from them, but could make money in other ways only through the more or less concealed agency of knights or their own freedmen, the knights were free to act as bankers, money-lenders, tax-farmers, and merchants or contractors in a large way, and to take charge of such third-rate provinces as the Caesar might think fit to entrust to them. Money-lending at Rome was an extremely profitable business. Not only was the nobleman often extravagant in his tastes, but when once elected to a public position he was practically compelled to spend money lavishly in giving shows and exhibitions of the kind which will be described immediately, or upon some public building, or otherwise. In consequence he often incurred heavy debts. Meanwhile the smaller traders and agriculturists, who were in competition with slave-labour and other false economic conditions, to say nothing of bad seasons, were frequently in the hands of the usurers. Though efforts were repeatedly made to check exorbitant rates of interest, they were apparently quite as ineffectual as with us. An almost standard charge was at the rate of one-twelfth of the loan, or $8\frac{1}{3}$ per cent, but another common rate was that of one per cent per month. Rates both higher and lower are known to us from particular cases. Naturally the question depended on the security, when it did not depend upon the greed of the one side and the ignorance of the other. Much, however, of what the books call money-lending was only what we should consider legitimate banking. Be this as it may, the knights made large fortunes from the practice. They were also the tax-farmers, who operated in the case of those imposts which were still left indirect. The practice was to make an estimate of the amount of such a tax derivable from a province, to purchase it from the government at as large a margin of profit as possible, and so relieve the state of the trouble and cost of collecting it. For this purpose "companies" were formed, with what we should call a "legal manager" at Rome. The managers would bid at auction for the tax, pay the purchase-money into the treasury, and proceed to get in the tax through local managers and agents in the provinces concerned. It has already been explained that the more important taxation of the empire was at this date direct — a community in Gaul, Spain, Asia Minor, or Syria knowing what its assessment was, taking its own measures, and using its own native or local collectors. The knights at Rome might still advance sums to such communities, but they were not in this case tax-farmers. It is unfortunate that the word "publicans" — bracketed with "sinners" — is used in the New Testament translation for the local collectors like St. Matthew. Not only does the word convey either no notion or a wholly incongruous one to the ordinary reader, but it is apt to mislead those who know its origin. Because the financial companies at Rome, in purchasing the taxes, were taking up a public contract, they were called *publicani*. But it is not these men who were themselves acting as petty collectors — in any case they had nothing to do with the native collectors appointed by the communities — and it is not these who enjoyed an immediate association with "sinners." The fact is that the Latin word applied to the great tax-farming companies, who were acting for Rome, was afterwards transferred to even the smallest collecting agent with opportunities for extortion and harshness.

The stratum of Roman society below the knights was extremely composite. The slaves, of course, are not included. They have no right to the Roman "toga," nor may they even wear the conical Roman cap, except at the Saturnalia, when everything is deliberately topsy-turvy. Omitting these, we may roughly divide the rest, as the Romans themselves divided them, into "people" and "rabble." The rabble are either persons without regular occupation, or *lazzaroni*, sheer idlers, loafers, and beggars. Doubtless many of them would execute an errand or carry a parcel for a small copper, otherwise they would be found hanging about the public squares, lounging on the steps or in the precincts of public buildings, such as temples, basilicas, porticoes, and baths, and playing at what the Italians call *morra* — a more clever and tricky species of "How many fingers do I hold up?" — or at "Heads or Tails." The poor of ancient Rome, like those of modern Italy, could subsist on very plain and simple food. Water, with a dash of wine when it could be got — and apparently at this date wine cost less than a penny a quart — and porridge or bread, however coarse, would suffice, so long as there were amusements, sunshine, and no need to work. Every considerable city of the empire round the Mediterranean would doubtless contain its proportion of such "lewd fellows of the baser sort," but it was naturally the imperial city that contained by far the most. Rome was by no means the only city in which doles of free corn were made and free spectacular exhibitions given. But in other places the distributions were occasional and depended on the bounty of local men of wealth or ambition, whereas at Rome the dole was regular, and the spectacles frequent and splendid. Rome was the capital, and the abode of the emperor. It claimed the privileges

R

of the Mistress City, including the enjoyment of the
surplus revenues.   Policy also demanded that the
rabble should be kept quiet by "bread and games."

It is for these reasons that the names of some
200,000 citizens stood upon a list to receive each
month an allowance of corn — apparently between
six and seven bushels — at the expense of the imperial
treasury.   This quantity they took away and made
into bread as best they could.   In many cases doubtless
they sold it to the bakers and others.   It must be
added that, apart from the free distribution, the
imperial stores contained quantities of grain which
could always be purchased at a low rate.   Occasionally a dole of money was added; in one case Nero
gave over £2 per man.   Meanwhile there was water
in abundance to be had for nothing, brought by the
carefully kept aqueducts into numerous fountains
conveniently placed throughout the city.   While,
however, we must recognise that the number of
idlers was very large, we must be careful not to
exaggerate.   It is absurd to assume, as some have
done, that because 200,000 citizens are receiving free
corn there are 200,000 unemployed.   The Roman
emperors never intended to put a premium on lazi-
ness, but only to deal with poverty.   In order to
receive your dole of corn it was not necessary to
show that you were starving, but only that you were
entitled, or in other words, on the list.   It is also
a mistake to think that any chance arrival among
the Roman *olla podrida* could claim his bushel and
a half of corn a week.   In any case only Roman

citizens could participate. All the poorest workers, whether actually employed or not, could take their corn with the rest. Nor must we forget that among the unemployed there were a considerable number who were, for one reason or another, only temporarily out of work. Nevertheless, it requires no study of political economy to know, nor were Roman statesmen blind to see, that the best way to make men cease to work is to show them that they can live, however shabbily, without. The really surprising thing is perhaps that the Roman government, with its immense funds and resources, stopped short where it did. An unsound economic system had brought about difficult conditions, with which the emperors and their advisers dealt as best they could.

It was inevitable that among so numerous a pampered rabble, and so many impoverished aliens who tried their fortunes in the capital, there should be beggars in considerable numbers. We cannot tell precisely how many they were. You might find them on the bridges, where they marked, as it were, a "stand" for themselves and crouched on a mat, or at the gates, or wherever carriages must proceed slowly on the highroads near the city, as for instance up the slope of the Appian Way as it passed over the south-western spur of the Alban Hills. Other towns would be infested in the same manner. Nor were thieves and footpads wanting in the streets or highwaymen upon the roads, especially in the lonelier parts near the marshes between Rome and the Bay of Naples. The city was, indeed, liberally policed, but Roman streets, as we have seen, were for the most part narrow, crooked, and unlighted at night. As usual, it was the comparatively poor who suffered from the street robber; the rich, with their torches and retinue, could always protect themselves.

After the "rabble" we will take the "people" in the sense current at this date. We must begin by adjusting our notions somewhat. The Romans made no such clear distinction as we do between trades and professions. To perform work for others and to receive pay for it is to be a hireling. Painters, sculptors, physicians, surgeons, and auctioneers are but more highly paid and more pleasantly engaged hirelings. Only so far do they differ from sign-painters, masons, undertakers, or criers. No doubt the theory broke down somewhat in practice, yet such is the theory. That which in our day constitutes a "liberal" profession — a previous liberal education and a high code of professional etiquette — can hardly be said to have existed in the case of corresponding professions at Rome. If the liberality departs from our own professional education and the etiquette is relaxed, we shall presumably revert to the same state of things. A surgeon was commonly a "sawbones," and a physician a compounder and prescriber of more or less empirical drugs. Their knowledge and skill were by no means contemptible, and their instruments and pharmacopoeia were surprisingly modern. Among the Greeks and Orientals their social standing was high, but at Rome, where they

were chiefly foreigners, for the most part Greeks,
the old aristocratic exclusiveness kept them in comparatively humble estimation, however large might
be their fees in the more important cases. Something
will be said later as to the state of science and knowledge in the Roman world. For the present it is
sufficient to note that artist, medical man, attorney,
schoolmaster, and clerk belong theoretically to the
common "people," along with butchers, bakers, carpenters, and potters.

Setting aside the aristocratic and wealthy classes

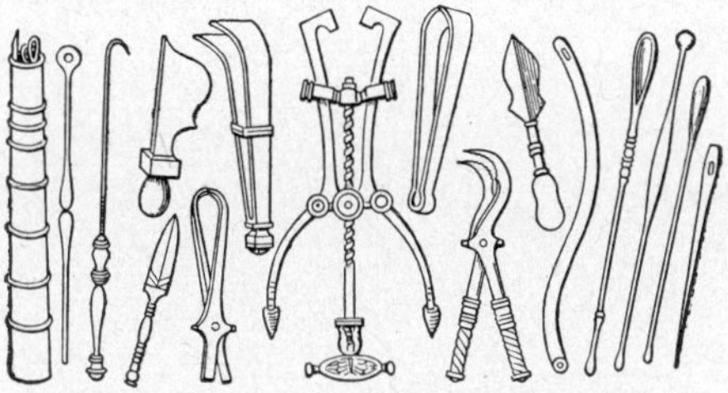

Fig. 69. — Surgical Instruments. (Pompeii.)

on the one hand, and the pauperised class on the
other, we have lying between them the workers,
whether native Romans or the emancipated slaves,
who are now citizens known as "freedmen." To
these we must add the rather shabby genteel persons
whom we have already described as "clients."
Among workers are found men and women of all the
callings most familiar to ourselves, with one exception.
They do not include domestic servants. Romans
who could afford regular servants kept slaves. It
is true that occasionally one of the poorer citizens,
and even a soldier on furlough, might perform some

menial task connected with a household, such as hewing wood or carrying burdens; but such services were regarded as "servile." With this exception there is scarcely an occupation in which Roman citizens did not engage. In such work they often had to compete with slave-labour. It is probable, doubtless, that the greater proportion of the slave body were employed as domestic servants. But many others tilled the lands of the larger proprietors. Others laboured under the contractors who constructed the public works. Others were used as assistants in shops and factories. It is obvious that such competition reduced the field of free labour, when it did not close it entirely, and the free labour must have been unduly cheapened. But to suppose that all the Roman work, whether in town or country, was done by slaves is to be grossly in the wrong. Romans were to be found acting as ploughmen and herdsmen, workers in vineyards, carpenters, masons, potters, shoemakers, tanners, bakers, butchers, fullers, metal-workers, glass-workers, clothiers, greengrocers, shop-keepers of all kinds. There were Roman porters, carters, and wharf-labourers, as well as Roman confectioners and sausage-sellers. To these private occupations must be added many positions in the lower public or civil service. There was, for example, abundant call for attendants of the magistrates, criers, messengers, and clerks. Unfortunately our information concerning all this class is very inadequate. The Roman writers — historians, philosophers, rhetoricians, and poets — have extremely little

to say about the humble persons who apparently did
nothing to make history or thought. They are
mentioned but incidentally, and generally without
interest, if not with some contempt, except where a
poet is choosing to glorify the simple life and therefore
turns his gaze on the frugal peasantry, who doubtless
did, in sober fact, retain most of the sturdy old
Roman spirit. About the soldiers we know much,
and not a little about the schoolmasters. The connection of the one occupation with history and of
the other with authors will account for this fact.
Something will be said of the army and also of the
schools in their special places. Keepers of inns are
not rarely in evidence in the literature of satire and
epigram, and no language seems too contemptuous
for their alleged dishonesty. But of inns enough
has been said. We learn that the booksellers made
money out of the works of which they caused their
slaves to make copies, and which they sold in "well
got up" style for four shillings, or, in the case of
slender volumes, for as little as fourpence-halfpenny.
But to this day we do not know how much profit
an author drew from the bookseller, or how it was
determined, or whether he drew any at all. It is
most reasonable to suppose that he sold a book
straight out to the publisher for what he could get.
Otherwise it is hard to see how any check could be
kept upon the sales. The only occupation upon
which literature offers us systematic information is
agriculture, including the pasturing of cattle and the
culture of the vine. For the rest we derive more

knowledge from the excavations of Pompeii than from any other source. From actual shops and their contents, from pictures illustrating contemporary life, and from inscriptions and advertisements, we are enabled to reconstruct some picture of commercial and industrial operations. We can see the fuller,

FIG. 70. — BAKER'S MILLS. (Pompeii.)

the baker, the goldsmith, the wine-seller, and the wreath-maker at their work. We can discern something of the retail trade in the Forum; or we can see the auctioneer making up his accounts.

The baker, for example, was his own miller. There are still standing the mills, with the upper stone — a hollow cylinder with a pinched waist — capable of revolving upon the under stone and letting

the flour drop into the rim below. Into the holes
in the middle of the upper or "donkey" stone, and
across the top, were fixed wooden bars, which were

FIG. 71. — CUPIDS AS GOLDSMITHS. (Wall Painting.)

either pushed by men or drawn by asses yoked to
them. The oven is still in place, and, charred as
they are, we are quite familiar with the round flat
loaves shaped and divided like a large "cross" bun.

The dough was kneaded by a vertical shaft with arms revolving in a receptacle, from the sides of which other arms projected inwards, so that there was little room for the dough to be squeezed between them. We have pictures of the fuller, to whom the woollen garments — the togas and tunics, and the mantles of the women — were regularly sent to be washed by treading in vats, to be beaten, stretched, and bleached with sulphur, and to have their naps raised with a comb or a bunch of thorns. The goldsmith is depicted

FIG. 72. — GARLAND-MAKERS.

at his furnace or his anvil. The garland-makers are at work fastening the blossoms or petals on a ribbon or a tough strip of lime-bark. Dealers in other goods are showing the results of their labour to customers, who carefully examine them by eye, touch, and smell. The tablets containing the receipts for sales and rents still exist as they were found in the house of the shrewd-looking Jucundus the auctioneer. They formally acknowledge the receipt of such-and-such sums realised at an auction, "minus commission," although unfortunately they do not happen to tell us how much the commission was. We see the

venders of wine filling the jars for customers from
the large wine-skin in the waggon. In conclusion
to this subject it should be observed that all manner

FIG. 73.—BUST OF CAECILIUS JUCUNDUS.

of descriptive signs were in use; and just as one may
still see a barber's pole or a gilt boot in front of a shop,
or a painted sign at a public-house, so one might
see the representation of a goat at the door of

a milk-vender, or of an eagle or elephant at the door of an inn.

Meanwhile out in the country we can perceive the farm, with its hedges of quick-set, its stone walls, or its bank and ditch. The rather primitive plough — though not always so primitive as it was a generation

FIG. 74. — PLOUGH.   (Primitive and later forms.)

or so ago in Italy — is being drawn by oxen, while, for the rest, there are in use nearly all the implements which were employed before the quite modern invention of machinery. It may be remarked at this point that the rotation of crops was well understood and regularly practised. Then there are the pasture-lands, on the plains in the winter, but in summer on the hills, to which the herdsmen drive their cattle along certain drove-roads till they reach the unfenced domains belonging to the state. There they form a camp of huts or wigwams under a "head man," and surround their charges with strong fierce dogs, whose business it is to protect them, not only from thieves, but also from the wolves which were then common on the Apennines — where, indeed, bears also were to be met. There was no want of occupation in the country in the time of haymaking, of the vintage, or of olive-picking. Even the city unemployed could gather a bunch of grapes or pick an olive, just as they can with us, or just as the London hop-picker can take a holiday and earn a little money in Kent. In the vineyards, where the vines commonly trailed upon low elms and other trees, various vegetables grew between the rows, as they still do about Vesuvius; on the hills were olive-groves, which cost almost nothing to keep in order, and which supplied the "butter" and the lamp-oil of the Mediterranean world.

We need not waste much compassion upon the life of the Roman working class. It is true that there was then no doctrine of the "dignity of labour," but that there was reasonable pride taken in a trade reputably maintained is seen from the frequent appearance of its tools upon a tombstone. In respect of the mere enjoyment of life, the labourers, of the Roman world were, so far as we can gather, tolerably happy. They had abundant holidays, mostly of religious origin; but, like our own, so frequently added to, and so far diverted from religious thoughts, that they were more marked by jollity and sport than by any solemnity of spirit. The workmen of a particular calling formed their guilds, "city companies," or clubs, in the interests of their trade and for mutual benefit. There was a guild of bakers, a guild of goldworkers, and a guild of anything and everything

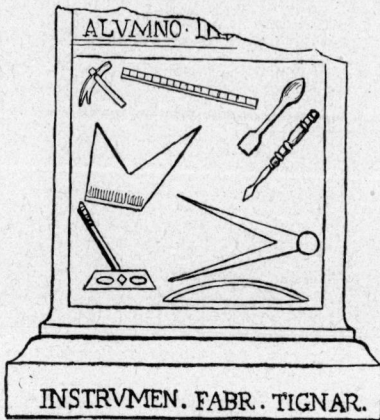

FIG. 75. — TOOLS ON TOMB.

else. Each guild had its special deity — such as Vesta, the fire-goddess, for the bakers, and Minerva, the goddess of wool-work, for the fullers — and it held an annual festival in honour of such patrons, marching through the streets with regalia and flag. Doubtless the members of a guild acted in concert for the regulation of prices, although the Roman government took care that these clubs should be non-political, and would speedily suppress a strike if it seriously interfered with the public convenience. The ostensible excuse for a guild, and apparently the only one theoretically accepted by the imperial government, was the excuse of a common worship. It is at least certain that the emperors jealously watched the formation of any new union,

and that they would promptly abolish any which
appeared to have secret understandings and aims, or
to act in contravention of the law.   In the towns
which possessed local government the municipal authorities were still elected by the people; and the
guilds, especially of shopkeepers, could and did play
their parts in determining the election of a candidate.
The elections might make a difference to them in
those ways in which modern town-councillors and
mayors may influence the rates, the conditions of the
streets, the rules of traffic, and so forth.   There are
sixteen hundred election notices painted in red and
black about the walls of Pompeii, and we find So-and-
So recommended by such-and-such a trade as being a
"good man," or "an honest young man," or a person
who will "keep an eye on the public purse."   It is
amusing to note that, in satirical parody of such
appeals as "the fruitsellers recommend So-and-So,"
we find that "the petty thieves recommend So-and-
So," or we get the opinion of "the sleepers one and
all."   Special objects connected with these and other
associations were the provision of "widows' funds,"
and of proper burial for the members.   Of the importance of the latter to the ancient world we shall
speak when we come to a funeral and the religious
ideas connected with it.

The most difficult task in dealing with antiquity
is to visualise the actual life as it was lived.   In the
life of the humbler citizens the remains of Pompeii
lend more help than anything else to the desired

sense of reality, but they are the remains of Pompeii,
not of Rome. Nevertheless there are many points
in which we may fairly argue from the little town
to the larger, and it is customary to adopt this
course.

We may, therefore, think of the common people

FIG. 76.—POMPEIAN COOK-SHOP.

among these ancients as very much alive in their
frank curiosity, their broad humour, their love of
shows, and their keen enthusiasm for the competitions,
their interest in petty local elections, their advertising
instincts, their insatiable fondness for scribbling on
walls and pillars, whether in paint or with a "style,"
a sort of small stiletto with which they commonly

wrote on tablets. The ancient world becomes very
near when we read, side by side with the election
notices, a line from Virgil or Ovid scrawled in a
moment of idleness, or a piece of abuse of a neighbouring and rival town — such as "bad luck to the
Nucerians" — or a pretty sentiment, such as "no one
is a gentleman who has not been in love," or an
advertisement to the effect that there are "To let,
from July 1, shops with their upper floors, a flat for a

FIG. 77. — IN A WINE-SHOP.

gentleman, and a house: apply to Prinus, slave of
So-and-So"; or "Found wandering, a mare with
packsaddle, apply, etc." — the latter, by the way,
painted on a tomb.

For places of social resort there were the baths,
the colonnades, the semicircular public seats, the
steps of public buildings, the shops, and the eating-
houses and taverns. The middle classes, in the
absence of the modern clubs, met to gossip at the
barber's, the bookseller's, or the doctor's. Those of a

humbler grade would often betake themselves to the establishments corresponding to the modern Italian *osterie*, where were to be obtained wine with hot or cold water and also cooked food. As they sat on their stools in these "greasy and smoky" haunts they might be compelled, says the satirist, to mix with "sailors, thieves, runaway slaves, and the executioner," but even men of higher standing were often not unwilling to seek low pleasures amid such surroundings, especially when, as was frequently the case, there was provision for secret dicing beyond the observation of the police.

From literature, meanwhile, we may fill in their vivacious language, the courteous terms the people apply to each other, such as "you ass, pig, monkey, cuckoo, chump, blockhead, fungus," or, on the other side, "my honey, my heart, my dove, my life, my sparrowkin, my dainty cheese." But to go more fully into matters like these would carry us too far afield.

We will end this topic with a last look at the ordinary free workman, who wears no toga, but simply a girt-up tunic, a pair of boots, and a conical cap, and who goes home to his plain fare of bread, porridge, lentil soup, goats'-milk cheese, "broad" and "French" beans, beetroot, leeks, salted or smoked bacon, sausages, and black-pudding, which he will eat off earthenware or a wooden trencher, and wash down with cheap but not unwholesome wine mixed with water. He has no pipe to smoke; he has never heard of tea, coffee, or spirits. He may have been told that certain remote barbarians drink beer, and he may know of a thing called butter, but he would not touch it so long as he can get olive-oil. However humble his home, he will endeavour to own a silver salt-cellar, and to keep it as an heirloom.

CHAPTER XV

THESE topics bring us naturally to the consideration of the chief amusements and entertainments of Rome and of those parts of the empire which were either fairly romanized or else contained a large number of resident Romans.

Holidays, some of them lasting over several days, were at this date liberally spread throughout the year. Most of them belonged to fixed dates, others were festivals specially proclaimed for victories or other causes of rejoicing. We may estimate their average number at Rome itself at about a hundred. At first sight this might indicate an astonishing waste of time and the prevalence of enormous indolence. But we must remember that the Romans had no such thing as Sunday. Our own Sundays and the weekly half-holidays make together seventy-eight days, and if to these we add the holidays at Christmas, Easter, and other Bank and public "closings," we shall find that our annual breaks in the working year are not very far from the Roman total, however differently they may be distributed. The difference between us and them lies rather in the way in which the holidays were employed. Originally the holidays did not imply any giving of shows and games in the way of chariot-races, gladiatorial combats, and the like. They were simply festivals of deities — of Flora, the goddess of flowers, Ceres, the goddess of crops, Apollo the god of light and healing, and other divinities — honoured by sacrifices, processions, and feasts. The feast of Saturn, for example, was at first held for only one day. Later it was extended over five and then over seven days, exactly as our Christmas celebrations — which are a Christian adaptation of it — tend virtually to spread over longer and longer periods. At this winter festival of the Saturnalia there was an interchange of presents — such as confectionery, game, articles of clothing, writing-tablets — and a general outburst of goodwill and merriment. For one day the slaves were allowed to put on the freeman's cap, the "cap of liberty," and to pretend to be the masters. This is the source of the mediaeval monkish custom of permitting one annual day of "misrule." Meanwhile the citizen threw off the toga and clad himself in colours as he chose. He played at dice publicly and with impunity. The cry of "Hurrah for the Saturnalia!" was heard everywhere. Later it became customary to hold public shows on these days, and the emperors gave gladiatorial games and acrobatic or dramatic entertainments, at which there were scrambled various objects, articles of food, coins or tickets entitling the holder to some gift which might be valuable, valueless, or comical. Similarly there was a holiday on New Year's Day, when presents were again interchanged, regularly including a small piece of money "for good luck." The gifts on this day frequently bore the inscription "a Happy and Prosperous New Year to you." Presents at all times played a prominent part in Roman etiquette and sociality. Not only were they given at holidays but also at all important domestic events. Even at a dinner-party, besides actual articles of food to be carried home, there were frequently gifts of a kind either expressly adapted to the recipient, or else drawn by a humorous lottery. Among numerous other articles of which one might be the recipient in various seasons and circumstances, there are mentioned books, pictures, tablets of ivory, wood, or parchment, cushions, mufflers, hats, hoods, sponges, soap, rings, flasks, baskets, musical instruments, balls, pens, lamps, tooth-picks, dice, money-boxes, satchels, parrots, magpies, and monkeys. On the Ides of March the poorer classes made their way to the Campus Martius beside the river, built themselves arbours or wigwams of boughs, and spent the day and evening in riotous song and jollity.

In general, however, the parts of these festivals to which the people looked forward with liveliest anticipation were those public entertainments, commonly known as "the games" or "sports," which were provided for them free of cost. The expense was theoretically borne by the state — whether from the exchequer of the emperor or from that of the senate

— and the state did indeed spend as much as six or
eight thousand pounds upon a particular celebration.
But, both in Rome itself and in the provinces, it was
practically obligatory that the public officer who had
charge of a given festival for the year should spend
liberally of his own upon it. No man either at Rome
or in a provincial city could permit himself to be
elected to such a public position unless he was prepared to disburse a sum perhaps as large as the sub-
vention given by the state. The more he gave,
particularly if he introduced some striking or amusing
addition to the ordinary shows, the more popular he
became for the time being. In the Roman world you
must pay for your ambitions, and this was the most
approved way of paying. We might moralise over
the enormous frivolity which could waste day after
day thousands and thousands of pounds upon such
transitory pleasures, instead of conferring lasting
benefits in the way of hospitals or schools. But it is
not the object of this book to moralise. We may feel
confident that the Roman populace, if offered the
choice, would have voted for the chariot-races or the
gladiators, not for the college or the hospital.

The entertainments provided were of several kinds,
by no means equally popular. There were plays in
the theatres; there were contests of running, wrestling,
boxing, throwing of spears and disks, and other
"events," corresponding to our athletic sports; there
were chariot-races in the Circus, answering to our
horse-races at Epsom or Newmarket; and there were

spectacles in the amphitheatre, to which, happily, we
have no modern parallel. These included huntings
and baitings of animals, fights with wild beasts — performances far more dangerous than those of the Spanish
bull-ring — and, above all, the combats of the gladiators
or professional "swordsmen." So far as there exists
a later analogue to the last it is to be found in the
more chivalrous tourney in the lists, but the resemblance is not very close. Least valued among the
real Romans were the athletic sports. For genuine
enjoyment of these we must look to the Greek part of
the empire. At Rome they appeared tame, for the
mind of the Roman populace was naturally coarse in
grain; what it delighted in was something sensa-
tionally acrobatic, or provocative of a rather gross
laughter, or else involving a thrilling anticipation of
danger and bloodshed. In taste the Romans were in
fact similar to those modern spectators who love to
see a man plunge from
a lofty trapeze into a
narrow tank, with a
reasonable chance of
breaking his neck. It
is a strange contradic-
tion with other Roman
attitudes when we find

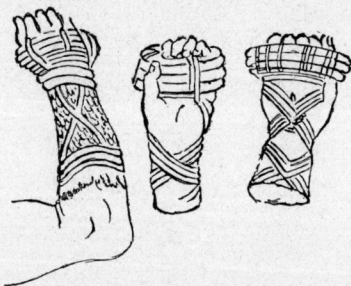

Fig. 78. — Boxing-Gloves.

that they objected to
the Greek wrestling or running on grounds of decorum,
because it was innocently nude. On the athletic
sports, although they were never wanting in the
"games" at Rome, we need not therefore dwell. It

may be sufficient to show by an illustration what
sort of notion the ancient world entertained of
interesting pugilism. It is only fair to say that the
"boxing-gloves" here given — thongs of leather
wrapped tightly round the arm and hand, and loaded
or studded with lead or iron — were a notion borrowed
from the professional pugilists of Greece.

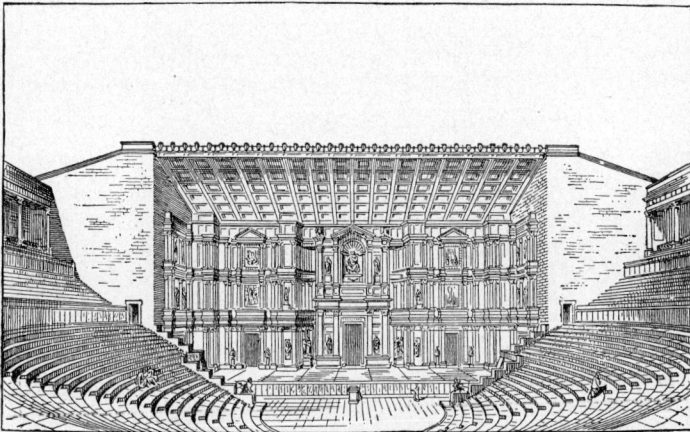

FIG. 79. — THEATRE AT ORANGE (restored).

Next lowest in esteem stood the plays given on
the theatrical stage. Mention has been made in a
previous chapter of the three great theatres of
Rome, one of them said, though somewhat incredibly,
to be capable of holding 40,000 spectators. Their
shape and arrangement have already been hinted at.
Huge structures of a similar kind existed in all the
great romanized towns of Italy and other provinces.
One at Orange in France is still well preserved, and two
of smaller dimensions — one without a roof for plays,
and one roofed for musical performances — are among

the most easily remembered of the remains extant at
Pompeii.   In the Grecian half of the empire the theatres
were not essentially different, the chief distinguishing
feature being that, while the Roman auditorium formed
half a circle, that of the Greek type formed over two-
thirds.   In the Roman type the level semicircle in
front of the stage, from which we derive the name
"orchestra," was occupied by the chairs of the senators,

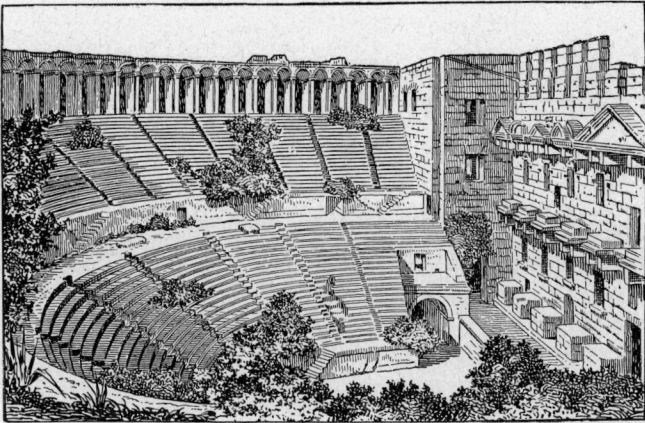

FIG. 80. — THEATRE AT ASPENDUS.

and the fourteen tiers of stone seats immediately
behind them by the knights; certain sections were
also set apart for special classes, one being for soldiers,
one for boys not yet of age, and one for women,
whose presence was not encouraged, and who, except
at the tragedies, would have shown more modesty
by staying away.   Facing the seats is a stage, higher
than among the Greeks, but somewhat lower than it
is commonly made in modern times; and at the back
of the stage is a wall architecturally adorned to

represent a house or "palace" front, and containing one central and two side doors, which served for separate purposes conventionally understood. Over the stage is a roof, which slopes backward to join the wall. The entrances to the ordinary tiers of seats are from openings reached by stairs from the outside arcade surrounding the building; those to the level "orchestra" are from right and left by passages under an archway, which supports a private box for the presiding official. The two boxes are approached from the stage, and when the emperor is present he is seated in the one to the spectators' left. Round the top of the building, inside above the seats, runs a covered walk, which serves as a lounge and a *foyer*. Over the heads of the spectators a coloured awning— dark-red or dark-blue by preference — may be stretched on masts or poles; when no awning is provided, or when it cannot be used because the wind is too strong, the spectator is permitted to wear a broad-brimmed hat, if he finds one desirable for his comfort. The whole building must be thought of as lined and seated with marble, gilded in parts, and decorated with pillars and statues.

The curtain, instead of being pulled up, as with us, when the play begins is pulled down, falling into a groove in the stage. Where we should say the "curtain is up" the Romans would say exactly the reverse, "the curtain is lowered." For plays in which the palace-front was not appropriate, scenery was employed to cover it, being painted on canvas or on boards which could be pulled aside; other scenes were stretched on frames, which could be made to revolve so as to present various faces.

The actors, however much admired for their art, and however influential in irregular ways, were looked upon as in a degraded position, and no Roman who valued social regard would adopt this line of life. Among the Greeks and such Orientals as were under Greek influence no such stigma rested upon the profession, and therefore many of the chief actors of the imperial city had received their training in this more liberal-minded part of the Roman world. The rest were mostly slaves or ex-slaves. If a Roman of any standing took part, it was either because he was a ruined man, or else because the emperor had capriciously ordered him to undergo this humiliation.

The plays themselves were certainly of no great merit from a constructive or literary point of view. We hear a good deal nowadays of the "decline of the drama," but perhaps in no civilised country has it declined so far as it had descended in Rome by the year A.D. 64. The regular and classical drama — that is to say, literary tragedy and comedy — was not likely to appeal to any ordinary Roman gathering. The philosopher Seneca indeed wrote tragedies in imitation of the Greek, but they were intended for the reader and the library, and there is little probability that they were ever performed, or even offered to the stage. Tragedies were, it is true, represented, but they were mostly Greek, and the performance was in the Greek style. The heroic actors wore masks, covering not only the face but the whole head, which

they raised considerably in height. About the body
fell long and trailing robes of splendid material and
colour, and on the feet were thick-soled boots which

FIG. 81. — TRAGIC ACTOR.

increased the height by several inches. The comedian
played in low shoes or slippers; and "boot" and
"slipper" were therefore terms in common vogue
to distinguish the two kinds of theatrical entertainment. Of Pliny's two favourite country-houses on

Lake Como one was called "Tragedy" as standing high, the other "Comedy" because on a lower site beside the water. The whole effect sought in the heroic play was the grandiose, and no attempt was made to reproduce the actualities of life. In the accompanying illustration will be seen the tragic hero as he appeared upon the Roman stage. In considering this somewhat amazing apparition it must be remembered that at Rome, as in Greece, the theatre was huge, effective opera-glasses were not known, and subtle changes of facial expression would have passed unnoticed. The make-up of the actor, like the painting of the scenes, was compelled to depend upon broad effects.

With its love of the false heroic, of rhetorical bombast, of sumptuous dress, magnificent scenes, and gorgeous accessories in the way of "supers" and processions, the Roman tragic drama of this period must have borne a striking resemblance to the corresponding English pieces of the Restoration or age of Dryden. Perhaps the most popular part of the performance was the music and dancing, whether by individual actors or as ballets, accompanied by the flageolet, the lyre, or the cymbals.

In comedy there was apparently no originality. As in the oldest days of their drama the Romans had copied the Greeks, so they copied them still. We may believe that the acting was often excellent, especially in respect of intonation and gesture, but little can be said for the play, whether from the point of view of literature or of morals. Since verbal description must necessarily be of little force, it will serve better to present here a few specimens of comic masks and a scene from comedy.

FIG. 82. — COMIC MASKS.

Much more in demand were theatrical performances of a lower kind. These were farces, interludes,

FIG. 83. — SCENE FROM COMEDY.

or character-pieces, and dumb-shows known as "pantomimes." The farce was a loosely constructed form of fooling comedy, containing much of the ready Italian improvisation or "gag," and regularly introducing the four stock characters which have lasted with little disguise for so many centuries. There was an old "grandfather," the forerunner of the modern pantaloon; a cunning sharper; a garrulous glutton with a fat face (known as "Chops"); and an amorous Simple Simon. Sometimes types of foreigners or provincials were introduced, with caricatures of their dress and language, after the manner, and probably with the veracity, of the stage Scotchman, Irishman, or Frenchman. All these parts were played in masks.

The interlude again was a slight piece with very little plot, and composed in a large measure of buffoonery, practical jokes, hitting and slapping, and dancing. Topical allusions and contemporary caricatures were freely introduced, and the whole performance, however coarsely amusing, was both vulgar and indecent. In these pieces no masks were worn and also no shoes, and the women's parts — taken in the other instances by men and boys — were actually played by females, whose posture-dances were no credit to their sex.

The dumb-shows or "pantomimes" were performances in which expressive and elaborate gestures and movements were left to tell the whole tale. For this kind of piece the actors naturally required not only uncommon cleverness but also great suppleness of body. As usual, these qualities, together with the qualities of voice, the magnificent dress, and the carefully cultivated long hair, won for the actor a

demoralising influence over too large a number of
the more impressionable and untrammelled Roman
dames.

Meanwhile the huge audience must not be conceived as sitting in quiet and restrained attention, but as roaring with laughter, applauding and
stamping, shouting approval and encores, hissing and
waving handkerchiefs. And meanwhile the *claqueurs*
will have been duly distributed by those interested in
the success of the performance. Every now and then
a fine rain of saffron perfume is shed over the audience
from pipes and jets distributed round the building.
It deserves remark also that in the theatre, as in
the other places of amusement, the gathering frequently broke out into demonstrations of its feeling
towards persons and politics. There was safety in
numbers, and the applause or hissing which greeted a
personage or a topical allusion — or a line which could
be twisted into such — could hardly be laid to the
account of any individual. A certain license was
conceded and fully utilised at the festivals : it served
as a safety-valve, and wise emperors apparently so
regarded it. At Rome the government was indeed
"despotism tempered by epigram," but it was no less
tempered by these demonstrations at the games and
spectacles.

More worthy of imperial Rome were the exhibitions of chariot-races held in the immense Circus
Maximus. That building, already described, would
at this date probably hold some 200,000 persons, but

T

it could never provide room enough for the excited
people, who not only gathered in multitudes from
Rome itself, but also from all the country, even all the
empire, within reach. For weeks the chances of the
parties have been discussed and betted upon; even
the schoolboys have talked chariots, chariot-drivers,
and horses. The fortune-tellers have been consulted
about them; dreamers have dreamed the winners;
and many an underhand attempt, sometimes including
the hocussing of men or horses, has been made to
corrupt the sport. The struggle is in reality not
between chariot and chariot, but between what we
should call stable and stable. There are four parties
— the white, red, green, and blue — whose drivers will
wear the respective colours, in which also the chariots
were probably painted. By some means the green
and blue have at this date contrived to stand out
beyond the others, and the chief interest commonly
centres upon these.

The day of the great spectacle arrives. Outside
the building and in the porticoes surrounding it the
sellers of books of the races and of cushions are plying
their trade along with venders of confectionery
and perfumes. The people are streaming into the
numerous entrances which lead by stairways to the
particular blocks or tiers of seats in which they are
entitled to sit, and for which they bear a ticket.
Full citizens are wearing the toga, or, if the emperor
has not forbidden the practice, the brightly coloured
cloak which has been already described. Seats are
reserved for officials, senators, knights, and Vestal

Virgins; and on the side under the Palatine is a large balcony-box for the emperor and his suite. At these games women have no special place set apart for them; they sit in their richest and showiest attire among the general body of the spectators, and flirting and love-making are part of the order of the day. A very crude form of field-glass or "spy-glass" was already in use, apparently consisting generally of a mere hollow tube, but occasionally provided with a magnifying lens. Nero himself, in consequence of his short-sight, had a "glass" in some way contrived of emerald.

At one end of the Circus is a building containing a curved line of stalls, equidistant from the starting-point, in which the drivers hold their chariots in readiness. These are all barred, and only at the signal will the doors be thrown open. The horses are commonly three-year-olds or five-year-olds. In some races there are two horses to the chariot, in others four. Less commonly there are three or six, or even a greater number. In the year 64 the number of cars running will be four, one for each club. How many races there are to be, and in what variety, will depend upon the presiding officer, who, as has been said, is paying a considerable portion of the expenses, and who will receive or lose applause according to the entertainment he affords to the spectators. Commonly there will be about twenty races run, although occasionally even that number may be increased.

Down the middle of the arena, though not quite

in its axis, runs a low broad wall called the "backbone," bearing various sculptures along its summit,
and in the middle an obelisk, now standing in the
Piazza del Popolo, which Augustus had brought from
Egypt after his conquest of that country. On the
extremities of the "backbone" are placed the figures
of seven dolphins and seven large eggs, and just free
of each end, on a base of their own, stand three tall
cones coated with gilt, round which the chariots are
to turn as a yacht turns round the buoy. Seven
times will the chariots race down the arena, round

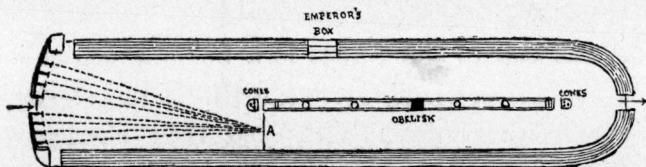

FIG. 84. — PLAN OF CIRCUS.

the end of the backbone, and back again. At each
lap a dolphin and an egg will be removed from the
wall, and as the last disappears the winning driver
makes straight on for the white line which serves as
the winning-post.

But they have not yet started. At the fixed hour
a procession starts from the Capitol, descends by the
temple of Saturn and past the face of the Basilica
Julia, turns along the "Tuscan Street," and enters
the Circus under a large archway in the middle of
the building which contains the stalls. In front go
a body of musicians with blare of the straight Roman
trumpet and the scream of the flageolets; behind
these comes the high official who has charge of the

particular festival. He is mounted high on a chariot,
and is clothed in a toga embroidered with gold and
a tunic figured with golden palm-branches: in his
hand he carries an ivory sceptre, and over his head
is held a crown of gold-leaf. Behind the chariot is
collected a retinue in festal array. The competing
chariots follow; after these are the effigies of deities,
borne on platforms or on vehicles to which are attached
richly caparisoned horses, mules, or elephants; in
attendance upon them are the connected priestly
bodies. As this procession passes round the Circus
the spectators rise from their seats, roar their acclama-
tions, and wave their handkerchiefs. When it has
made the circuit, its members retire to their places, and
the chariots are shut in their stalls. Soon the president
takes his stand in his box, lifts a large handkerchief
or napkin, and drops it. Immediately the bolts of
the barriers are withdrawn, and the chariots dash
forward towards the point marked A. The drivers,
clothed in a close sleeveless tunic and wearing a skull-
cap, all of their particular colour, lean forward over
their steeds, and encourage them with whips and
shouting. At their waists you will see the reins
gathered to a girdle, at which also hangs a knife, in
readiness to cut them away in case of accident. The
chariot is a low and shallow vehicle of wood covered
with ornament and as light as it can well be made, and
it requires no little skill for the charioteer to maintain
his footing while controlling his team. Down the
straight they rush, each endeavouring to gain an
advantage at the turn, where the left rein is pulled,

and the left horse — the pick of the team — is brought as closely round the end of the wall as skill and prudence can contrive. It is chiefly, though by no means only, here that the accidents occur, and that the chariots lose their balance and collide with each other, or strike against the end of the wall and are overthrown. How readily collision might happen may be seen from the following diagram, where the courses of two chariots, A and B, are indicated.

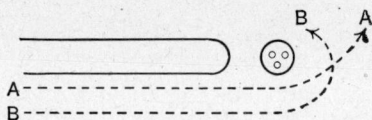

FIG. 85.—THE TURN IN THE CIRCUS.

Sometimes the teams get out of hand and general disaster may result. Round and round they go, the spectators yelling in their excitement for the blue or the green, the red or the white, and making or revising their bets. "Too far out!" "Well turned!" "The green wins!" "Well done, Hirpinus!" Shouts like these form a roar to which perhaps we have no modern parallel. One by one the eggs and dolphins disappear from the wall; the chariots are reduced in number; the four or five miles are completed; and an enormous shout goes up for the winner, whose name — of man and horse and colour — will be for days in everybody's mouth. For his reward he will not only obtain the honour of the palm-branch; he will receive presents in money, gold and silver wreaths, clothes, and various articles of value. Socially he

may be but a slave or a person in base esteem; the
occupation, however reputable in the Greek portion of
the empire, is not for a free-born Roman; nevertheless, like the jockey who wins the Derby, he is the
hero of the moment.

Race follows race, with an interval for the mid-
day meal. During that time there will be interludes of acrobatic and other performances. One

FIG. 86. — CHARIOT-RACE.

rider, for example, will stand upright on the back
of two or more horses, and will spring continually
from one to the other while they are at the gallop.
Most of the company will take their refreshments
where they are. When a man of some standing
was reproached by Augustus for this rather undignified proceeding, he replied: "That is all very well
for you, Sire, but your place is sure to be kept."
We need not proceed further into details concerning

the "events" in the Circus. It may however be worth while to add that the Romans cared nothing for the modern form of race by jockeys on single horses.

The Circus is quite a different thing from the oval amphitheatre, a structure for once of native Roman devising, without which no Roman town could consider itself complete. Though the Colosseum was not yet built, there already existed an amphitheatre in the Campus Martius, and such buildings were to be found in all considerable towns which contained a large Roman element. There is one, though of later date than Nero, still to be seen in fair preservation at Verona; the well-known amphitheatre at Pompeii was in full use in the year 64, and other cities — Capua, Puteoli, Nîmes, Antioch, or Caesarea — were provided with the joys of the gladiatorial shows and the beast-fight. Only in the thoroughly Greek or thoroughly Oriental part of the empire was the amphitheatre absent. Where there was no fixed building of stone or wood, a temporary structure was erected and a company of gladiators would perform in the place at the expense of some local officer or of some wealthy citizen with social ambitions. Whatever may be thought of the Greeks in other respects, they felt no liking, but only an openly expressed repulsion, for the barbarous exhibitions of bloodshed in which the Roman revelled. Outside Jerusalem an amphitheatre was built by the romanizing Herod, but it was done to the horror of all orthodox Jews.

FIG. 87. — AMPHITHEATRE AT POMPEII.

281

The performances were of two main kinds; fights between men and beasts — occasionally between two kinds of wild beast — and fights between men and men. There was no make-believe about these combats; they meant at least serious wounds, even when they did not mean death. Those who fought with beasts might in some cases be volunteers; in general they were captives or condemned criminals, and it perhaps hardly needs pointing out that, when St. Paul says he had "fought with beasts at Ephesus," he is merely speaking in metaphor adapted to the times. It was not intended that the criminal should escape death, but only that he should be able to make a fight for his life. Meanwhile the gladiators who fought with men and not with beasts were in the position of professionals, who might be slaves, condemned brigands, mutineers, prisoners of war, or volunteers. The picture drawn by Byron, although the so-called "Dying Gladiator" which inspired him is in reality no gladiator but a Gaulish warrior, perhaps fairly represents one class of combatant, but it represents only one. In the case of these "swordsmen" a number of successful fights might in the end secure freedom and something more for slave or prisoner, and a competence for the volunteer. It was not unnatural that men of courage and strength should frequently offer themselves for this service. Their physical training was indeed severe both in the way of exercise and of diet, and their personal treatment was harsh and ignominious; but their fame, such as it might be, was wide, and their rewards often solid. Contemporary

Fig. 88. — Barracks of Gladiators. (Pompeii.)

writers also complain that, however brutal and ugly they were, there were always women ready to adore them and to consider them as beautiful as Adonis. At Pompeii a scribbling calls one of them "the sigh of the girls." Nevertheless no Roman with much self-respect, unless forced by a malignant emperor, would bear the stigma of having appeared as a gladiator, any more than in modern times one would choose to be known as a professional pugilist. Moreover these same heroes, after their glorious day in the arena, were carefully stripped of their showy armour, imprisoned in barracks, and, if disobedient or troublesome, chastised with the lash and put in irons or the stocks.

The prelude to a beast-fight was frequently rather a "hunt," amounting to a demonstration of skill in dealing with wild animals which could hardly be said to fight, but which were difficult to capture or kill. Success with javelins or arrows required somewhat more skill and daring than the "big game" shooting of modern times. To give a greater air of naturalness to the performance the arena was sometimes temporarily planted with shrubs and trees, and diversified with rock-work. After the beast "hunt" came the beast "fight," which might be against bisons or bulls, wild boars or wolves, lions or tigers, a rhinoceros or an elephant. In such contests the man commonly wore no body-armour. He took his sword or spear, swathed his right arm and his legs, and went out to meet the enemy in his tunic. The beasts were either let loose from the end of the arena, or, as later in the Colosseum, they were brought up in cages from their underground dens by means of lifts worked by pulleys. Indirectly, it may be observed, the mania for this sport produced one distinctly beneficial result, inasmuch as the more dangerous wild beasts became almost exterminated from the Roman world. The number killed was enormous, hundreds of lions or panthers being produced and slain during the shows of a single festival. It may be added that on the top of the wall or platform surrounding the arena there was placed — at least in the Colosseum — a metal

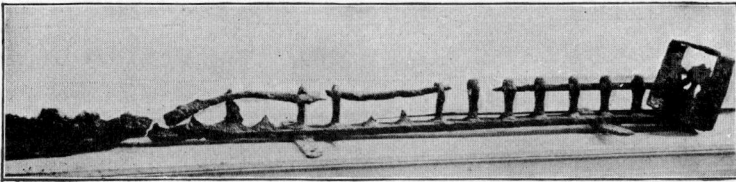

FIG. 89. — STOCKS FOR GLADIATORS. (Remains from Pompeii.)

grating or screen, of which the top bar revolved, so that if a wild beast managed to spring so high and take a grip, the feat was of no use to him. To keep him at a further distance a trench surrounded the arena and separated it from the platform.

But *the* great entertainment of the amphitheatre was the combats of men with men. After the beast-fights, which were held in the mornings, and amounted in estimation to a *matinée*, there followed the fights of the gladiators. Outside the building are being sold the books which catalogue the pairings, together with some record of the men, the name of their training-school, and a statement as to the weapons with which they will fight and as to whether they have made previous appearances. At the appointed time the procession enters from one end of the arena, and the combatants parade and salute the emperor, if he is present, or the presiding officer. Their weapons are examined, and there is a preliminary sham-fight, partly for exhibition of skill and to influence bets, partly for practice. The men then return to their places, a trumpet blows, and a pair commences the

FIG. 90. — GLADIATORS FIGHTING.

real fighting. Sometimes a man is in full and heavy armour from head to foot; sometimes he is lightly equipped with a half-shield and a spear; sometimes he carries only a sharp three-pronged spear and a casting-net, in which he endeavours to enmesh an enemy fully armed. Besides combats on foot, there may be fights upon horseback, or even in chariots of the kind then best known in Britain. To encourage the participants, and to lend more spirit to the scene, there is a blowing of horns and trumpets while the fight proceeds. All around the people are shouting their comments and their advice; they applaud and adjure and curse. "Get up to him!" "Kill him!" and the like are heard on every side. A man falls, not dead, but disabled, and the spectators shout "He has it." He holds up his finger in sign of defeat, but he utters no cry. Shall he be killed, or shall he not? The answer depends on the president or "giver" of the exhibition. He looks round, and if he perceives that the great majority are giving an upward flick of the thumb, and hears them call "Give him the steel!" the man is doomed; if, on the contrary, handkerchiefs are waved, his life is spared. A good fight or a good record may save him to fight again another day. The formal presentation of a wooden sword would mean that he was discharged for life from the necessity of further fighting. If his enemy's dagger must be pressed into his throat, or if he has been slain out-right, there is a passage under the middle of the side of the amphitheatre through which the body will be dragged by a hook into the mortuary. Another combat follows between another pair — sometimes between two sides — and should the arena become too sodden with blood, it is raked over and fresh sand is scattered.

It is amazing in what a cold-blooded manner all this was carried out. When one reads the notices written up at Pompeii, that on such-and-such a date there will be exhibited so many pairs of gladiators, that "there will be a beast-hunt," and that "awnings will be provided and perfume sprinkled," it is difficult at first to realise that it means all that it does mean. To the credit of the Romans — so far as they deserve

any at all — let it be stated that the presence of women
was not encouraged at these shows; that if they
appeared at all, it must be in the upper tier, as far as
possible from the arena; and, strangely enough, that
only the six Vestals, in virtue of their religious claims,
could be placed in any position of honour. These sat
upon the lowest platform, in line with the special
seats of the emperor or president and the highest
officials of the state, but it is probably a libel for an
artist to depict them as so many Maenads lusting for
the blood of the vanquished.

The only other form of public entertainment which
it seems desirable to mention was that of a naval
battle, in which the sea was either represented by
flooding the amphitheatre, or by means of a permanent
lake, such as that which Augustus created artificially
across the Tiber. The proceedings bore all the appearance of reality. Ships were rammed, sunk, over-
turned, and boarded, and, so far as the men were
concerned, the battle might be as grim and bloody as
any other kind of gladiatorial contest.

CHAPTER XVI

THE WOMEN : MARRIAGE, THE ROMAN MATRON, AND HER DRESS

WE will assume that Silius is a married man, and that his wife is a typical Roman dame worthy of his station in life. Her name shall be Marcia, or, if she possesses more than one, Marcia Sabina. Marriage does not confer upon her the name of her husband, and if she requires further identification in connection with him, she will be referred to as "Silius's Marcia." At an earlier date a woman owned but a single name, but already practical convenience and pride of descent had combined to make it desirable that she should bear a second, which might be taken from the family either of her father or of her mother. Thus if Silius and Marcia themselves have a daughter, she may in her turn perhaps be called Silia Bassa, perhaps Silia Marcia.

If now we proceed to describe the position of Marcia in her conjugal and family relations, to speak of her way of life, and to suggest her probable character, it must be understood that the description would by no means necessarily fit every Roman matron. Women are said to be infinitely various, and in this respect the ancient world was precisely like the modern. And not only has it further to be borne in mind that there were several strata of Roman society, and that city life differed widely from country life; there was also an actual difference in the legal position of a wife, according to the terms upon which she had chosen to enter the state of wedlock. In other words, there were two forms of matrimony. According to the old-fashioned style a wife passed into the power of the husband; her legal position — though not, of course, her domestic standing — was the same as that of his daughter. Once on a time he had even possessed the right of putting her to death, but at our date that privilege no longer existed. It was enough that she should be subject to his authority. In that position she managed the home and family, and often managed him as well. How far this time-honoured style of marriage was still maintained among the lower classes of Roman society it is impossible to tell; our information is almost entirely restricted to the higher, or at least the wealthier, orders. It is, however, probable that among the artisans and labourers, where the dowry of a wife cannot have amounted to anything very considerable, this more stringent state of matrimony was the rule. Paterfamilias was the head and lord of the house, while mater-familias held in practice much the same position as she did in Anglo-Saxon households of two or three generations ago.

Meanwhile among the upper classes, but in no

way legally limited to them, an alternative and easier
form of marriage had become increasingly popular.
It was one which gave to both parties the greatest
amount of freedom of which a conjugal union could
reasonably allow. The woman did not pass into the
power of the man, and, short of actual infidelity, she
lived her own life in her own way, although naturally
conforming to certain recognised etiquette as a
partner in a respectable Roman *ménage*. If neither
affection nor moral suasion could preserve harmony
or proper courses, either party might formally
repudiate the contract, and, after a short interval,
seek better fortune in some other quarter. There
was, of course, a public sentiment to be considered;
there was family influence; there was the characteristic Roman pride; there was often a fair measure
of mutual esteem and even affection; and there were
obvious joint interests which made for stability; but
beyond these considerations there was nothing to
hamper the inclination of either husband or wife.
Yet it is a grave mistake to imagine, because there was
much, and sometimes appalling, looseness of life under
a Nero, that the race of noble and virtuous Roman
matrons — the Cornelias and Valerias and Volumnias
— was extinct; and it is equally a mistake to suppose
that Rome no longer produced its honourable gentlemen filled with a sense of their responsibilities to
family and state. The satirist should not here, nor
elsewhere, be our chief, much less our only, guide.
The England of Charles II. is not to be judged in
its entirety by the comedies of the time nor by the

Memoirs of Grammont. On this matter, however, it will be more convenient to touch in a later paragraph. It will be best to deal first with the system in vogue, and then to consider the sort of woman whom it produced.

It cannot be denied that at this date, though marriage was regarded as the normal and proper condition for men and women who desired to do their duty by the state, and though the wise emperors did everything in their power to encourage it, a very large proportion of the men of the upper classes regarded it as a burden and a vexatious interference with their liberty. It was not necessarily that they had any desire to be vicious, nor indeed would marriage be much of a hindrance to vice; it was that they desired to be free. The cause of their disinclination was the same as it is sometimes alleged to be now — the increasing demands of women, their increasing unwillingness to bear the natural responsibilities of matrimony, their extravagant expectations, and the impossibility of there being two masters in one house claiming equal authority. But whereas we recognise that love is a possible adjuster of all the difficulties, it was no tradition of the Romans that marriage should be based on love. With them it very seldom began with love, or even with direct personal choice, but was in most instances entirely a *mariage de convenance* and arranged for them as such. Even after marriage we are told by a contemporary writer that the proper feeling for a man to entertain for his wife is rational respect, not emotional affection. Experience has shown that the result was too often unsatisfactory.

It is unfortunate that the only satires or criticisms on married life which have come down to us were written by men; one would like to hear what the women might have said, if a woman had ever been a satirist. There is nearly always some basis of truth in a classic satire, but the question is "How much?" Juvenal belongs to a later generation than that of Nero, but what he says is doubtless equally applicable to that age. It is therefore interesting to note one or two of his objections to contemporary woman, regarded as a wife. In the first place she is too interfering and even dictatorial. "What madness is it," he asks of the man whom he supposes himself to be addressing, "that drives you to marry? How can you bear with a tyrannous woman, when there are so many good ropes in the world, when there are high windows to throw yourself out of, or when there is the bridge quite handy?" "Why should you be made to wear the muzzle?" "Why take into your house some one who will perhaps shut the door in the face of an old friend whom you have known ever since he was a boy?" "When you displease her, she weeps, for she keeps tears always ready to fall, but when you try to prevent her from displeasing you, she tells you it was agreed that each should have liberty, and that she is a human being." He goes on to attack her faithlessness, her extravagance, her superstition, her loquacity, and so forth. Let us by all means discount his fierce invectives; nevertheless we must take them as but a heightened way of putting circumstances which had a real and all too frequent existence, and which encouraged the growing fancy for bachelordom. We shall, however, soon look at a very different picture of domestic relations, and it is only fair to assume that these also were by no means uncommon.

A Roman girl with a reasonable dowry might expect to be married at any age from about 13 to 18. The Italian of the south, like the Greek, ripens early. The legal age was 12; on the other hand to be unmarried at 19 was to be distinctly an old maid. In the northern provinces of the empire maturity was less early, whereas south of the Mediterranean it was even earlier. The legal age for the bridegroom was that at which his father or guardian allowed him to put on the "toga of the man" and enter the Forum. Thus theoretically a Roman youth might become a benedict when about sixteen, and Nero was only at that age when he married his first wife Octavia. Generally speaking, however, if Marcia was as old as 16, Silius would hardly be under 26 or 27.

The marriage, as has been said already, would commonly be a matter of arrangement between families, sometimes effected by their own members, sometimes by an interested friend or some other go-between. "You ask me," writes Pliny to Mauricus, "to look out for a husband for your niece. There is no need to look far, for I know a man who might seem to have been provided on purpose. His name is Minicius. He is well-connected, and comes from Brescia, which you know to be a good old-fashioned place retaining the simple and modest manners of the country. He is a man of active energy and has held high public office. In appearance he is a gentleman, well-built, and with a wholesome ruddy complexion. His father has ample means, and though perhaps your family is not much concerned on that point, we have to remember that a man's income is one of the first considerations in the eyes, not only of our social system, but of the law."

A marriage of the full and regular type could only be contracted between free citizens. There were varying degrees of the morganatic about all others, such as marriage with a foreigner or emancipated slave. A non-Roman wife meant that the children were non-Roman. A man of the senatorial order could not marry a freedwoman, if he wished to have the union recognised; also no complete marriage could be contracted with a person labouring under degradation publicly inflicted by the authorities or degraded *ipso facto* by certain occupations. For this reason the actress on the "variety" stage could not aspire to become even an acknowledged Roman wife, much less a member of the order which more or less corresponded to our peerage. Nor could a Roman marry a relative within certain prohibited degrees. He might not, in fact, marry any woman whom he already possessed what was called "the right to kiss."

We are, however, dealing with two persons entirely beyond exception, namely Quintus Silius Bassus and Marcia Sabina. A match has been made between these parties, perhaps several years before the actual

marriage can take place, and while the intended
bride is a mere child of ten: even the future groom
may be but a boy. When the go-between has done
his or her work to the satisfaction of both families,
there takes place a betrothal ceremony, of which the
original purpose was, of course, to bind each party
morally to carry out the contract, but which, by the
year 64, might mean very little.

In theory the Roman law required the consent of
both participants; a father could not absolutely
force son or daughter to marry a particular person,
nor, indeed, any person at all. But on the other
hand, according to the Roman law, neither sons nor
daughters were free to act independently of the
father's will, nor to possess independent property,
so long as the father lived, or until he chose to
"emancipate." It naturally follows that paternal
pressure was the chief factor in determining a
marriage, and only those men or women whose fathers
were dead, or who had been formally freed from
tutelage, were in a position absolutely to please
themselves. We need not suppose either that sons
were always very amenable, or that parents were
invariably self-willed and autocratic, but it is obvious
that marriages based on mutual attraction must
have been extremely few. We will suppose that
Silius is his own master, while Marcia has a father
or a guardian still alive.

At the betrothal ceremony the friends of both
houses are in attendance, a regular form of words is

interchanged between Silius and the father of Marcia,
a ring is given by the man to his *fiancée*, to be worn
on the fourth finger of her left hand, and he adds
some other present, most probably some form of
that jewellery of which the Roman women were and
still are so extraordinarily fond. A feast naturally
follows.

You would think this performance sufficiently
binding, and binding no doubt it was from a moral
point of view, so long as there was reasonably good
behaviour on either side, or so long as neither Silius
nor Marcia's father was prepared wantonly to flout
general opinion or to offend a whole connection by
simply changing his mind. On the other hand, there
was no legal compulsion whatever to carry out the
contract. The Roman world knew nothing of actions
for breach of promise. If either party chose to
repudiate the engagement, they were free so to do.
In that case they were said to "send back a refusal"
or to "send a counter-notice." A family dispute,
a breath of suspicion, a change of circumstances,
and even an improved prospect might be sufficient
excuse, or no excuse need be offered at all.

In the present instance, however, no such ugly
missive passes between the house of Silius on the
Caelian Hill and that of Marcius on the Aventine,
and the wedding takes place in due course. It will
not be in May nor in early March or June, nor on
certain other dates which, for reasons mostly long
forgotten, were regarded as inauspicious. It is a
social ceremony, and neither state nor priest will

have anything to do with sanctioning or blessing it. The pillars at the sides of the vestibules of both houses are wreathed with leaves and boughs, and the friends and clients of both families proceed in festal array to the house of the bride. If Marcia is very young she has taken her playthings — dolls and the like — and has dedicated them to the household gods as a sign that she now puts away childish things and devotes herself to the serious tasks of life. She has then been carefully dressed for the occasion. Her hair, however she may have worn it before or may wear it afterwards, is for to-day made up into six plaits or braids, which are wound into a coil on the top of her head. As an initial rite it is parted by means of an instrument resembling a spear, a survival of the time when a bride was a prize of war, and when her long locks were actually divided by a veritable spear in token of her subjection. Round this coiffure is placed a bridal wreath, made of flowers which she must have gathered with her own hands, and over her head is thrown a veil — more strictly a cloth — of some orange-yellow or "flame-coloured" material, which does not, however, like the Grecian or Oriental veil, conceal her face. On her feet are low yellow shoes. Meanwhile the bridegroom arrives, escorted by his friends, and he also wears a festal garland. As with all other important undertakings of Roman life, a professional seer will be in attendance to take care that the auspices are favourable. Peculiar portents, very unpropitious behaviour of nature, a very strange

appearance in the entrails of a sacrificial victim, are
omens which no properly constituted Roman can
afford to overlook. The auspices being favourable —
and there is reason to believe that no undue insistence
was laid on their unpropitious aspects — the bride is
led into the reception-hall, and the contract of
marriage is signed and sealed. That there should
be a dowry, and a considerable one, goes without
saying. In some cases it is actually settled on the
husband, who is to all intents and purposes purchased
by it; but in most it is available for his use only so
long as the marriage continues unbroken. For the
rest, the wife's property is and remains her own.
Her guardian is still her father and not her husband:
her legal connection is still with her own family and
not with his. She is a Marcia and not a Silia. If
the marriage is dissolved, at least without sufficient
demonstrable provocation on her part, her father
will see that her dower is paid back. To such terms
as these the parties affix their names and seals, and
a certain number of friends add their signatures as
witnesses.

This done, one of the younger married women
present takes the bride and leads her across to Silius
who holds her right hand in his. Both repeat a
prescribed formula of words, and all the company
present exclaims "Good luck to you!" and offers such
other congratulations as seem fit. A wedding-dinner
is held, generally, but not necessarily, in the house
of the bride, and a wedding-cake, served upon bay-
leaves, is cut up and divided among the guests.

It is now evening, and a procession is formed to
bring Marcia home to the house of Silius. In front
will march the torchbearers and what we should call
"the band," consisting in these circumstances of a
number of persons playing upon the flageolet.
Silius goes through a pretence of carrying off Marcia
by force — another practice reminiscent of the ancient
time when men won their brides by methods similar
to those of the Australian aborigine with his waddy.
Both groom and bride are important people, and
along the streets there is many a decoration; many
a window and doorway is filled with spectators;
shouts, not always of the most discreet, are heard
from all sides, and loud above all rings the regular
Io Talasse — whatever that may have meant, for no
man now knows, and almost certainly no one knew
then.   In the midst of the procession Marcia, followed
by bearers of her spindle and distaff, is being led by
two pretty boys, while a third carries a torch; Silius
meanwhile is scattering nuts or walnuts, or *confetti*
made like them, to the crowd. Arrived on the
Caelian, the bride is once more seized and lifted over
the threshold; when inside the hall, Silius presents
her with fire and water in token of her common share
in the household and its belongings; and she offers
prayers to various old-fashioned goddesses who are
supposed to preside over the introduction to married
life.

If we have given with some particularity the
orthodox proceedings of a fashionable wedding, it

must again be remembered that not all weddings
were fashionable, and that one or other of these details
might be omitted as taste or circumstances required.
Among the poorer folk there must often have been
practically no ceremony at all beyond the "bringing
home." And if there are certain items which appear
to us trivial and meaningless, it is probably un-
familiarity which breeds our contempt. Perhaps a
far-off generation may wonder how civilised folk in
the twentieth century could perform absurd antics
with rice and slippers.

Marcia is now what was known as a "matron."
Her position is far more free than it could ever have
been in Greece or the Orient, more free indeed than it
would be in any civilised country at the present time.
The Romans had at all times placed the matron in
a position of dignity and responsibility, and to this
is now added the greatest liberty of action. Her
husband salutes her in public as "Madam." Since he
is a senator, and it is beginning to be the vogue to call
such men "The Most Illustrious," she also shares that
title in polite reference to herself. She is not confined
to any particular portion of the house, nor, within
the limits of decorum, is she excluded from masculine
company. She is the mistress of the establishment,
controlling, not only the female slaves, but also the
males, in so far as they are engaged in the work of
the household. She keeps the keys of the store-rooms.
Theoretically at least she has been trained in all the
arts of the housekeeper, and thoroughly understands

domestic management, together with the weaving and spinning which her handmaids are to perform. The merits of the wife, as summed up in the epitaphs of the middle classes, are those of "good counsellor, good manager, and good worker in wool." She walks or is carried abroad at her pleasure, attends the public games in the Circus, and goes with her husband to dinner-parties, where she reclines at the meal just as he does. When her tutelage is past she can take actions in the law-courts, or appear as witness or surety. Her property is at her own disposal, and she instructs her own agent or attorney. It is only necessary that she should guard the honour of her husband. So long as he trusts her he will not interfere. It is only a very tyrannical spouse who will insist that her litter or sedan-chair shall have the curtains drawn when in the streets. We will assume that Marcia is a lady of the true Roman self-respect and dignity, and that Silius and she live a life of reasonable harmony.

But though there were many such Marcias, there were other women of a very different character. There is, for instance, Flavia, who has a perfect frenzy for "manly" sports, and practises all manner of athletic exercises, wrestling and fencing like any man, and perhaps becoming infatuated and practically running away with some brawny but hideous gladiator. She also indulges frankly in mixed bathing. There is Domitia, who is too fond of promenading in the colonnades and temples, where

a *cavaliere servente*, ostensibly her business man —
though he does not look like it — may regularly be
seen carrying her parasol. When at home, she
neglects her attire and plasters her face with dough
in order to smooth out the wrinkles, so that she may
give to anybody but her own family the benefit of
her beauty. There is the ruinously extravagant
Pollia, whose passion for jewels and fine clothes runs
her deeply into debt, for which, fortunately, her
husband is not responsible. There is Canidia, who
is shrewdly suspected of having poisoned more than
one husband and who has either divorced or been
divorced by so many that she has had eight of them
in five years, and dates events by them instead of in
the regular way by the consulships: "Let me see.
That was in the year in which I was married to So-
and-So." There is Asinia, whose selfishness is so
great, and her affection so frivolous, that she will
weep over a sparrow and "let her husband die to
save her lap-dog's life." All these women are most
likely childless, and many a noble Roman house
threatens to become extinct.

There are others, again, whose foibles are more
innocent. Baebia, for example, is merely a victim
to superstition. She is always consulting the
astrologers, the witches, and the dream-readers; she
is devoted to the mystic worship of the Egyptian
Isis, with its secret rites of purification, or she is a
proselyte to the pestilent notions of the Jews. She
is too much under the influence of some squalid
Oriental who carries his pedlar's basket, or whose

business is to buy broken glass for sulphur matches.
Meanwhile Corellia is a blue-stocking, as bad as
a *précieuse* with a *salon*. As soon as you sit down
to table she begins to quote Homer and Virgil and
to compare their respective merits. She cultivates
bright conversation in both Greek and Latin, and her
tongue goes loudly and incessantly like a bell or gong.
Her poor husband is never permitted to indulge in
an expression which is not strictly grammatical.
Worse still, she probably even writes little poems
of her own. She may keep a tame tutor in philosophy, but she makes no scruple about interrupting
his lesson on morals while she writes a little billet-
doux. Pomponia is an ambitious woman, whose
mania is to interfere in elections by bringing to bear
upon the senators what has been called in recent
times the "duchesses'" influence. If her husband
becomes governor of a province, she will endeavour
to be the power behind the throne, and her meddling
will in any case prove harmful to the strict administration of justice.

The remedy in such cases was divorce. In the
lower orders of society a mild personal castigation
was quite legal and probably not uncommon; but
then in these lower orders divorce was by no means
so convenient. Among the upper classes its frequency
made it scarcely a matter of remark. Nothing like
it has been seen until modern America. There was
no need of an appeal to the courts or of a decree
nisi; there was not even need of a specific plea,
although naturally one would be offered in most cases.

The husband or wife (or the wife's father, if she had one), might send a formal and witnessed notice declaring the marriage dissolved, or, as it was called, "breaking the marriage lines." The man had only to take this step and say with due deliberation "Take your own property"—or, as the satirist puts it, "pack up your traps"—"give up the keys, and begone." The woman on her side need only give similar notice and "take her departure." The only check lay in family considerations, in public opinion, which was extremely lenient, in financial convenience, or in the possibility of particularly wanton conduct being so disapproved in high quarters that a senator or a knight might perhaps find his name missing from the list of his order at the next revision.

It has appeared necessary to give this darker side of the social picture, for, though assuredly not so lurid as might be gathered from the moralists, it was dark enough. For obvious reasons it is desirable not to elaborate. It is perhaps more profitable, as well as refreshing, to consider the brighter side. That there were noble women and good wives, and that the froth and scum and dregs of idle town-life did not make up the existence of the contemporary Roman world, may be seen from passages like the following, which are either quoted or condensed from a letter of Pliny concerning a lady named Arria. The events belong to the reign of Nero's predecessor Claudius. Pliny writes: "Her husband, Caecina Paetus, was ill; so also was her son; and it was

x

expected that both would die. The son, an extremely
handsome and modest youth, succumbed. His mother
arranged for his funeral and carried it out, the husband
meanwhile being kept in ignorance. Not only so, but
every time she came into his room she pretended that
the son was alive and better, and very often, when
he asked how the boy was getting on, she answered,
"He has slept well, and shown a good appetite."
Then, when the tears which she had so long kept
back proved too much for her, she used to leave the
room and give herself up to grief. When at last she
had dried her eyes and composed her countenance she
returned to the room." When her husband had taken
part in an intended revolt against Claudius, he was
to be carried as a prisoner across the Adriatic to Rome.
"He was on the point of embarking, when Arria
begged the soldiers to take her on board with him.
'I presume,' she said, 'you mean to allow an ex-
consul a few attendants of some kind, to give him
his food, and to put on his clothes and shoes. I will
do all that myself.'" Her request being refused,
"she hired a fishing-smack and followed the big
vessel in this tiny one." When Claudius ordered
the husband to put himself to death, Arria took a
dagger, stabbed herself in the breast, drew the weapon
out, and handed it to him with the words: "Paetus,
it does not hurt. It is what you are about to do that
hurts."

Arria doubtless is a rare type of heroine. But also
of the quiet domesticated wife we have a description
from the same writer. Unfortunately the letter is one

of the most priggish of all the rather self-complacent
epistles written by that thoroughly respectable and
estimable man; but that fact takes nothing from the
information for which we are looking. Pliny is writing to his own wife's aunt. "You will be very glad
to learn that Calpurnia is turning out worthy of her
father, of yourself, and of her grandfather. She has
admirable sense and is an excellent housekeeper; she
is fond of me, which speaks well for her character.
Through her affection for me she has also developed
a taste for literature. She possesses my books and
is always reading them; she even learns them by
heart. When I am to make a speech in court, she
is all anxiety; when I have made it, she is all joy.
She arranges a string of messengers to let her know
what effect I produce, what applause I win, and what
result I have obtained. If I give a reading, she sits
in the next room behind a curtain and listens greedily
to the compliments paid to me. She even sets my
verses to music and sings them to the harp, with
no professional to teach her, but only love, who is
the best of masters. I have therefore every reason
to hope that our harmony will not only last but grow
greater every day."

And all this time, away in the country homestead
and cottage, the good Marsian or Sabine mother is a
veritable pattern of domestic probity and discipline.
If she possesses handmaids, she teaches them their
work in the kitchen or at the loom; if she possesses
none, she brings up her big daughters in the right
ways of modesty, frugality, and obedience to the gods;

and her tall sons religiously obey her when she sends
them out to chop the firewood in the rain and cold of
the mountain-side.

One subject of perpetual interest where women are
concerned is that of dress and personal appearance.
The Roman woman emphatically pursued the cult of
beauty and personal adornment. Perhaps the first
prayer which a mother offered for an expected daughter
was that she should be beautiful. Whether she proved
so or not, no pains were spared to correct or supple-
ment the work of nature. It is true that fashion,
except in the dressing of hair, underwent none of
those rapid and astonishing changes which perplex the
unsophisticated male of to-day. Above all, there were
no hats. But all that gold and jewels, colours — blue,
green, yellow, violet — and varied stuffs — woollen,
linen, muslin, and silk — could do for dress was done
by every typical woman of means; and every device
for improving the complexion, the teeth, the hair, the
height, and the figure — which, by the way, never
sought the wasplike waist — was fully exploited. We
need not go too closely into details. It will be
enough to describe the ordinary attire and the ordinary
methods of beautification.

The conventional indoor dress consisted of, first,
an inner tunic, short and sleeveless, with a band
passing over or under the breast, so as to produce
something resembling what is called the Empire
figure; second, an outer tunic of linen or half-silk,
less often of whole silk, which fell to the feet. The

outer tunic was fastened on the shoulders with brooches; it had sleeves over the upper arm, and, in the case of adults but not of young girls, a flounce or furbelow at the bottom. A girdle produced a fold

FIG. 91. — TOILET SCENE. (Wall Painting.)

under the breast. The garment was commonly white, but might be bordered with coloured fringes and embroidery; for ladies of senatorial rank it bore the broad stripe worked in purple or gold. On the feet sandals were often worn, but for out-of-doors these were replaced by soft shoes of white, coloured,

FIG. 92.—WOMAN IN FULL DRESS.

or gilded leather, sometimes studded with pearls or
other gems.

When a lady left the house she threw over the indoor dress a large mantle or shawl, much resembling the toga of the men, except that its colour was apparently what she pleased. This article was passed over the left shoulder and under the right arm, which was left free; it then fell in graceful folds to the feet. Works of art show that a fold of the shawl was frequently laid over the top and back of the head, for which no less becoming covering had yet been introduced.

The hair alone was subject to innumerable vagaries either of fashion or of individual taste. It might have a parting or no parting; it might be plaited over the head and fastened by jewelled tortoise-shell combs, or by pins of ivory, silver, or bronze with jewelled heads, as varied and ornamental as the modern hatpin; it might be carried to the back and rest in a knot on the neck, where it was bound with ribbons; it might be piled into a huge pyramid or "towers of many stories," so that a woman often looked tall in front and ap-

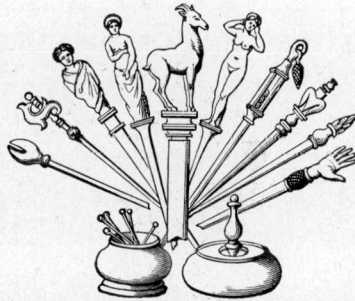

FIG. 93. — HAIRPINS.

peared quite a different person at the back; it might be encased in a coloured cloth or in a net of gold thread, for which poorer people substituted a bladder. But in all cases it was preferred that the hair should be wavy, and this was a matter which was attended to by a special *coiffeur* kept among the slaves. No handmaid had a harder or more ungrateful task than the tiring-woman, who built up and fastened the reluctant locks while the mistress contemplated the effect in her bronze or silver mirror. There was no rule for a woman's treatment of herself in this respect. "Consult your mirror," is the advice of the poet Ovid, who has hopelessly lost all count of styles, since they were "more numerous than the leaves on the oak or the bees on Hybla." To full dress belonged a coronal or tiara, consisting of a band of gold and precious stones.

But who shall dare to speak of the jewellery that bedecked a Roman matron *en grande tenue* — of the pearl and pendant earrings, the necklaces of pearl and diamonds, the gold snake armlets with their emerald eyes, the bangles and finger-rings, the brooches and buckles on the shoulders and down the sleeves, the gems scattered among the hair, the chains and châtelaines strung with all manner of glittering articles? Says one who lived at the time: "I have seen Lollia Paulina covered with emeralds and pearls gleaming all over her head, hair, ears, neck, and fingers to the value of over £300,000." If Rome is the eternal city, it is eternal in this respect at least as much as in any other.

Who, still more bold, shall pry into her apparatus for the beautification of her person, examining her patch-box and the innocent little pots of rouge, vermilion, and white lead for the complexion, and of soot to rub under the eyes? Who shall scrutinise

too closely that delicate blue which tinges her
temples? Who shall dare to question whether that
yellow hair of the most approved tone, then best seen
in Germany, grew where you find it or came from
some head across the Rhine? Who shall venture to
ask whether that smooth skin was preserved by her
wearing last night a mask of meal, which she washed
off this morning with asses' milk? Petronius, indeed,
says that the "lady takes her eyebrows out of a little
box," and probably Petronius knew. For her artificial
teeth there is an obvious and sensible excuse, and it
is no reproach to her if, as the poet declared, "she
puts her teeth aside at night, just as she does her
silks." Probably she scents herself far too heavily,
but there are many Roman men who are just as bad.

She is ready now for all emergencies, and we may
leave her, sitting in her long-backed cushioned chair,
waving in one hand a fan of peacock's feathers or of
thin wood covered with gold-leaf, and holding in the
other a ball of amber or glass to keep her hands cool
and dry.

CHAPTER XVII

CHILDREN AND EDUCATION

UNLIKE too many couples of the same class, Silius
and Marcia are blessed with children. We will assume
that there are two, a boy, whose full name shall be
Publius Silius Bassus, and a girl, who is to be called
Silia Bassa. It is perhaps to be regretted that there
is not a third, for in that case the father would enjoy to the full certain privileges granted by law
to parents who so far do their duty by the state. As
it is, he will in the regular course of things receive
preference over childless men, when it comes to
candidature for a public office or to the allotting of
a governorship. The decline in the birthrate had
become so startling at the close of the republic that
the first emperor, Augustus, had decided that it was
necessary on the one side to penalise persons who
remained either unmarried or childless, and on the
other to grant fixed concessions to all who were the
parents of three. A bachelor could not, for instance,
receive a legacy from any one but a near relative; a
married man without children could only receive half
of such a legacy; a man with three children could
not only enjoy his legacy in full, but could take the

shares forfeited by any bachelor or childless legatee
who figured in the same will. It does not appear
that the law produced any great effect, and, to make
it still more futile, the later emperors began to bestow
what was called the "privilege of three children" on
persons who actually had either fewer or none at all.

The power of the father over the children is
theoretically almost absolute. Even when a son
is grown up and married he legally belongs to his
father; so does all his supposed property. The same
is the case with a daughter, unless she becomes a
Vestal Virgin, or unless she marries according to the
stricter of the two kinds of matrimony already
described. In the older days of Rome the father
could, and sometimes did, put his children to death if
he chose. Though too free an exercise of so extreme an
authority was no longer recognised, it was still quite
legal to make away with an infant which was badly
deformed. Says Seneca, in the most matter-of-fact
way, "We drown our monstrosities." It was quite
legal also to expose a child, and leave it either to
perish or to be taken up by whosoever chose. In
most such instances doubtless the child became the
slave of the finder. Not only was this allowable at
Rome and in the romanized part of the empire; it
was a frequent practice throughout the Greek or
Eastern portion. Again, a father might sell his child
as a slave, particularly for continual disobedience.
All these things the parent might legally do; but it
is extremely difficult to discover how far they were
actually done, inasmuch as our information in this

respect hardly touches the lower classes, while among
the upper classes there was naturally far less tempta-
tion to be rid of the burden of maintaining such few
children as most families produced. On the whole it
appears highly improbable that in the truly Roman
part of the empire there was any considerable
destruction of infant life or exposure of infants. It
does not follow that, because the strict law does not
prevent you from doing a thing, you will therefore
do it, in the face of public disapproval and of all the
promptings of natural affection. In their family
relations the ancient Romans possessed at least as
much natural feeling as is commonly shown in modern
times. The fact is that in matters of law the Romans
were eminently conservative; they left as much as
possible to the silent working of social opinion. In
the oldest times the patriarchal system existed in the
family, and new Roman legislation interfered with
parental power only just so far as experience had
loudly demanded such intervention. There can have
been no very pronounced abuse of the powers of the
father, and, as the discipline of the family was regarded
as essential to the discipline of the state, the law was
always unwilling to weaken in any way the hold of
such family discipline. The strictly legal authority
of the father was therefore maintained, while its
abusive exercise was limited by the risk, if not the
certainty, that it would meet with both public and
private censure.

Nevertheless, to return to the point which called
for this explanation, it is quite in the power of Silius

to expose or sell little Publius or little Silia. But
for a man in his position to do anything of the kind
would bring the scorn of all Roman society about his
ears; and, among other humiliations, almost undoubtedly his name would be expunged from the
senatorial list. Moreover Silus, though a pagan, is
a human being, and his affection for his children
would certainly be no less warm than that of the •
average Christian man of to-day.

Immediately after birth there is a little ceremony.
The babe is brought and laid upon the hearth or floor
before the household gods for the father to inspect it.
As has been said already, if it is a monstrosity, he
may order it to be made away with. Otherwise it is
still open to him either to acknowledge the infant or
to refuse to have anything to do with it. The act of
acknowledgment consists in stooping down and lifting
up the child from the ground. For this reason the
expression used for acknowledging and undertaking
to rear a child was "lifting" or "picking up." In
our instance the little son and daughter are, of course,
not only picked up, but welcomed as the young hopes
of the proud house of Silii Bassi.

On the ninth day in case of the boy, or the
eighth in that of the girl, the child is named, after
certain ceremonies of purification. The whole proceeding bears much resemblance to a christening, except
that there is no calling in of the services of a church.
The relations and friends gather in the hall, each
bringing his present, and even the slaves make

their little inexpensive offerings. The gifts are chiefly little trinkets of gold, silver, and ivory — rings, miniature hands, axes, swords, or crescents — which are to be strung across the baby's breast. The original purpose of all these objects was to act as charms against the blighting of the child by evil powers, or, more definitely, by the "evil eye," that malignant influence which still troubles so many good Italians, both ignorant and learned. With the same intention the father hangs upon the child's neck a certain object which it will carry till it comes of age. If a few years later you met the boy Publius in the Roman streets, you would find him wearing a round case or locket in gold, some two inches in diameter and resembling the modern cased watch. Inside is shut his protecting amulet. When he is sixteen and puts on the man's toga, his amulet will be laid aside. In the case of the little Silia it will be worn until she marries. Poorer folk, for whom gold is too expensive, will enclose the amulet in a case of leather.

The naming over, the child is registered. The Romans were adepts in the art of utilising a religious or superstitious practice for purposes of state, and the development of the registration of births and deaths is but one instance. In older times it had been a custom, on the occasion of a birth, to pay a visit to the shrine of "Juno the Birth-Goddess," and to leave a small coin by way of offering. It is easy for a state to convert an already established general custom into a rule; and at our date this shrine of Juno had become practically a registration office, where a small fee was paid and the name of the child entered upon the rolls.

We need not follow with any closeness the infancy of either boy or girl till the seventh year. The ancient world was very much like the modern. Suffice it to glance at them cutting their teeth on the teeth of wolves or horses, rocked in cradles decorated with gold and purple, or running about and calling their parents by the time-honoured *mamma, tata* — words, if we can call them words, which came from those small Roman mouths precisely as they have come from time immemorial from so many others. Their slave nurse, who is a Greek and talks Greek to them, tells them the old wives' tales and fables. They play with rattles, balls, and little carts, with pet birds and monkeys, and the girl with dolls of ivory or wax or of painted terra-cotta. They have swings, and ride on sticks and build houses. When bigger, the boy has his tops and hoops, with or without bells, and he plays marbles with nuts. Meanwhile attempts are made, somewhat after the kindergarten pattern, to teach them their alphabet by means of letters shaped in wood or ivory. Whether or not it is modern kindergarten method to tempt children to learn by offers of sugar-plums, that course was often adopted in the world of both Greece and Rome.

On the whole the life of the child, though strictly governed, appears to have been pleasant enough until schooldays began. Though many children were taught at home by a more or less learned slave acting as private tutor, the great majority, at least of the boys, were sent to school. There was at this date no compulsory education; the state dictated nothing and provided nothing in connection with the matter; many children must have received no education at all, and many only the barest elements. Nevertheless the average parent realised the practical utility of at least reading, writing, and simple arithmetic, and schools of the elementary type sprang up according to the demand. What the higher education was like will be set forth in its place.

The ideal education, as understood in the older days of Rome, was a training which should fit a man for his duty to the gods, the state, and the family. It was above all things a moral and practical training. A man has certain domestic, political, and religious functions to perform: let him learn how best to perform these. Under this system there was little room for accomplishments or for purely intellectual pursuits. Little by little, however, such liberal elements, artistic and philosophical, struggled into the sphere of Roman education, but never to the extent or with the intellectual effect which belonged to them in Greece. Even by A.D. 64 the education of a Roman boy was very narrow, and, in the direction in which it sought some liberality, it often went sadly astray. The clearest course will be for us to take young Publius Silius through a course typical of the time. We will assume that he does not receive all his lessons at home, but that, through an old-fashioned preference on the part of his father, he goes to a school, along with boys who are mostly but not necessarily of the same social standing with himself.

We have unfortunately almost no information as to any social grading of schools, or as to their size. All we know is that some schools were taught entirely by one man, while others employed an undermaster or several. In some cases the school is entirely a private enterprise, the master charging a monthly fee — amounting in the elementary schools to a penny or twopence a week — together with small money presents on certain festivals. The more select establishments naturally charged more. Probably most of the schools in Rome and the larger towns were upon this private footing. In other instances a number of parents in a smaller town would club together and subscribe sufficient money to provide the salary of a schoolmaster for their children. In yet others some benefactor, generally a wealthy local magnate, had given or bequeathed an endowment fund, from which a school was either wholly or partially financed. At a rather later date Pliny writes a letter, of which the following is a passage, interesting in this connection. "When I was lately in my native part of the country (that is to say, at Como), a boy — the son of a fellow townsman — came to pay his respects. I said, 'Are you at school?' 'Yes,' he replied. 'Where?' 'At Milan.' 'And why not here?' At this his father said, 'Because we have no teachers here.' 'And why have you none? It

Y

is of the greatest importance to any of you who are
fathers — and it happened that several fathers were
listening — that your children should be taught here
rather than anywhere else. . . . How small a thing
it is to put money together and engage teachers,
and to apply to their salary the amount which you
now spend on lodgings, travelling expenses, and the
articles that have always to be purchased when one
is away from home.'" Whereupon he proceeds
himself to offer to contribute one-third of whatever
sum the parents collect. He does not believe in
giving the whole, because experience has taught him
that endowments of this kind are commonly misused.
The parents must themselves retain an interest in
preventing corruption; and this will be the case so
long as they are themselves paying their share. In
this instance we are, however, to think rather of a
high school or school of rhetoric than of the primary
school. Como would not lack a primary school, nor
would parents send very young children to lodge
in Milan. There is no trace of real boarding-
schools.

To whatever school Publius goes he will be accompanied by a sedate slave, generally elderly and also
generally a Greek, whom you may call his "guardian,"
or his "governor," or his "mentor," according to your
fancy. The function of this worthy is to look after
the morals and behaviour of the boy when in the
streets, and also to supervise his manners when at
home. Publius will not be free of this incubus until
the day when he puts on the adult's toga; and he

must be prepared to accept, at least in his younger days, not only scolding, but also corporal punishment from him. In poorer families the mother corrected her children with a slipper. The "guardian" of Publius is nevertheless a slave, and will carry the young master's books and school requisites for him, while the sons of poorer parents are marching along, freer and happier, with their tablets and writing-case slung over their left arm. When, in the New Testament, we are told that the "Law hath been our school-master unto Christ," the word employed does not

FIG. 94. — WRITING MATERIALS.

at all mean schoolmaster. It means this slave who keeps the pupil under salutary discipline until he reaches the schoolmaster, and who superintends his conduct until he is of age.

School age regularly begins at seven for the elementary stage, which commonly includes writing, reading, and arithmetic. The first lessons in writing are done upon wax tablets, which correspond to our slate. For school purposes they are flat pieces of wood, with a rim, their surface being covered with a thin layer of wax. The pupil takes a "style," or metal stiletto, pointed at one end and flat at the other; with the point he scratches, or "ploughs" as the Romans called it, the writing in the wax; with the other end he flattens the wax and so makes the necessary erasures when he desires to correct a word or to "clean his slate."

His first efforts will probably consist either of tracing letters through a stencil, or of forming them from a copy while the master guides his hand. He will next write a series of words — the good old copy-book method with the good old copybook maxims. It is only when he has gained some proficiency that he will be allowed to write upon paper or parchment with ink and with a split reed for pen. In such a case the backs of useless documents come in handy, and particularly serviceable are the rolls containing the poems of the numerous authors whom no one wants to read, but whose books thus find one of their ultimate uses, another being to wrap up spices or salt fish. His arithmetic will be merely such as will enable him to make up accounts. The Roman numerals did not lend themselves easily to the method now adopted of calculating on paper, and the Roman pupil therefore reckoned partly with his fingers, partly by means of counters laid or strung upon a board. At this he became remarkably proficient, and at mental arithmetic there is reason to believe that he could beat the modern boy hollow. Along with the reckoning he would also necessarily learn his tables of weights and measures. "Two-and-a-half feet one step; two steps one pace; a thousand paces one mile." So he said or sang, and a mile — *mille*, "a thousand" paces — remains our own word to this day, even though it has come to signify an eccentric 1760 yards.

That Roman boys bore no love to school or school-master is little wonder. Perhaps Publius may be fortunate; but if his schoolmaster is of the ordinary type he will be an irascible loud-voiced person, who bawls and scolds and thrashes. It will be a common thing to find, as Seneca puts it, a man "in a violent passion teaching you that to be in a passion is wrong." The doctrine went that "he who is not flayed is not educated." The methods of the military centurion may have had something to do with creating this behaviour, but there is perhaps another excuse to be found for the Roman pedagogue. His school, if of the inferior kind, is like any other shop, a place open to the street, whether on the ground floor or in the balcony-like *entresol*. There is no cloistered privacy about his instruction. To such a place at a very early hour come the boys "creeping unwillingly." When the days are short the school opens before daybreak, and the smoky lamps and lanterns create an evil smell and atmosphere in the raw and chilly morning. That is no time to be amiable towards inattention or stupidity. There were many other circumstances to try the temper, and the Roman temper, except among the highest classes, was, as it still is, quick and loud. No real boy who had been at a Roman school but knew what it was to have his ears pinched and to take his punishment on his hands with the cane or the tawse. Many had been "horsed," in the way depicted in the illustration.

There is also no cause for surprise that boys often shammed illness and did little things to their eyes, so that mother or father might keep them from their books for a while.   There were of course academies of a better class than these schools open to the street, and probably Publius Silius would be taken to one where his "guardian" waits with others in an antechamber, while he is himself being taught in a room where the walls are pictured with historical or mythological scenes, or with charts or maps, and where there stand busts of eminent writers.

FIG. 95. — HORSING A BOY.
(After Sächs.)

The boys are seated on benches or forms, and the master on a high-backed chair.   When the pupil is called upon to repeat a lesson, he stands up before the teacher; when the whole class is to deliver a dictated passage it rises and delivers it all together, in orthodox sing-song style.

Somewhere towards eleven o'clock there is an interval, and the boys go home for lunch or buy something from the seller of rissoles or sausages in the street.   In the afternoon — when the schoolmaster has taken his own luncheon and probably his short siesta — they return to school, putting in altogether about six hours of lessons in the day.

That boys and girls went to the same elementary schools is not absolutely provable from any explicit statement to that effect; but there are one or two passages in literature which point almost certainly to that conclusion. It is at least undeniable that girls, and even big girls, went to school, and that in those schools they were taught by men. One school-master is addressed by the poet as "detestable to both boys and girls." We have seen that in maturity the Roman woman lived in no sort of seclusion; and it is reasonable to suppose that as a girl she was treated in much the same way as girls in a mixed school of to-day. Nevertheless it is also almost certain that such mixed schools were only those of the common people, or of the lower middle classes: the daughters of the better-circumstanced would be instructed at home by private tutors. There they would learn to read and write both Greek and their native Latin, to play upon the lyre or harp, to dance — Roman dancing being more a matter of gesture with hands and body than of movement with the feet — and to carry themselves with the bearing fit for a Roman lady. To teach the household duties was the function of the mother.

At Rome, as with us, there was, first, a primary education, pure and simple, given in the schools of those who would nowadays be registered as teachers of primary subjects. Next there was what we should call a secondary or high-school education, given by a "grammar master," in which the education was almost wholly literary. The same school might doubtless employ a special arithmetic master, and also a teacher of music, but mainly the business of such an establishment was theoretically to prepare the boy for a proper and effective use of language, whether for social or for public purposes. In the Rome of the republic a man of affairs or ambitions required above all things to be an accomplished speaker, and this tradition had not weakened under the empire. Moreover, for the training of the intellectual faculties as such, the Romans had no better resource than grammatical and literary study. Science was purely empirical, mathematics was mainly arithmetic and mensuration, and there was no room in these subjects for that exercise of discernment and acumen as well as of taste which was provided by well-directed study of the best authors. In the secondary education, therefore, the chief object sought was "the knowledge of right expression," and the acquirement of "correct, clear, and elegant diction." This was to be achieved by the most painstaking study of both the Greek and the Latin poets; and it is worth noting that the Romans had the good sense to begin with the best. Every boy must know his Homer, and steep himself in the easy style and sound sentiments of Menander; he must also know his Virgil and his Terence. He must know how to read a passage with proper intonation and appreciation of the sense, and he must learn large quantities of such poetry by heart. In the early stages the master's part is first to read aloud a certain passage with what he thinks to be the right articulation and expression; he then explains the meaning or the allusions, and does whatever else he considers necessary for the understanding and appreciation of the piece. It is then the pupil's turn to stand up and repeat the passage so as to show that he has caught the true sense and can impart the true intonation. No doubt there were bad and indifferent teachers as well as good ones, and doubtless there was much mere parroting on the part of the learner. It was then, as it is now, chiefly a question of the sort of teacher. It is probable that in many schools the action of the mental faculty as well as of the voice became pure sing-song. Julius Caesar once made the comment: "If you are singing, you are singing badly; if you are reading, you are singing."

The more advanced stage of this higher education was that of the "school of oratory." The pupil has already acquired a correct grammatical style, and a reasonable amount of literary information; he now trains himself for the actual practice of the law-courts or the deliberative assembly. He is to learn how to argue a case; how to arrange his matter; by what devices of language to make it most effective; and how to deliver it. At a later date there were to be public professorships of this art, endowed by the emperor, but there are none of these at Rome itself under Nero. The "professor of oratory" receives his fee of some £20 or so per annum from each pupil. At this stage the study of the great prose-writers is substituted for that of the poets; themes are set for

330 LIFE IN THE ROMAN WORLD

essays to be written upon them; and those essays will
then be delivered as speeches. Sometimes a familiar
statement or maxim from a poet is put forward
to be refuted or supported, or for you to argue
first against it and then for it. Or some historical situation may be proposed, and the student
asked to set forth the wisest or most just course
in the circumstances. "Hannibal has beaten the
Romans at Cannae: shall he or shall he not proceed directly to attack Rome? Examine the
question as if you were Hannibal." Much of this
appears theoretically sound enough. Unfortunately
the subjects were generally either hopelessly threadbare or possessed no bearing upon real life. "We
are learning," says Seneca, "not for life, but for the
school." The only novelty which could be given to
the treatment of old abstract themes or puerile questions was novelty of phrase, and the one great mark
of the literature of this time is therefore the pursuit of
the striking expression, of something epigrammatic or
glittering. A speech was judged by its purple patches
of rhetoric, not by the soundness of its thoughts.
Prizes, apparently of books, were offered in these
Roman schools, and a prize would go to the youth
who could tell you in the most remarkable string of
brilliant language what was your duty towards your
country, or what were the evils of anger, or for what
reasons it is right for a father to disown his son.
Meanwhile parents would look in at the school from
time to time and listen to the boys declaiming, and it
is easy to see with the mind's eye the father listening,

like the proud American parent at a "graduation" day, to his gifted offspring "speaking a piece."

Education commonly stopped at this point. If the rhetorical training is taken early, the boy is now about sixteen; but there was nothing to prevent the oratorical course from following instead of preceding the "coming of age." In this case we will suppose that it has preceded. The youth has now received a good literary training and considerable practice in the art of speech-making. He knows enough of elementary arithmetic to keep accounts, or, in special cases — where he is intended for certain professional careers — he may understand some geometry and the principles of mechanics and engineering. He may or may not have learned to sing, and enough of music to play creditably on lyre or harp. Unlike the young Greek, he will not necessarily have been made to recognise that gymnastic training is an essential part of education. He may indulge in such exercises by way of pastime or for health; he may, and generally will, have been taught athletics; but he does not acknowledge that they have any practical bearing upon his aptitude for either warfare or civil life.

It is hard to gauge the intellect of the average Roman youth of sixteen; all we know is that, while the best of literature, science, art, and philosophy was left to be undertaken by Greeks, the Romans seized upon whatever learning had an appreciable practical bearing, and that, as men capable of administering and directing, they left their intellectual and artistic superiors far behind.

Up till this time the boy has worn a toga with a purple edge, and also the gold amulet-case round his neck. The time has, however, come for him to be regarded as a man — not indeed free of his father's authority, but free to walk about without a bear-leader, to marry, if his father so desires, or to decide upon a career. Accordingly, on the 17th of March by preference, he will put away the outward insignia of boyhood, dedicate his amulet to the household gods, and will don the all-white toga of a man. The relatives, friends, and clients will gather at the house, and, after offering their congratulations, will escort the youth to the Capitol, and thence down to the Forum, where his appearance in this manner will be accompanied by introductions and a recognition on all sides that he is now "of age." At the Record Office the name of "Publius Silius Bassus, son of Quintus," is recorded with due fulness of description, and he ranks henceforth as one of the citizens of Rome.

After this little ceremony of coming of age, a number of the young men apparently did nothing. The sons of poorer parents have long ago gone to their work in their various trades. Those of the more well-to-do may — and, if they are afterwards to seek public office, they must — now undertake military service amid the conditions which are to be described in the next chapter. Others, being of a more studious turn, will proceed to complete their education by going abroad to one or other of the great seats of philosophic study which corresponded to our universities. Philosophy meant to the Roman a guide to the

direction of life. Roman religion, upon which we
shall hereafter dwell in some detail, consisted of a
number of forms and ceremonies, or acts of recognition
paid to the deities; it embodied certain traditional
principles of duty to family and state; but otherwise
it exercised very little influence on the conduct of
life. So far as such guidance was supplied at all, it
was by moral philosophy, the treatment of which, as
it was understood at this date, is bound up with that
of religion and must wait till we reach that subject.
It is true that there were professional teachers of
philosophy at Rome itself, but the metropolis was not
their chief resort, any more than, until recently,
London would have been recognised as a seat of
university learning of the front rank. It is also true
that many great houses maintained a domestic
philosopher, who not only helped in moulding the
tone of the master of the house and afforded him
intellectual company, but might act as private
philosophic tutor to his son. But for the most part
this highest instruction was rather to be sought in
cities specially noted for their assemblage of professors
and lecturers. Chief among these figured Athens,
Rhodes, Tarsus, Antioch, Alexandria, and Marseilles.
At Naples also might be found a large number of
men of learning, but they were chiefly persons who
had retired from professional life, and who chose that
city because of its pleasant climate and surroundings,
and because they could there enjoy each other's society.
In some of the cities named — particularly Athens
and Alexandria — there were endowed professorships

(though not endowed by the Roman emperors) of which the benefit was enjoyed, not only by the local student but also by those from other parts of the Roman world who chose to resort to such established teachers. This does not mean that such students paid no fee, nor that there was any lack of lecturers unendowed. The student was free to take his choice. Where there was endowment, as at Athens, there was control by the local authorities over the behaviour of students and also of their teachers; but it is evident that a professor's audience was by no means always a very well-ruled or docile body. As in the German universities, the visiting students were men, and some of them fairly advanced in years, and, also as in Germany, they followed their own tastes in study and changed from university to university at will. They, as it were, "sampled" the professors and made their own election. The teacher not only lectured to them, but also lectured them; while, on their side, they were entitled to catechise, and in a sense "badger," the lecturer, to propound difficulties, and to make more or less pronounced exhibition of their sentiments.

In the philosophic lecture-room the student, possessing his share of the vivacity and excitability of the south, would stamp, spring from his seat, shout and applaud, calling out in Greek "splendid!" "inimitable!" "capital!" "prettily said!" and so forth. Plutarch writes a little essay on the proper manner of behaving in the lecture-rooms, and he tells us: "You should sit in a proper manner and not lounge;

you should keep your eyes on the speaker and show
a lively interest; maintain a composed countenance
and show no annoyance or irritation, nor look as if you
were thinking of other things." Such an attitude
was the ideal and orthodox; but he tells us also that
there were some who "scowled; their eyes wandered;
they sprawled, crossed their legs, nodded and whispered
to their neighbour, smiled, yawned sleepily, and let
their heads droop." This was not necessarily because
the lecturer was dull, but because he might be giving
lessons which were unwelcome to some among his
audience. The cap fitted them too well, as it sometimes does when offered by a modern preacher. But,
says the same Plutarch, if you did not like these
direct and rough-tongued monitors, you could find
other professors, *poseurs*, who were all suavity;
gentlemen whose philosophical stock-in-trade was
grey hair, a pleasant voice and delivery, graceful
language, and much self-appreciation. These were
the Reverend Charles Honeymans of the period, and
their following was like unto the following of that
popular pulpiteer.

Since mention has been made more than once
of reading and libraries, it is well to realise the form
commonly taken by books. We must not think of
the modern bound volume standing on its shelf or
open in the hand. At our date any books made up
in the form of leaves — or what the Romans called
"tablet" form — consisted only of some four or six
pages. The regular shape for a book was that of a

roll, or, if the work was a large one, it might consist
of several such "rolls" or "sections." The material
was either paper — in its original sense of papyrus — or
the skin known as parchment. Papyrus was naturally
the cheaper and the less durable. Prepared sheets
of a given length and breadth — the "pages" — were
written upon and then pasted to each other side
by side until a long stretch was formed. The last
sheet was then attached to a thin roller, commonly
of wood, answering to that used in a modern wall-
map. Round a roll of any pretensions there was

FIG. 96. — PAPYRI AND TABULAE. (From Dyer's *Pompeii.*)

wrapped a cover of coloured parchment, red, yellow,
or purple. The ends of the roll were rubbed smooth
with pumice-stone and dyed, and a tag or label was
affixed to bear the name of the author and the work.
A number of such rolls, related in subject or authorship, were placed on end in a round box, with the
labels upwards ready for inspection. In the library
such a box would stand in a pigeon-hole or section of
shelf, from which it might be carried where required.
Sometimes the rolls themselves lay in a heap horizon-
tally in a pigeon-hole without a box, but this was
manifestly a less convenient practice. To keep away

the bookworms cedar-oil was rubbed upon them, giving them a yellowish tinge.

The reader, taking the body of the roll in one hand, begins to unwind the long strip with the other. After reading the first column or page thus exposed, he mechanically re-winds that portion, while the width of another page is pulled into view.

The writing itself was done by means of a reed, sharpened and split like a quill-pen, and dipped in ink made in various ways, but mostly less "biting" than our own. This made it comparatively easy to sponge out what was written, and to use the same roll over again — as a "palimpsest" — for some work more desired. It is perhaps needless to say that the writing was regularly to be found upon one side only. If the back was used, it was for economy, for unimportant notes, or as an exercise book for schoolboys.

We may imagine a fine library copy, or *édition de luxe*, of Virgil as consisting of a number of rolls, each a long strip of the best parchment rolled round a staff of ivory with gilded ends. Its "cover" is a wrapper of parchment richly dyed and bearing coloured bands of leather to serve as fasteners. From the smoothed and dyed end stands out a scarlet label, marked "Virgil Aeneid Book I." (or as the case may be). When opened, the first page will reveal a painted portrait of the poet, and the writing will be found to be in a beautifully clear and even calligraphy. Beside the shelf on which the work is placed there most likely stands a lifelike bust of Virgil in marble or in bronze.

z

CHAPTER XVIII

THE ARMY : MILITARY SERVICE : PUBLIC CAREER

In the older days of Roman history the fighting forces had been a "citizen army," called out for so long as it was needed, and levied from full and true Roman citizens. In the imperial times with which we are here dealing it had become a standing army. Soldiering was a profession, for which the men volunteered, and, so far as Roman citizens were concerned, it was now seldom, if ever, the case that military service required to be made compulsory on their part. It is true that a young man of the higher classes who proposed to follow a public career, leading to higher and higher offices of state, must have gone through some amount of military training, but no other Roman was actually obliged to serve. The empire was so vast and the total of the standing forces comparatively so small that it was always possible to fill up the legions with those who had some motive or inclination that way. Theoretically the state possessed a claim upon every able-bodied man, but the population of the empire was probably a hundred millions, and to collect a total of some 320,000 soldiers, made up of Roman or romanized "citizens" and of

provincial subjects in about equal shares, was a
sufficiently easy task, and the recruiters could therefore afford to pick and choose. Above all we must
clear our minds of the notion that the Roman soldiers
necessarily came from Rome, or even from Italy.
They were drawn from the empire at large, and a
legion posted in Spain, for example, might be recruited
from a special class of Spaniards.

Roughly speaking, the regular army, extending
along the frontiers from Chester to Jerusalem and
from Jerusalem to Algeria, was composed of two
main divisions, called respectively the "legions"
and the "auxiliaries." Other special or detached
forces — such as the twelve regiments of Imperial
Guards and the six of the City Guard — came under
neither of these headings, and we may leave them
out of the question for the present.

A legion was a brigade of about 6000 infantry,
with 120 horsemen attached to it. It was recruited
from any convenient part of the empire, but only
from men already enjoying the rights of Roman
citizens, or else from those other provincials who were
considered sufficiently homogeneous with the Roman
civilisation to stand shoulder to shoulder with such
citizens. In being permitted to serve on these terms
a man regularly becomes *ipso facto* a citizen. The
qualifications required were that you should be free-
born — that is to say, neither slave nor ex-slave —
your physique must be good, and your height about
5 feet 10 inches: there must be nothing serious
against your record or character as viewed from the

Roman standpoint; and, if you were not already a citizen, you must belong to one of those organised communes which were the units of administration and of taxation within the empire. You undertake to serve for twenty years, after which time you will receive an honourable discharge and either a sum of money — at this date apparently about £50 — or a grant of land. By ability and character you may rise from private soldier to centurion, that is to say, commander of a hundred, but in ordinary circumstances you can climb no further up the military ladder. If at the end of your term you are still robust and are considered useful, you may, if you choose, continue to serve in a special detachment of "veterans," with lighter duties and with exemption from common drill. The Roman legions would thus be made up for the most part of troops from about 18 to 38 years of age, although a considerable number might be somewhat older.

A legion once formed had a perpetual existence; its vacancies were filled up as they occurred; and it is obvious that it must have consisted of respectable men of picked physique, mostly in the prime of life, and perfectly trained in all the qualities of a soldier. When not on actual campaign they were drilled once a day, and the recruits twice. They practised the hurling of spears and all the attitudes of attack with sword and pike, and of defence with the shield. Now and then there was a review or a sham fight. They learned how to fortify a camp, how to attack it or to defend it. Every month they put on full armour,

marched out with steady Roman tramp for ten miles
and back again to camp for the sake of practice.
Meanwhile they were made useful in building the
military roads, bridges, and walls. Add to this the
strict Roman discipline, and it is difficult to conceive
of any training more capable of turning a body of
6000 men into a stubborn and effective fighting
machine. The half-naked German across the Rhine
was physically as strong and as brave; the woad-
dyed Celt of Britain was probably more dashing in
his onset; the mounted Parthian across the Euphrates
was more nimble in his movements; but neither
German nor Celt cultivated the organisation or
solidarity of action of the Roman, nor could the
Parthian equal him for steady onward pressure or
determined stand.

To each legion was given a number and also
a name of its own, acquired by some distinguished
feat or some conspicuous campaign, or adopted
in vaunt or compliment. Thus it might be the
"Victorious" Legion, the "Indomitable," or the
"Spanish" Legion, or it might, for example, wear a
crested lark upon its helmet and be called the Legion
of the "Lark." The commander of the whole legion
is a man of senatorial rank; its standard is a silver
eagle on the top of a staff, commonly holding a
thunderbolt in its claw. To each legion there are ten
regiments, called "cohorts," averaging six hundred
men, and every such regiment has its colonel, or, as
the translation of the Bible calls Claudius Lysias, "its
chief captain." The regiment in its turn consists of

six companies or "hundreds," with a "centurion" at the head of each, and every pair of hundreds, if not every company, possesses a standard of its own, con-sisting of a pole topped with large medallions, metal disks, wreaths, an open hand, and other emblems.

FIG. 97.— ROMAN STANDARDS.

Let us imagine a cer-tain Seius to become a private soldier in a legion. He was born in Gaul, in the district of Lugdunum or Lyons, and he is either a full Roman or sufficiently romanized to rank with Romans. He is drafted to the Twentieth Legion, otherwise known as the "Victorious Valerian," and finds himself stationed in the island of Britain at that farthest camp of the north-west which has since grown into the city of Chester. On joining his company he is made to take a solemn oath that he will loyally obey all orders of his commander-in-chief, the emperor, as represented by that emperor's sub-ordinates, his immediate officers. That oath he will repeat on each 1st of January and on the anniversary of the emperor's accession. For full military dress he will first put on a tunic reaching nearly to his knees, and, since he is serving in the northern cold, a pair of fustian breeches covering the upper leg. On his feet will be a pair of strong sandals, of which the thick

soles are studded with hobnails. Over his breast, and
with flaps over the shoulders, he will wear a corslet
of leather covered with hoop-like layers, or maybe
scales, of iron or bronze. On his head will be a plain
pot-like helmet or skull-cap of iron. For the rest he
will possess also a thick
cloak or plaid to be used
as occasion needs. In
his right hand he will
carry the famous Roman
pike. This is a stout
weapon, over 6 feet in
length, consisting of a
sharp iron head fixed in
a wooden shaft, and the
soldier may either charge
with it as with a bayonet,
or he may hurl it like a
javelin and then fight at
close quarters with his
sword. On the left arm
is a large shield, which
may be of various shapes.

FIG. 98. — ARMED SOLDIER.

One common form is curved inward at the sides like
a portion of a cylinder some 4 feet in length by
$2\frac{1}{2}$ in width : another is six-sided — a diamond pattern,
but with the points of the diamond squared away.
Sometimes it is oval. In construction it is of wicker-
work or wood, covered with leather, and embossed
with a blazon in metal-work, one particularly well
known being that of a thunderbolt. The shield is

not only carried by means of a handle, but may be
supported by a belt over the right shoulder. In
order to be out of the way of the shield, the sword —
a thrusting rather than a slashing weapon, approaching 3 feet in length — is hung
at the right side by a belt
passing over the left shoulder.
Though this arrangement may
seem awkward to us, it is to
be remembered that the sword
is not required until the right
hand is free of the pike, and
that then, before drawing, the
weapon can easily be swung
round to the left by means
of the suspending belt. On
the left side the soldier wears
a dagger at his girdle. The
writer of the Epistle to the

FIG. 99. — A ROMAN GENERAL. Ephesians is thinking of all
this equipment when he bids the Christian put on
"the whole armour of God," including the "belt
of truth," the "breast-plate of righteousness," the
"shield of faith," the "helmet of salvation" and the
"sword of the spirit." The officer, of course, wears
armour, cloak, and helmet of a more ornamental
kind, and must have presented a very martial and
imposing figure.

Our friend Seius goes through the drill, the exercises, and the hard work already mentioned. His pay
will be somewhere about £8 a year, or a little over

three shillings a week, and his food will consist mainly
of wheaten porridge and bread, with salt, and a drink
of thin sour wine little better than vinegar. His
wheat — the price of which is deducted from his pay —
is measured out to him every month, and it is his
own business to grind it or get it ground and converted into bread. Vegetables he will procure as he
likes or can; but meat, except a limited amount of
bacon, he will commonly neither get nor very much
desire. On one occasion indeed we find the soldiers
complaining that they were being fed altogether too
much upon meat. It deserves to be remarked that
the results speak well for the wholesomeness of this
simple diet of the legionary. For his quarters he will
be one of ten sharing the same tent under the supervision of a kind of corporal. There are no married
quarters. Not only are women not permitted in the
camp, but the soldier cannot legally marry during his
term of service.

Seius will meet with no gentle treatment while in
his pupilage. The grim centurion, or commander of
his company, is a man of iron, who has risen from the
ranks; his methods are sharp and summary, and he
carries a tough switch of vine-wood, with which he
promptly belabours the idle or the stupid. Any neglect of duty or act of disobedience is inevitably
punished, sometimes by hard labour in digging
trenches, sometimes by a fine, sometimes by stripping
the soldier of his armour and making him stand for
hours in civilian attire as a butt for ridicule in the

middle of the camp, sometimes by a lowering of his rank corresponding to the modern taking away of a man's "stripes." If a soldier proves a hopeless case, he is expelled with ignominy from the camp and army. If he deserts or plays the traitor he may either

FIG. 100. — CENTURION.

be decapitated or beaten to death with cudgels. If a whole company or regiment gets into disgrace, it may have to put up with barley instead of wheat for its rations, and if it is guilty of gross insubordination, or of some crime which cannot be sheeted home to the individual, it may be "decimated," or, in other words, every tenth man, drawn by lot, may be con-

demned to death. The last, of course, is an extreme
measure, and is only mentioned here as belonging to
extreme cases.

On the other hand, if Seius is a smart soldier he
will gradually gain recognition as such. He may

Fig. 101. — Standard Bearer.

become the head man in his mess of ten; or be made
an orderly, to carry the watchword round to the
messes; or he may be chosen by the centurion as his
subaltern. As he gains maturity and steadiness, and
wins confidence, he may be elected to bear the
standard of his company, in which case a bear's skin
will be thrown over his shoulders, and the top of his

helmet will be concealed beneath the head of that beast, worn as a hood. Being a saving man, and taking a pride in himself, he will gradually decorate his sword-belt and girdle, and perhaps his scabbard, with silver knobs and ornaments. Also behaving well in the victorious brushes with the Britons, he will acquire, besides occasional loot and booty-money, a number of metal medallions or disks, to be strung across his breast somewhat after the manner of the modern war-medals. Gradually, as he becomes a veteran, he may rise to be centurion, when he will wear a crest upon his helmet and greaves upon his shins, have his corslet of scale-armour covered with medallions, and will himself carry the vine-rod of authority. If he should ever succeed in becoming, not merely the centurion of his company, but the first or senior of all the sixty centurions belonging to the whole legion, he will rank practically as a commissioned officer, will retire on a competence if he does retire, and will in all probability be made a knight. In that case he may proceed to higher commands, as if he had been born in that order to which he has at last attained.

But all this promotion is yet a long way off. One morning, while Seius is still a private, he hears, not the "taratantara" of the long straight trumpet which calls to ordinary work, but the sound of the military horn, which means that the legion is to march. He helps to pack up the tent, the hand-mills, and other indispensable needments, and to place them on the mules, packhorses, or waggons. He then puts on

his full armour, although, if it is hot, and if there is
no immediate danger, he may sling his helmet over
his shoulder, while his shield, marked with his name
and company, may perhaps be stacked with others
in a baggage-waggon. His food-supply for sixteen
days — the Roman fortnight — is wrapped in a parcel,
and this, together with his eating and drinking
vessels and any other articles such as would appertain
to a modern knapsack, is carried over his shoulder

FIG. 102. — BAGGAGE-TRAIN.

on a forked stick. It is known that to-night the
army will be obliged to camp on the way, and it is
a binding rule of the service that no camp arrangements shall be left to chance. Surveyors will ride
on ahead with a body of cavalry, and will choose a
suitable position easily defended and with water near.
They will then outline the boundaries according to
a certain scale, and will parcel out the interior,
according to an almost invariable system, into blocks
or sections to accommodate certain units. When
the legion arrives, it marches in with a perfect understanding as to where each company of men and each

part of the baggage-train is to quarter itself. Being in an enemy's country it is not enough simply to post sentries. A trench must be dug and a palisade erected round the camp, and for that purpose every soldier on the march has carried a couple of sharpened stakes and a sort of small pickaxe. It may therefore

FIG. 103. — SOLDIERS WITH PACKS.

be readily understood that Seius is heavily laden. Besides the weight of his body-armour and his shield, pike, and sword, his orthodox burden is about forty-five English pounds.

Before entering upon this description of the service and armour of the legionary troops, it was stated that the legions made up but one-half of the

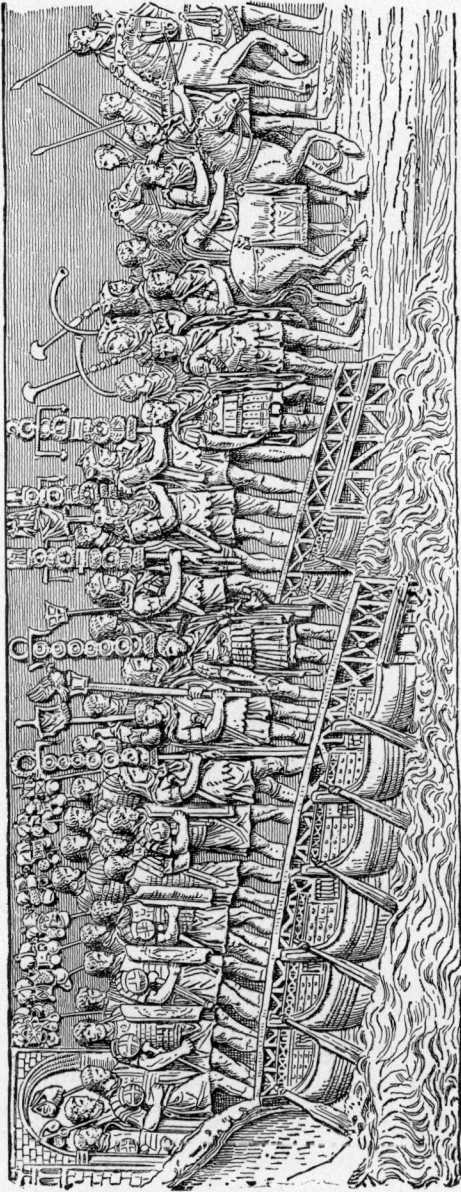

FIG. 104. — ROMAN SOLDIERS MARCHING. (Scheiber.)

351

Roman army, the other half consisting of what were known as "auxiliaries." If there were in the whole Roman empire 150,000 soldiers of the kind described, there were also about 150,000 of a different type. Just as it is a natural part of the British policy to raise bodies of Indian or African troops from among the non-British subjects of the empire, so it was an obvious course for the Romans to raise native troops in Africa, Syria, Spain, Gaul, Britain, or the German provinces on the western bank of the Rhine. And just as the British bring their non-British regiments into connection with the regular army, and put them under the command of British officers, so the Romans associated their "auxiliary" soldiery, mostly under Roman officers, with the regular force of the legions. To every legion of 6000 men there was attached, under the same general of division, a force of about 6000 men of non-Roman standing. The subject people of a province was called upon to recruit a certain quota of such troops, and, when so recruited, the soldiers of this class were required to serve for twenty-five years. At the expiration of their term they became Roman citizens, and their descendants ranked as such in the enjoyment of Roman opportunities. Such forces were not themselves formed into "legions" under an "eagle"; they served in separate regiments. Some of them were infantry almost indistinguishable from the Roman; others were armed in a different manner as to shield, spear, and sword; others were light skirmishing troops using their native weapons, such as javelins, slings, and bows. A very large proportion were cavalry, and whereas a legion possessed only 120 Roman horsemen, the auxiliary cavalry attached to it would number one or more regiments of either 1000 or 500 men each. But it was also part of the Roman policy to employ such auxiliary troops, not in the region in which they were raised and among their own people, but elsewhere, and sometimes even at the opposite extremity of the empire. Thus in Britain might be found, not only Germans and Batavians, but Spaniards or Syrians, while in Syria there might be quartered Africans or Germans, and in Africa troops from the modern Austria. We cannot call this custom an invariable one, but it was usual, and obviously it was politic.

To these two co-operating forces — legions and auxiliaries — we must add the Imperial Guards, twelve regiments of 1000 men each, quartered in Italy, and generally congregated in a special camp just outside the gate at the top of the Quirinal and Viminal Hills beyond the modern railway station. Like other "Guards," these were a picked body, containing many volunteers from Italy itself, while

FIG. 105. — IMPERIAL GUARDS.

others came from the most romanized parts of Gaul or elsewhere. They enjoyed many privileges, wore a more gorgeous armour, served only sixteen years, and received double pay. Frequently it came to be the case that this particular body of troops was the one which made and unmade emperors, chiefly under the influence of pecuniary promises or largess. Besides these, 6000 City Guards were in barracks inside the metropolis for the protection of the town; 7000 *gendarmerie*, already mentioned, served as

FIG. 106. — BESIEGERS WITH THE "TORTOISE."

night-watch and fire-brigade, but perhaps scarcely rank as soldiers. Here and there in the empire there also existed separate volunteer detachments of various dimensions serving on special duty, and it was to one of these that belonged the Cornelius of the Acts of the Apostles, who is there described as a centurion of the "Italian band."

It would carry us too far afield if we entered into detailed descriptions of Roman warfare — of Roman marches, Roman camps, and fortifications,

Roman sieges, and military engines. Otherwise it would be highly interesting to watch the attack made upon an enemy's wall or gate by a band of men pushing in front of them a wicker screen covered with hide, or holding their shields locked together above their heads, so as to form a roof to shelter them from the spears, stones, firebrands, and pots of flame which rained down from the walls.

Or we might see moving up on wheels a shed, from the open front of which protrudes the great iron head of a ram affixed to a huge beam. If you were under the shed, you would see that the beam was perhaps as much as 60 feet in length, and that it was suspended on chains or ropes by which it could be swung, so that the

Fig. 107. — Roman Artillery.

head butted with a deadly insistence upon the masonry of the wall. Meanwhile the enemy from the ramparts are doing their best to set the shed on fire, to break off the ram's head with heavy stones, to pull it upwards by a noose, or to deaden the effect of the shock by lowering stuffed sacks or other buffer material between it and the wall. At another point, in place of the shed, there is rolled forward a lofty construction like a tower built in several stories. When this approaches the wall it will overtop it, and a drawbridge with grappling irons may be dropped upon the parapet. Elsewhere there is mining and countermining. From a safer distance the artillery of the time is hurling its formidable missiles. There is the "catapult," which shoots a giant arrow, sometimes tipped with material on fire, from a groove or half-tube to a distance of a quarter of a mile. The propelling force, in default of gunpowder or other explosive, is the recoil of strings of gut or hair which have been tightened by a windlass. There is also the heavier "hurler," which works in much the same manner, but which, instead of arrows, throws stones and beams of from 14 pounds to half a hundredweight, doing effective damage up to a distance of some 400 yards.

Seius joins his legion as a private infantry soldier. He is in the "hobnailed" service. But if our young noble, Publius Silius Bassus, enters upon a military career, he will probably become one of the 120 Roman horsemen attached to the legion, and will be serving as a "knight" or "gentleman," with servants to relieve him of his rougher work. The cavalrymen among whom he serves do not ride upon a saddle with stirrups, but on a mere saddlecloth. On their left arm is a round shield or buckler; they carry a spear of extreme reach, wear a longer sword than the infantrymen, and on their back is a quiver containing three broad-pointed javelins, very similar to assegais, which serve them as missiles. If by good service they obtain medallions like the infantry, they will fasten them to the bridles and breast-straps of their horses, and altogether will make a fine and jingling show. Through the influence of his family, Publius will most likely be taken under the personal supervision of the general in command, will frequently mess with him, and will perhaps act as a kind of

FIG. 108. — AUXILIARY CAVALRYMAN.

honorary aide-de-camp. After a sufficient initiation into military business, he will be appointed what may be called colonel of an infantry regiment of auxiliaries, then colonel of a regiment of the legion, and subsequently, if he is following the profession, colonel of a regiment of the auxiliary cavalry. He does not at any time pass through the rank of centurion, any more than the British officer passes

through that of sergeant-major. The class distinction
is at least as great in the case of the Romans.

When the young noble has completed this series
of services — although the whole of it is not absolutely
necessary, and it will be sufficient if he has been six
months titular colonel of a regiment of the legion —
he may perhaps return to Rome, and at the age of
twenty-five may enter upon his first public position,
and so become himself a senator. His duties may be
connected with the Treasury at Rome itself, or more
probably .he will accompany a proconsul who is on
his way to govern a province for a year — perhaps
Andalusia, or Macedonia, or Bithynia. To his chief
he stands for that year in a kind of filial relation.
His main business will be to supervise the financial
affairs, to act as paymaster, and to keep the accounts
of the province, but he will also, when required,
administer justice in place of the governor. In this
capacity he learns the methods of provincial government in readiness for the time when he himself may
be made a governor, whether by the senate or by the
emperor. His next step upward will be to the post
of aedile, one of the officials who control the streets,
public buildings, markets, and police of Rome. By
the age of thirty he may arrive at the second highest
step on the official ladder, in a position which qualifies
him to preside over a court of law. Or it may bring
with it no greater function than that of presiding
over "games" in the circus or amphitheatre, and of
spending a liberal sum of money of his own upon

making them both magnificent and novel. After
this he may receive from the emperor the command
of a brigade — the 12,000 men composed of a legion
and its auxiliaries — perhaps at Cologne or Mainz,
perhaps at Caerleon-on-Usk, perhaps near Antioch.
In this position his movements are subject to the
authority of the governor of the province, who is
the "lieutenant" or "deputy" of His Highness in the
larger capacity, while he himself is but a " lieutenant"
of Caesar as commanding one of his legions.

He may now himself be appointed governor to
a province, but hardly yet to those which are the
"plums" of the empire. There is still one highest
post for him to fill. This is the consulship. Under
the republic the two consuls had been the highest
executive officers of the state, and the year was
dated by their names. Nominally they were still in
the same position, and the sane emperors made a
point of treating them with all outward respect.
They took precedence of all but "His Highness the
Head of the State." But whereas under the republic
there had been but two consuls holding joint office
for the year, under the emperors the post had
become to such a degree complimentary, and there
were so many nobles who desired the honour or to
whom the emperor was minded to grant it, that it
became the custom to hold the position only for two
months, so that twelve persons in each year might
boast of being ex-consuls or having "passed the
consul's chair."

Publius Silius, we may suppose, passes up each

step of the ladder, or what was called the "career of
honours," and becomes senatorial governor of no less
important a province than "Asia" — that nearer
portion of Asia Minor which contained flourishing
cities like Smyrna, Ephesus, and Rhodes. In that
office, as in any other which he may hold, it behoves
him to comport himself with caution and modesty.
If he is a man of unusual influence or popularity he
will do well to keep the fact concealed. There must
be nothing in his demeanour or his speech to lay him
open to a charge of becoming dangerous to the
emperor. That emperor is Nero; and even stronger
and saner emperors than Nero watched suspiciously
the behaviour of aspiring men.

CHAPTER XIX

To undertake to set forth with any definiteness the religious ideas of "a Roman" of A.D. 64 would be an extremely difficult task. Those ideas would differ with the individual, being determined or varied by a number of considerations and influences — by locality, education, and temperament. Silius would not hold the views of Seius and probably not those of Marcia. We may speak of the "State religion" of Rome, as distinct from various other religions tolerated and practised in different parts of the empire, but it is scarcely possible to define the contents of that "State religion." There were certain special priests and priestly bodies who saw to it that certain rites and ceremonies should be performed scrupulously in a prescribed manner and on prescribed dates; but these were officers of the state, whose knowledge and functions were confined to the ritual observances with which they had to deal. They were not persons trained in a system of theology, nor were they preachers of a code of doctrines or morals; they had no "cure of souls," and belonged to no church; they had no *credo* and no Bible or corresponding authority to which to refer. Though most well-informed persons could have told the names of the prominent deities in the calendar—such as Jupiter, Mars, Apollo, and Ceres—perhaps scarcely any one but an encyclopaedist or antiquarian could have named one-half of the total. It is not merely that the deities on the list were so numerous. There were other reasons for ignorance or vagueness. In the first place, the line between the operations of one deity and those of another was often too fine to draw, and deities originally more or less distinct came to be confused or identified. Secondly, it was often hard, if not impossible, to make up one's mind whether a so-called deity — such as Virtue, Peace, or Health — was supposed to have a real existence, or whether it was simply the personification of an abstract quality. Thirdly, many of the ancient divinities had fallen out of fashion, and to a large extent out of memory, while many new ones — Isis and Serapis for example — had come, or were coming, into vogue.

The state possessed its old-established calendar of days sacred to a number of deities, and its code of ritual to be performed in their honour. There were ancient prescriptions as to what certain priests should wear, what they should do or avoid in their priestly character, what victims — ox, sheep, or pig — they should sacrifice, what instruments they should use for the purpose, and in what formula of words they should pray in particular connections. There was a standing commission, with the Pontifex Maximus — at this date that excellent religious authority, the

emperor Nero — at its head, to safeguard the state
religion, to see that its requirements were carried out,
and that no one ventured to commit an outrage
towards it. But the state could not have told you
with any precision that you must believe in just so
many deities and no others; it could not have told
you precisely what notions to entertain concerning
those deities whom it did officially recognise; it
dictated no theological doctrines; neither did it dictate
any moral doctrines beyond those which you would
find in the secular law. It reserved the right to
prevent the introduction of foreign or new divinities
if it found sufficient cause; but so long as the
temples, the rites and ceremonies, the cardinal moral
axioms of the Roman "religion," and the basic
principles of Roman society were respected, the state
practised no sort of inquisition into your beliefs or
non-beliefs, and in no way interfered with your
particular selection of favourite deities.

Polytheism in an advanced community is always
tolerant, because it is necessarily always indefinite.
What it does not readily endure is an organised attack
upon the entire system, whether openly avowed or
manifestly implied. Even undisguised unbelief in
any deity at all it is often willing to tolerate, so long
as the unbelief is rather a matter of dialectics than
anything else, and makes no attempt at a crusade.
When a state so disposed is found to interfere with a
novel religion, it will generally be easy to perceive
that the jealousy is not on behalf of the deities nor
of a creed, but on behalf of the community in its

political, economic, or social aspect. This, however, is perhaps to anticipate. Let us endeavour to realise as best we can the religious situation among the Roman or romanized portion of the population.

Though we are not here directly concerned with the steps by which the Roman religion had come to be what it was, we can scarcely hope to understand the position without some comprehension of that development. The Romans were a conservative people, and many of the peculiarities of their worship were due to the retention of old forms which had lost such spirit as they once possessed.

In the infant days of the nation there had been no such things as gods in human shape, or in recognisable shape at all. There were only "powers" or "influences" superior to mankind, by whose aid or concurrence man must work out his existence. The early Romans and such Italian tribes as they became blended with were, as they still are, extremely superstitious. In a pre-scientific age they, like other peoples, were at a loss to understand what produced thunder and lightning, rain, the fertility or failure of crops, the changes of the seasons, the flow or cessation of springs and streams, the intoxication or exhilaration proceeding from wine, and a multitude of other phenomena. Fire was a perplexing thing; so was wind: the woods were full of mysterious sounds and movements. They could comprehend neither birth nor death, nor the fructification of plants. The consequence was a feeling that these things were due to unseen agencies; and the attempt was made to bring those powers into some sort of relation with mankind, either by the compulsion of magical operations and magical formulae, or by sacrifices and offerings of propitiation, or by promises. A superhuman power might be placed under a spell, or placated with food and drink, or persuaded by a vow. Such "powers" were exceedingly numerous. Greatest of all, and recognised equally by all, was the power working in the sky with the thunder and the rain. Its presence was everywhere alike, and its operations most palpable at every season. Countless others were concerned with particular localities or with particular functions. Every wood, if not every tree, and also every fountain, was controlled by some such higher "power"; every manifestation or operation of nature came from such an "influence." There was no kind of action or undertaking, no new stage of life or change of condition, which did not depend for help or hindrance upon a similar power. At first the "powers" bore no distinctive names, and were conceived in no definite shapes. They were not yet gods. The human being who sought to work upon them to favour him could only do, say, and offer such things as he thought likely to move them. But in process of time it became inevitable that these superhuman agencies should be referred to under some sort of title, and the title literally expressed the conception. Hence a multitude of names. Not only was there the ever-prominent Jupiter or "sky-father"; there was a veritable multitude of powers with provinces

great and small. Among the larger conceptions the
power concerned with the sowing of seed was Saturn,
that with the growth of crops was Ceres, that with
the blazing of fire was Vesta. Among the smaller,
the power which taught a babe to eat was Edulia,
that which attended the bringing home of a bride was
Domiduca. The ability to speak or to walk was
supposed to be imparted by separate agencies named
accordingly. Flowers depended on Flora and fruits
on Pomona.

But to assign a name is a great step towards
creating a "power" into a "god," and such agencies
began to take shape in the mind of those who named
them. This was the second stage. Jupiter, Ceres,
Saturn, and almost all the rest became "gods." The
powers in the woodlands — a Silvanus or Faunus —
became embodied, like the more modern gnomes and
kobbolds. Once imagine a shape, and the tendency
is to give it visible form in an image "like unto man,"
and to honour it with an abode — a temple or shrine.
The earliest Romans known to us erected no images
or temples, but they were not long in creating them.
Particularly rapid was the reducing of a god to
human form when they came into close contact with
the Etruscans and the Greeks. For all the important
deities poetry and art combined to evolve an
appropriate bodily form, which gradually became
conventional, so that the ordinary notion of a Jupiter,
a Juno, a Mercury, or a Ceres was approximately that
which had been gathered from the statue thus
developed. This trouble was not taken with all the

most ancient divinities. Many of the old rural and
local deities, and many of those with quite minor
provinces, were left vague and unrealised. They
were represented in no temples and by no statues.

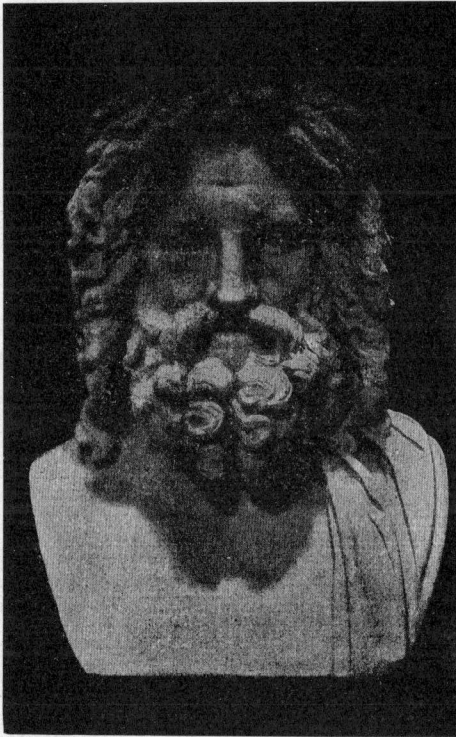

FIG. 109. — JUPITER.

Naturally as the Roman state grew from a set of
neighbouring farms into a great city, and from a small
settlement into a vast empire, the little local gods fell
into the background. The deities which concerned
the state, and to which it erected temples, were those
with the more far-reaching operations — such as the

gods identified with the sky and its thunders, with
war, with fertility, with the sea, with the hearth-fire
of all Rome. The rest might well be left to localities
or to domestic worship.

From the early days of Rome there existed a
calendar for festivals to certain divinities important
to the little growing town, and a code of ceremonies
to be performed in their honour, and of formulae of
prayer to be offered to them. The later Romans, in
their characteristic conservatism, adhered to those
festivals, to that ritual, and to those formulae, even
when some of the deities had ceased to be of appreciable account, and when neither the meaning of the
ritual nor the sense of the old words was any longer
understood by the very priests who used them.

Reflect a moment on this situation. First, we
have a number of deities of the first rank, housed in
temples, embodied in statues, and recognised in all
the Roman world; next a number of minor divinities
whose operations and worship may be remotely rural
or otherwise local, and whose functions are by no
means always distinguishable from those of the
greater gods; then a series of more or less un-
intelligible ceremonials carried out by ancient rule
in honour of divinities often practically forgotten;
outside these a number of vague powers presiding
over small domestic and other actions; finally, a
peculiar Roman tendency — in keeping with the last
— to erect into divinities, and to symbolise in statues
housed in temples, all manner of abstract qualities

and states, such as Hope, Harmony, Peace, Wealth, Health, Fame, and Youth.

Reflect again that, when the Romans, as they spread, came into contact with Greeks, Egyptians, or other foreigners, they met with deities whose provinces were necessarily often identical with or closely akin

FIG. 110. — A SACRIFICE.

to their own. Then remember that there is no church and no official document to define the complete list of Roman gods. Does it not follow, as a matter of course, on the one hand, that the importation of new gods was an easy matter, and on the other, that no individual Roman could draw the line as to the number of even the old-established deities in whom he should or should not believe?

2 B

The guardians of the public religion were satisfied
if the due rites were paid by the state to those deities,
on those dates, and precisely in that manner, which
happened to be prescribed in the official religious
books. For the rest they left matters to the
individual.

So much it has been necessary to say in order to
account for existing attitudes. We must use the
plural, since the attitude of the state officials is but
one of several, and, inasmuch as the state officials
themselves were not a theological caste but only
secular servants of the community administering
the regulations for external worship as laid down in
the records, it often happened that their official
attitude had nothing to do with their individual
beliefs. Often they did not know or care whether
there was a real religious efficacy in the acts which
they performed; sometimes all that they knew was
that they were doing what the state required to be
done properly by some one.

Cicero quotes a dictum of a Pontifex Maximus
that there was one religion of the poet, another of
the philosopher, and another of the statesman. This
is true, but it is hardly adequate. We must at least
add that of the common people. A well-known
statement of more modern birth puts the case — rather
too strongly — that at our period all religions were
regarded by the people as equally true, by the philosopher as equally false and by the statesman as
equally useful. We may begin with the ordinary
people of whatever station, who were not poets

nor thinkers nor magistrates. It is an error to
suppose that such Romans of the first century were
either atheistic or indifferent to religion. Their fault
was rather that they were too superstitious, ready to
believe too much rather than too little, but to believe
without relating their belief to conduct. They did
not question the existence of the traditional gods,
nor the characters attributed to them; they were
ready to perform their dues of worship and to make
their due offerings, but all this had no bearing
upon their own morality. They believed with the
terror of the superstitious in omens and portents, and
in rites of expiation and purification to avert the
threatened evil. They were alarmed by thunder and
lightning, earthquakes, bad dreams, ravens seen on
the wrong side of the road, and other evil tokens.
They commonly accepted the existence of malign
spirits, including ghosts. They were prepared to
believe that on occasion a statue had bled or turned
round on its base; that an ox had spoken in
human language; or that there had been a rain of
blood. There were doubtless exceptions, and superstition was less dire and oppressive than once it
was. More than fifty years before our date Cicero
had said that even old women no longer shuddered
at the terrors of an underworld, and fifty years
after it the satirist asserts the same of children.
But both writers are speaking somewhat hyper-
bolically. Doubtless it had been wondered how
two augurs could look at each other without a
smile, but there is nothing to show that even a

minority of augurs were acutely conscious of anything to smile at.

In the multiplicity of deities the ordinary people
were prepared to accept as many more as you chose
to offer them, especially if the worship attaching to
them contained mystic or orgiastic ceremonies. By
this date the populace had become exceedingly mixed,
especially in the capital, and the cool hard-headed
Roman stock had been largely replaced or leavened
by foreign elements, especially from the East. The
official worship of the state was formal and frigid; it
offered nothing to the emotions or the hopes. Many
among the people felt an instinct for something more
sacramental, and especially attractive was any form
of worship which promised a continued existence,
and probably a happier existence, after death. Even
the mere mysteriousness of a form of worship had its
allurements. Hence a tendency to Judaism, still
more to the Egyptian worship of Isis and Osiris.
The latter made many proselytes, particularly among
the women, and contained ideas which are by no
means ignoble but to our modern minds far more
truly "religious" than anything to be found in the
native Roman cults. To pass through purification,
to practise asceticism, to feel that there was a life
beyond the grave apportioned to your deserts, to go
through an impressive form of worship held every
day, and to have the emotions thus worked upon —
all this supplied something to the moral nature which
was lacking in the chill sacrifices and prayers to
Jupiter and the other national divinities. In vain

had the authorities, in their doubt as to the moral effects, tried on several occasions to suppress this foreign worship; it always revived, and it now held its established place both in the imperial city and in

Fig. 111. — Isis Worship. (Wall-Painting.)

the provinces, particularly near the sea, for it was especially a sailors' religion. Rome, like Pompeii, had its temple of Isis and her daily celebrations. There was, however, no necessary conflict between this worship and the official religion. It was quite possible to accept Isis while accepting Jupiter. Nor,

though this particular cult has required mention,
must it be taken as belonging to more than a section
of the Roman population. Most Romans would look
upon it and other deviations with acquiescence, some
with contempt, and perhaps some with a shake of the
head, while themselves satisfied with an indifferent
conformity to the more established customs of the
state.

Setting aside the devotees of the mystic, the more
ordinary point of view was that between Romans and
the established gods of Rome there is an understanding.
The gods will support Rome so long as Rome pays to
them their dues of formal recognition. Their ritual
must not be neglected by the authorities; it is not
necessary for an individual member of the community
to concern himself further in the matter. The
state, through its appointed ministers, will make the
necessary sacrifices and say the necessary words;
the citizen need not put in an appearance or take
any part. He will not do or say anything dis-
respectful towards the deities in question, and he will
enjoy the festivals belonging to them. If remarkable
portents and disasters occur, he will agree that there
is something wrong in the behaviour of the state,
and that there must be some public purification or
other placation of the gods. If the state orders such
a proceeding, he will perform whatever may be his
share in it. So far he is loyal to the "religion of
the state."

In his private capacity he has his own wants,
fears, and hopes. He therefore betakes himself to

Fig. 112. — Household Shrine. (Pompeii.)

whatever divinity he considers most likely to help
him; he makes his own prayers and vows an offering
if his request is granted.   Reduced to plain commercial
language his ordinary attitude is — no success, no
payment.   A cardinal difference between the religion
of the Romans and our own is to be seen in the nature
of their prayers.   They always ask for some definite
advantage — prosperity, safety, health, or the like.
They never pray for a clean heart or for some moral
improvement.   Of more importance than the man's
moral condition will be his scrupulous observance
of the right external practices.   Unlike the Greek,
he will cover his head when he prays.   He will raise
his hand to his lips before the statue, or, if he is
appealing to the celestial deities, he will stretch his
palms upwards above his head; if to the infernal
powers, he will hold them downwards.   These are
the things that matter.

At home, if he belongs to the better type of
representative citizen, our Roman has his household
shrine and his household divinities, whom he never
neglects.   If he is very pious, he may pray to them
every morning, or at least before every enterprise.
In any case he will remember them with a small
offering when he dines.   There are the "gods of the
stores" — his "penates" — certain deities whom he
has selected as guardians of his belongings, and who
have their little images by the hearth in the
kitchen.   There is the household "protector," or
more commonly there are two, who may be painted
under the form of lightly-stepping youths in a

little niche or shrine above a small altar. To these he will offer fruits, flowers, incense, and cakes. And there is the "Genius" of the master of the house, who is also painted on the wall, or who may be represented by his own portrait bust or by the picture of a snake. That "Genius" means the power presiding over his vitality and health and well-being. If he is an artisan and belongs to a guild, he will pay special worship to the patron god or goddess of that guild — to Vesta, if he is a baker, to Minerva, if he is a fuller. Out of doors he will find a street shrine in the wall at a crossing, pertaining to the tutelary god of what may be called his "parish," and this he will not neglect. Like all other orthodox Romans he will not undertake any new enterprise — betrothal, marriage, journey, or important business — without ascertaining that the auspices are favourable.

In a general way he has a notion that the gods are displeased at certain forms of crime, and that they approve of justice and the carrying out of compacts. The gods overlook the state, because the state engages them so to do, and therefore to break the laws of the state is to anger the gods of the state. But this is rather subtle for the common man, and there is generally no understood immediate relation between these gods and his moral conduct, unless he has sworn an oath by one or other of them. The purpose of calling a god to witness is to bring upon a perjurer the anger of the offended deity. But he entertains no such conception as the modern one of "sin" or of "remorse for sin." "Sin" is either a breach of the secular law or breach of a contract with a deity, and "remorse" is but fear of or regret for the consequences.

His morality is determined by the laws of the state, family discipline, and social custom. For that reason his vices on the positive side will mostly be those of his appetites, and on the negative side a want of charity and compassion. He may be guiltless of lying and stealing, murder and violence; he may be honest and law-abiding; but there is nothing to make him temperate, continent, or gentle. His avowed code is "duty," and duty is defined by law and tradition.

If this is the religious condition of the commonplace man or woman — a blend of superstition, formalism, and tolerance — it is by no means that of the educated thinker. Such persons were for the most part freethinkers. Many of them, finding no better guide to conduct, conform to the "religion" of the state without any real belief in its gods or attaching any importance to its ceremonies. They do not feel called upon to propagate any other views, and they probably think the current notions are at least as good for the ignorant as any others. If they are poets, like Horace or Lucan, they will dress up the mythology, mostly from Greek models, and write fluently about Jupiter and Juno, Venus and Mercury, either attributing to them the recognised characters and legends, or varying them so as to make them more picturesque and interesting — perhaps even improving them — but all the time believing no more in

the stories they are telling, or in the deities themselves, than Tennyson need have believed in King
Arthur and Guinevere. The gods are good poetic
material and are sure to afford popular, or at least in-
offensive, reading. The poets doubtless do something
to humanise and beautify the popular conception of
a deity, but they seldom deliberately set out with any
such purpose. If the educated are not poets, but
public men of affairs, they may believe just as little,
and yet regard the established cult of the gods as an
excellent discipline for the vulgar and the best known
means of upholding the national principle of "duty."
If they are philosophers they may not, and the
Epicureans in reality do not, believe in the gods at all
— certainly not as they are generally conceived — and
will openly discuss in speech and in writing the question of their existence or non-existence, and of their
character and nature if they do exist. They will
endeavour to substitute for the barren formalism of
rites and ceremonies, or the inconsistent or incomplete
traditional morality of duty, another set of principles
as a sounder guide to life and conduct. Some are
monotheists, some are simply in doubt. Says Nero's
own tutor, Seneca, "Do you want to propitiate the
gods? Then be good. The true worshipper of the
gods is he who acts like them." "Better," remarks
Plutarch, "not believe in a God at all than cringe
before a god who is worse than the worst of men."
In the actual worship of images none of them believe.
One conspicuous writer of the time says: "To look for
a form and shape to a god, I consider to be a mark of

human feebleness of mind." Concerning the schools
of thought and in particular the tenets of those Stoics
and Epicureans whom St. Paul met at Athens, and
whom he could meet in educated circles all over the
Roman Empire, we shall have to speak in a following
chapter, when summing up the intellectual and moral
condition of the time.   Meanwhile it should be understood that, though a profound or anything approaching a professional study of philosophy was discouraged
among the true Romans — more than once the professional philosophers were banished from the capital —
there were few cultivated persons who did not to
some extent dabble in it, and even go so far as
to profess an adherence to one school or another.
None of these men believed in the "Roman religion"
as administered by the state, although many of
them were administering it themselves. The same
man could one day freely discuss the gods in conversation or a treatise, and the next he might be
clad in priestly garb and officially seeing that the
rites of sacrifice were being religiously carried out in
terms of the books, or that the auspices were being
properly taken.

It does not, however, follow at all that because
poet or public man cared nothing for the pantheon
and all its mythology, he was therefore without his
superstitions. He might still tremble at signs and
portents, at comets, at dreams, and at the unpropitious behaviour of birds and beasts. He might
believe in astrology and resort to its professors, called
the "Chaldaeans." On the other hand he might

laugh at such things. It was all a matter of temperament. It certainly was not every man who dared to
act like one of the Roman admirals. When it was
reported that the omens were unpropitious to an
imminent battle because the sacred chickens "would
not eat," he ordered them to be thrown into the sea
so that at least they might drink. The freethinkers
were in advance of their times. "Science" in the
modern sense hardly existed, and until phenomena
are explained it is hard to avoid a perplexity or
astonishment which is equivalent to superstition.

Consider now these various states of mind — that
of the people, ready to add almost any deity to the
large and vague number already recognised; that of
the poet, who finds the deities such useful literary
material; that of the magistrate or public man, who,
without enthusiasm or necessary belief, regards
religion as a thing useful to society; and that
of the philosopher, who thinks all the current religious conceptions unsound, if not absurd, and
morally almost useless.

Manifestly a society so composed will be one of
unusual tolerance. The Romans had no disposition
to force their religion on the subject provinces of the
empire. Their religion was the Roman religion; the
religion of the Greeks might be left Greek, the Jewish
religion Jewish, and the Egyptian religion Egyptian.
Any nation had a right to the religion of its fathers.
Nay, the Jews had such peculiar notions about a
Sabbath day and other matters that a Jew was

exempted from the military service which would
have compelled him to break his national laws. All
religions were permitted, so long as they were national
religions. Also all religious views were permitted to
the individual, so long as they were not considered
dangerous to the empire or imperial rule, or so long as
they threatened no appreciable harm to the social
order. If a Jew came to Rome and practised Judaism,
well and good. It was, in the eyes of the Romans, a
narrow-minded and uncharitable religion, marked by
many strange and absurd practices and superstitions,
but if a misguided oriental people liked to indulge in
it, well and good. Even if a Roman became a
proselyte to Judaism, well and good, so long as he did
not flout the official religion of his own country. If
the Egyptians chose to worship cats, ibises, and
crocodiles, that was their affair, so long as they let
other people alone. In Gaul, it is true, the emperor
Claudius, predecessor of Nero, had put down the Druids.
Earlier still the Druids had already been interfered
with; but that was because the Druids — those weird
old white-sheeted men with their long beards and
strange magic — were performing human sacrifices —
burning men alive in wicker frames — and such
conduct was not only contrary to the secular law of
Rome, but even to natural law. And when Claudius
finally suppressed them, or drove the remnant out of
Gaul into Britain, it was not simply because they
worshipped non-Roman gods and performed non-
Roman rites, but because they were, as they had
always notoriously been, a dangerous political in-

fluence interfering with the proper carrying out of the Roman government.

And when we come to Christianity it must be remarked that, so long as that nascent religion was regarded as merely a variety of Judaism, it was actually protected by the Roman power, and owes no little of its original progress to the fact. In the Acts of the Apostles it is always from the Roman governor that St. Paul receives, not only the fairest, but the most courteous treatment. It is the Jews who persecute him and work up difficulties against him, because to them he is a renegade and is weaning away their people. To the philosophers at Athens he appears as the preacher of a new philosophy, and they think him a "smatterer" in such subjects. To the Roman he is a man charged by a certain community with being dangerous to social order, to wit, causing factious disturbances and profaning the temple; and since he refuses to let the local authorities judge his case, and has exercised his citizen privilege by appealing to Caesar, to Caesar he is sent. And, when a prisoner in somewhat free custody at Rome, note that he is permitted to speak "with all freedom," and that in the first instance he is acquitted.

True, but the fact remains that Nero burnt Christians in his gardens after the great fire of Rome, and that certain later emperors are found punishing Christians merely for avowing themselves such. Why was Christianity thus singled out? It was not through what can be reasonably called "religious

intolerance," for, as has been said, the Romans did
not seek to force Roman religion on other peoples,
nor did they make any inquisition into the beliefs of
Romans themselves. The reasons for singling out
Christianity for special treatment are obvious enough.
The question is not whether the reasons were sound,
whether the Romans properly understood or tried to
understand, whether they could be as wise before the
event as we are after it, but whether the motive was
what we should call a "religious" one. To allow
Epicureans to deny the existence of gods at all, and
to make scornful concessions to the peculiar tenets of
Jews, could not be the action of a people which was
bigoted. If there was bigotry and intolerance, it was
political or social bigotry and intolerance, not religious.
To prevent any possible misconception let the present
writer say here that he considers the principles of
Christianity, as laid down by its Founder and as spread
by St. Paul, to have been the most humanizing and
civilising influence ever brought to bear upon society.
But that is not the point. The early Christians were
treated as they were, not because they held non-
Roman views, but because they held anti-Roman
views; not because they did not believe in Jupiter
and Venus, but because they refused to let any one
else believe in them; not because they threatened to
weaken Roman faith, but because they threatened to
weaken and even to wreck the whole fabric of Roman
society; not because they were known to be heretics,
but because they were supposed to be disloyal; not
because they converted men, but because they

appeared to convert them into dangerous characters. As it has been put, the Christians were regarded as the "Nihilists" of the period. We are apt to judge the Romans from the standpoint of Christianity dominant and understood; it is fairer to judge them from the standpoint of a dominant pagan empire looking on at a strange new phenomenon altogether misunderstood and often deliberately misrepresented. Moreover — and the point is worth more attention than it commonly receives — we have only to read the Epistles to the Corinthians, to perceive that the early Christian gatherings were by no means always such meek, pure, and model assemblages as they are almost always assumed to have been. Some of the members, for instance, quarrelled and "were drunken." There were evidently many unworthy members of the new communion, and of course there were also many manifestations of insulting bigotry on their part. The class of society to which the Christians belonged was closely associated in the Roman mind with the rabble and the slave, if not with criminals. What the pagan observer saw in the new religion was "a pestilent super-stition," "hatred of the human race," "a malevolent superstition." He thought its practices to be connected with magic. The *intransigeant* Christian refused to take the customary oath in the law courts, and therefore appeared to menace a trustworthy administration of the law. He took no interest in the affairs of the empire, but talked of another king and his coming kingdom, and he appeared to be an enemy to the Roman power. He held what appeared to be secret

meetings, although the empire rigidly suppressed all
secret societies. He weakened the martial spirit of
the soldier. He divided families — the basis of Roman
society—against themselves. He was a socialist
leveller. He threatened with ruin all the trades
connected with either the established worship — as
amongst the silversmiths at Ephesus — or with the
luxuries and amusements of life. Those amusements
in circus or amphitheatre he hated, and therefore
appeared misanthropic. He not only stood aloof
from the religious observances of the state and the
household, but treated them with contempt or
abhorrence.

Moreover, at this date, he refused to acknowledge
the one great symbol of the imperial authority. This
was the statue of the emperor. When that statue
was set up in every town it was not understood by
any intelligent man that the emperor was actually a
god, or that, when incense was burnt before the statue,
it was being burned to the emperor himself as deity.
But just as every householder had his attendant
"Genius" — the power determining his vital functions
and well-being — which was often represented as a
bust with the man's own features, so the statue of
the Augustus, "His Highness," represented the Genius
of that Head of the State, and the offering of incense
was meant as an appeal to the Genius to keep the
emperor and the imperial power "in health and
wealth long to live." The man who refused to make
such an offering was necessarily considered to be ill-
disposed to the majesty and welfare of the Head of the

State, and therefore of the state itself. The Roman attitude towards the early Christians was partly that of a modern government towards Nihilists, and partly that of a generation or two ago to a blend of extreme Radical with extreme atheist.

We are not here concerned with the whole story of the persecution of the Christians, but only with the situation at and immediately after the date we have chosen. It is at least quite cer ain that when Nero burned the Christians in the year 64 he was treating them, not as the adherents of a religion, but as social criminals or nuisances. How far his notions of Christianity may have been influenced by Poppaea we do not know. At least he believed he was pleasing the populace.

CHAPTER XX

STUDY AND SCIENTIFIC KNOWLEDGE
AMONG THE ROMANS

IN describing the education of a Roman youth, and also in setting forth the various religious attitudes of the time, mention has been made of the pursuit of philosophy. Religion supplied no real guide to moral conduct, and education provided little exercise for the cultivation of the higher intellectual faculties. It was left for philosophy to fill these blanks as best it could. Unlike the Greeks, the Romans, great as they were in law-making and administration, had little natural gift or taste for abstract thought. All the philosophic sects had been founded and continued by Greeks, and it was still to the Greek half of the empire that the contemporary world looked for the best schools and teachers of philosophy. The genuine Roman spirit at all times felt some mistrust of such studies, especially if they tended to carry the student away from practical life into the "shade" and the "corner," or if they tended to subvert the traditional notions of "duty" as inculcated by Roman law, Roman custom, and the religion of the state. Nevertheless, not only did many Romans, even of mature years, resort

388

to the philosophic "Universities" of the time, but
wealthy houses often maintained a domestic philosopher, whose business it was to supply moral teaching
and intellectual companionship to his employer.
Some, indeed, preferred merely a *savant*, who might
"post" them with information concerning Greek
writers, explain difficulties, and act in general as a
literary *vade mecum*. In many cases, if not in
most, the Roman aristocrat or plutocrat treated such
a retainer as a social inferior.

The Roman attitude towards thought and learning
too often reminds one of a certain modern type which
has been irreverently described as being "death on
culture." While the Greek and graecized oriental
loved research, discussion, dialectics, ethical and
scientific conversation, and literary coteries for their
own sake, the Roman more commonly regarded such
things as means for sharpening his abilities and for
imparting distinction in social intercourse. Doubtless there were, and had been, exceptions. No Greek
philosopher could be more in earnest than Lucretius,
the Roman poet of the later republic, and doubtless
there were no few Romans unknown to fame who
both grappled seriously with Greek philosophy and
also endeavoured to carry it religiously into practice.
Yet for the most part the Roman, even when he is a
writer upon such subjects, carries with him the
unmistakable air of the amateur or the dilettante.
In reading Seneca, as in reading Cicero, we feel that
we are dealing with an able man possessed of an

excellent gift for popular exposition or essay-writing, but hardly with a man of original philosophic endeavour or of strong practical conviction. And when we read the letters of the younger Pliny, we perceive a genuine admiration for men of thought and a genuine liking for "things of the mind," but we also discern that his dealing with philosophers and philosophy is strictly such as he deems "fit for a gentleman."

In his own way and for his own ends the Roman could be intensely studious. He was eager to know and to possess information; but his native taste was for information of a positive kind, for definite facts more or less encyclopaedic — the facts of history, of science, of art, of literature, or even of grammar. His natural bent was not towards pure speculation. The elder Pliny was in his prime in the later days of Nero, and though he is perhaps an extreme type, he is nevertheless a type worth contemplating. His nephew writes a letter to a friend in which he gives a formidable list of works which the uncle had written or rather compiled, culminating in that huge miscellany known as his *Natural History* — a book dealing, not only with geography, anthropology, physiology, zoology, botany, mineralogy, but also with fine art. How did he lead the ordinary Roman official life and yet accomplish all this before he was fifty-six? Here is the explanation. "He had a keen intellect, incredible zeal, and the greatest capacity for wakefulness. The end of August had not come before he began to work by

lamplight long before dawn; in winter he began as
early as one or two o'clock in the morning. It is
true that he could readily command sleep, which
visited and left him even during his studies. Before
daylight he used to go to the emperor Vespasian —
who also worked before day — and thence to his
appointed duty. Returning home he gave the
remainder of his time to his studies. After his
déjeuner — which, like any other food that he took in
the daytime, was light and digestible in the old-
fashioned style — if it was summer, some leisure
moments were spent in lying in the sun; a book was
read, and he marked passages or made extracts. He
never read anything without making excerpts, for
he used to say that no book was so bad as to contain
no part that was useful. After sunning himself he
generally took a cold bath. He then took a snack
and a very brief siesta, subsequently reading till
dinner-time as if it were a new day. During dinner
a book was read and marked, all very rapidly. I
recall an occasion on which a certain passage had
been badly delivered by his reader, whereupon one
of the company stopped him and made him read it
again. Said my uncle, 'I suppose you had caught
the meaning?' The friend nodded. 'Then why did
you call him back? We have lost more than ten
lines by this interruption of yours.' So economical
was he of time. In summer he rose from dinner
while it was still light, and in winter within an hour
after dark, as if compelled by some law. Such was
his day amid all his work and the roar of the city.

But when on holiday the only time he was not studying was bath-time. By bath I mean when he was actually right inside; for while he was under scraper and towel he would be read to or dictate. When travelling he thought of nothing else: at his side was a shorthand writer with a book and his tablets. In winter the writer's hands were protected by mittens, so that not even the sharpness of the weather should rob him of a moment. For the same reason even at Rome he used to ride in a sedan-chair (and not in a litter). I remember how he once took me to task for walking. Said he, 'You need not have wasted these hours;' for he considered as wasted all hours not spent upon study. It was by application like this that he completed all those volumes and also left to me a hundred and sixty note-books full of selections, written in very small hand on both sides of the paper. He used himself to say that, when he was the emperor's financial agent in Spain, he could have sold these note-books to Largius Licinus for £3000, and at that time they were considerably less numerous." . . . "And so," writes the nephew, "I always laugh when certain people call *me* studious, for, compared to him, I am a most indolent person."

And yet what does this "most indolent person" himself do in the course of a lifetime? After a complete oratorical education of the typical Roman kind he enters upon a full public career. He undergoes his minimum military service with the legions in Syria. He returns to Rome and passes right up to the consulship, acquiring particular ability in connection with the Treasury. Often he acts as adviser to other officers. Apart from his public position he is a pleader before the courts. He takes a prominent part in the debates of the senate. He belongs to one of the priestly bodies. He does his share in providing the public games. He is appointed "Minister for the regulation of the Tiber and of the Sewerage." He is afterwards made governor of Bithynia, which has fallen into financial disorder and requires reorganisation. He possesses numerous estates and has many tenants to deal with. He writes speeches, occasional poems, and a large number of letters carefully phrased with a view to publication. His social or complimentary duties are numerous and exacting. One day he goes out hunting wild boar on one of his estates, and kills three of them. How, think you, does he pass the time while the beaters are driving the animals towards the net? He is thinking up a subject and making notes, and actually finds the silence and solitude helpful. He concludes his short letter on the subject by advising his friend "when you go hunting, 'take my advice and carry your writing-tablets as well as your luncheon-basket and flask : you will find that Minerva roams the hills no less than Diana." Pliny the Younger is writing, it is true, a generation after Nero, but there had been no appreciable change in Roman intellectual tastes during that short interval.

The Roman may have had little inclination towards

abstract thinking, but he was not an idle-minded man.
Even the emperors often cultivated the muse. Nero,
we have seen, wrote verses, while his predecessor
Claudius bore a strangely near resemblance to our
own James I., not only in respect of his weakness of
character, but also of his pretensions to erudition and
authorship. We can hardly read the literature of
this and the next half-century without being amazed
at the number of names of writers who gained or
sought some share of repute, although few of them
have left works important enough to have been kept
alive till now. It is true that through all the writing
of this time there runs what has been called the
"falsetto" note, a fact which is due partly to the
absence of live national questions or the freedom
to discuss them, and partly to the false principles
of the rhetorical training already described. The
general desire was to show cleverness, wide reading,
and information; there was no impulse to great
creation or to exhibitions of profound feeling.
Epigram and "point" are no less compassed in the
overstrained epic of Lucan, and in the philosophic
essays of Seneca, than in the satires of Persius. It
is probable that what have been called intellectual
"interests" were never more widely spread than
in the *pax Romana* of the first and second centuries
A.D. We gather from literature that books innumerable were produced on subjects often as special and
minute as those selected for a German thesis, and
that almost every town worth the name, at least in
the Greek-speaking part of the empire, produced an

author of sorts. But when we look into the symposia
or chat of Plutarch or Aulus Gellius, we cannot fail
to note that a large proportion of this intellectual
and literary activity was being frittered away on
questions either stereotyped and threadbare, or of no
appreciable utility either to knowledge or conduct.
As for dilettante production at Rome itself Pliny
remarks in one letter: "This year has produced a
large crop of poets: there was scarcely a day in the
whole month of April on which some one did not
give a reading." During the generation into which
Nero was born and that which followed him, we meet
with no great creative work in either prose or poetry,
no great contribution to the progress of science or
thought. The most generally interesting writer of
the whole period was the Greek Plutarch, but though
the *Parallel Lives* which he was preparing are immortal in their kind, and though his *Moral Essays*
are often most excellent reading, it cannot be said
that he is a profound original thinker or a creator of
anything more than a taking literary form. Next
to him in value, earlier in date, stands Seneca, who,
like Plutarch, is a lively thinker and a deft essayist,
with the same love for a quotation and the same wide
interests, but assuredly not a considerable enlarger
of the field of human thought. To those who know
Montaigne, the best notion of Seneca and Plutarch
will be formed by remembering that his essays are
admitted by himself to be "wholly compiled of
what I have borrowed from them." The elder Pliny
supplies us with extracts and summaries of the

knowledge or the notions then extant, and we have writings on agriculture by Columella. The youthful and rather awkward satirist Persius sees the life which he criticises rather through the medium of books than through his own eyes. Such works of the period as have gained any kind of immortality are certainly interesting and often instructive, but they indicate a period in which reading is chiefly a cultivated amusement, and knowledge rather sought as a pastime and an accomplishment than as a power. The favourite reading must contain matter or sense, not too deep or exacting; and it must possess a style. Perhaps writers as various as Dryden, Pope, Horace Walpole, Samuel Johnson, De Quincey, Macaulay, or, on a lower platform, the authors of collections like the *Curiosities of Literature* would have been quite at home in this period: but it would have produced no Shakespeare, Milton, or Wordsworth. The agreeable poem, the well-expressed essay, are the approved reading for men of indolent bent: the informative collection for the more curious, serious, or practical-minded. If the early empire is "despotism tempered by epigram," it is perhaps not altogether untrue that the contemporary literature was pedantry tempered by epigram, or at least by quotation.

Science, though its matter was attractive enough to the practical Roman, was at a standstill. So far as it existed it was Greek. The Greeks had done almost all that could be done by sheer brain-power

and acumen. They could hardly proceed further
without those finer instruments which we possess, but
which they did not. Though they knew of certain
magnifying glasses, they had no real telescopes or
microscopes, no mariner's compass or chronometers, no
very delicate balances. They possessed a magnificent
thinking apparatus and put it to admirable use. The
modern scientist has generally nothing but admiration
for their keen insight, and for the brilliant hypotheses
which they invented and which were frequently but
unverified anticipations or partial anticipations of
theories now in vogue. Where they stopped short
was at experiment in test of hypothesis. Of all
exploits of pure thinking in the domain of science
perhaps the greatest has been the conception that the
earth, instead of being a flat disk, is a sphere. This
theory was held before the age of Nero by ancient
astronomers and geographers, who had derived the
notion partly from the eclipses of the moon — of which
they well understood the cause — and partly from the
rising of objects above the horizon. They understood
also that in a sphere there was gravitation to the
centre, and were able so to comprehend the level
surface of water on the globe. The geographer
Strabo, more than a generation before our chosen
date, readily conceives that, if one sailed straight
westward out of the Mediterranean through the Straits
of Gibraltar, he would ultimately come back round
the world by way of the East — that is to say, by India.
It was not left for Columbus to invent that doctrine.
It is true that in calculating the circumference of

the earth they had made it as much as one-seventh too large, but the wonder is that they came so near as they did. In regard to the distance of the moon they were not more than $\frac{1}{12}$th from the modern estimate. The possibility of error in dealing with the sun was much greater, and their 51,000,000 miles is little more than half of what it should have been. Exactly how far this doctrine of the sphericity of the earth was popularly entertained we cannot tell; it was probably almost confined to those directly interested in the question. A theory, anticipating Galileo, that it is the earth which moves round the sun, had been mooted, but certainly had very little currency. Nor was speculation confined to such astronomical conclusions. In the region of physical geography rational attempts were made to account for various phenomena, such as the existence of deltas or the risings of the Nile, or the appearance of sea-shells high on dry land. Strabo, in dealing with the Black Sea, has his theories of the elevation or subsidence of land. He also suggests previous volcanic conditions of certain districts which had been quiescent from before the memory or tradition of the inhabitants.

Sound methods of discovering latitude and longitude were not yet in use, and therefore a map of the world according to ideas current in the first century would present a strange aspect to us. There is much error in the placing of towns or districts upon their parallels; and coasts or mountain ranges, particularly, of course, on the outskirts of the empire or in the less familiar lands beyond its bounds, are perhaps made to

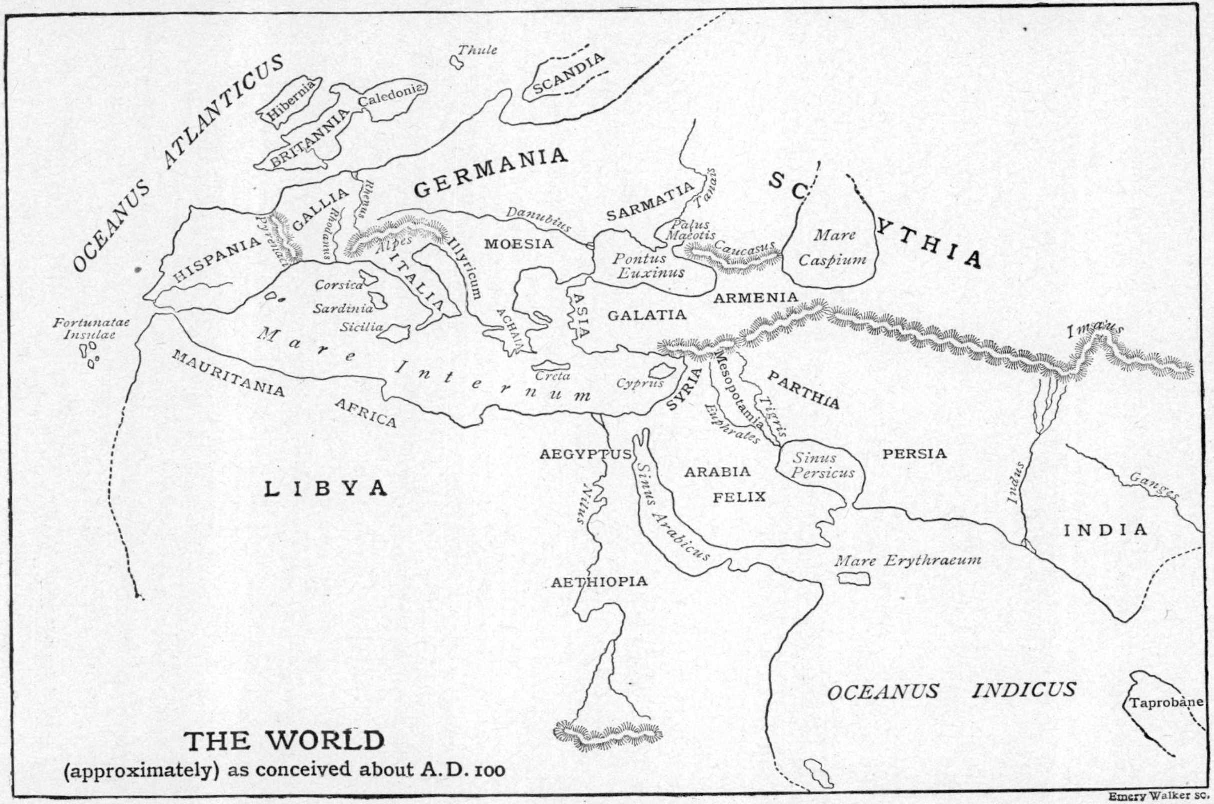

THE WORLD
(approximately) as conceived about A.D. 100

Fig. 113.— World as conceived about A.D. 100.

399

run north instead of north-west, or east instead of south-east. It follows that measurements of distances, especially across the wider seas, were often very in-accurate, although within and about the Mediter-ranean there was so much traffic and such close observation of the stars that the errors were gradually reduced. The mariner, when he did not follow the coast and guide his course by familiar landmarks, steered by the stars, but of these he had a very intimate knowledge, to which he joined a close ob-servation of the prevailing direction of the winds at the various seasons. There was a well-ordered system of lighthouses, and charts and mariners' guides were not wanting. In the winter months navigation over long distances was regularly suspended, and ships waited in port for the spring.

So far as acquaintance with the world was con-cerned, we have sufficient evidence that the trader knew his way very well down the African coast as far as Zanzibar, and along the southern shores of Asia as far as Cape Comorin. With Ceylon his acquaintance was vague, and only by tradition did he know of Further India by way of the sea and of China by way of the land. In the interior of Africa the caravans reached the Oases, and by way of Nile or caravan there was trade with the Soudan. Outside the Straits of Gibraltar, the Canary Islands and Madeira—known indiscriminately as the "Fortunate Isles," or "Isles of the Blest"—were in touch with the port of Cadiz. The shape of Great Britain beyond England was indefinite, although it was known to be an island, with the Shetlands lying beyond. Ireland was also recognised as an island and its relative size was not greatly misconceived. The chief misconception in this corner of Europe was that of orientation, Britain being placed either far too near or far too parallel to Spain (through a large error as to the shape of the Bay of Biscay). Meanwhile the coast of the Netherlands and Germany was made to run in a line much too closely parallel to the eastern shores of Britain. Scandinavia was known from navigating explorers and from the amber trade, but was commonly regarded as a large island. Knowledge of the Baltic did not extend beyond about the modern Riga, and of the whole region thence to the Caspian only the dimmest notions were entertained.

From what has been said concerning the calculation of the earth's diameter and of the distances of the sun and moon, it may be readily understood that the ancient mathematician had arrived at great proficiency in the geometrical branch of mathematics. This should cause no surprise when we remember what is meant by "Euclid." That eminent genius had lived at Alexandria three centuries and a half before the age of Nero, and he by no means represents all that was known of such mathematics at the latter date. The ancients were quite sufficiently versed in the solution of triangles to have made the necessary calculations in geography and astronomy, if they had but possessed the right instruments. Perhaps only an expert should deal — even in the few sentences required

2 D

for our purpose — with such matters as the calculation
of the capacity and proportional relations of cylinders,
or with the mechanics and hydrostatics of Archimedes.
That philosopher so far understood the laws of applied
force that he had boasted: "Give me a place to stand
on and I will move the world." What he and others
had learned concerning fluid pressure, or concerning
pulleys, levers, and other mechanical devices, had
not been lost by the Greeks and had been borrowed
from them for full practical use by the Romans.
They knew how to lift huge weights, and how to hurl
heavy missiles by the artillery previously mentioned.
Experiments had been made at Alexandria in the
use of steam-power, but had led to nothing
practical. It is obvious also from their buildings
and works of engineering, even without explicit
statement, that they well understood the distribution
of weight and the laws of stability. The laws of
acoustics were understood with sufficient clearness
to make them applicable with success to theatres.
In practical mensuration — a daily necessity for men
who were perpetually allotting lands or marking out
camps — the Romans were experts. In pure arithmetic
the contemporary world had made some considerable
advance, such as in the extraction of square-roots and
cube-roots; but, as has been already said, the Roman
interest was virtually confined to such arithmetic or
mathematics as appeared to possess some bearing on
actual use.

Of chemistry, in the modern scientific sense,
the ancients knew almost nothing. Empirically they

were aware of certain properties exhibited by sub-
stances, and could perform certain manipulations;
but, like moderns down to a very recent time, they
had no real understanding of the quantitative or
qualitative relations of elements. Long ago Greek
philosophy, followed by the Epicurean school, had
set forth an "atomic theory," which on the surface
is surprisingly like the modern chemical hypothesis;
but this contained strange and illogical features and
had no connection with actual practice. In this
department the chief proficiency of the world of
this date lay in metallurgy, in which the processes
empirically discovered, chiefly by Egyptians and
Phoenicians, were closely similar to those now
employed. They thoroughly understood the smelt-
ing of ores, but could render no scientific account of
the processes. Botany was in a very crude condition,
scarcely extending beyond such knowledge as was
required on the one hand for farming and horticulture,
and on the other for the vegetable medicines used by
contemporary physicians.

The doctoring of the time was also, of course,
largely empirical, but assuredly hardly more so than
it was a century or so ago, and distinctly more
rational than it became in the Middle Ages. We
cannot conceive of a reputable doctor at Rome pre-
scribing the nauseous mediaeval absurdities. Practical
surgery must have been surprisingly advanced, and
there is scarcely a modern surgeon who does not
exclaim in admiration of the instruments discovered
at Pompeii and now preserved in the Naples Museum

(see Fig. 69). In physic it is, of course, tolerably
certain that many of the remedies or methods of
treatment were of the sound and simple kind discovered by the long experience of mankind and often
put in use by our grandmothers. The defect of
contemporary medicine was that it was almost wholly
empirical. The ancient surgeon could doubtless
perform ordinary operations — amputations and ex-
cisions — with neatness, and the ancient physician
knew perfectly well what to do with the ordinary
complaints — the fevers and agues, the bilious attacks,
the gout, or the dropsy — but he was baffled by any
new conditions. Moreover, if he could diagnose
and cure, he could seldom prevent, inasmuch as he
had little understanding of the causes of maladies.
He had everything to learn in regard to sanitation
and the preventing of infection. A plague would
sometimes kill half the people in a town or district,
and the loss of 30,000 persons in the metropolis
would probably appear to most Romans as a visitation
of the gods, nor is it certain that the doctors would
generally disagree with that view. Though there
were many quacks, it is not the case that the
reputable medical men — most of them Greek, some
of them Romans, who borrowed a Greek name
because it "paid" — lacked the scientific spirit or
such knowledge as the time afforded. They went to
the medical school at Alexandria or elsewhere, and
studied their treatises on physic and anatomy, but, at
least in the latter subject, they were sadly hampered.
Dissection of human bodies was forbidden by law

as being a desecration of the dead, and though it might sometimes be practised *sub rosa*, it was the general custom to perform the dissections on other animals, particularly monkeys, and to argue thence erroneously to mankind.

CHAPTER XXI

PHILOSOPHY — STOICS AND EPICUREANS

WITH such an unsatisfactory equipment of science, and with such a vague and morally inoperative religion, it was no wonder that the higher minds of the contemporary world turned to the study of philosophy. Of such studies there had been many schools or sects, but at this date we have chiefly to reckon with two — the Stoics and Epicureans. There were, it is true, the Academics, who disputed everything, and held no doctrine to be more true than its contrary. There were Eclectics, who picked and chose. But the majority of those who affected a positive philosophy attached themselves either to the Stoic or else to the Epicurean system, not necessarily with orthodox rigidity on every point, but as a general guide — at least in theory — to the conduct of life. Where we belong to a certain religious denomination or church, and "sit under" a certain class of preachers, they belonged to a certain school of philosophy, and attended the lectures of certain of its expounders. Instead of a chaplain or parish clergyman they engaged or associated with an expert in their special system. But just as the Frenchman remarked, "*Je suis*

catholique, mais je ne pratique pas," so might one be
in principle a good Stoic without much exercise of the
accepted doctrines.   The distinction between the tenets
of the two great schools was wide, but within each
school itself individuals might differ as widely as
"Broad Church" from whatever its opposite may be
called. The choice between the two schools was
mainly a matter of temperament. Persons of the
sterner type of mind, caring comparatively little for
the physical comforts and gracious amenities of life,
and possessed of a strong sense of duty and decorum —
inclined, perhaps, not only to piety and self-abnegation,
but also to be somewhat dour and uncompromising —
were naturally attracted to Stoicism. Those of the
complementary character preferred the doctrines of
Epicurus.   The Stoics were the Pharisees, the
Epicureans the Sadducees, of pagan philosophy. As
the Pharisees were the most Hebraic of the Hebrews,
so it was Stoicism that came to be the characteristic
Roman creed.   The ordinary Roman had been brought
up in the tradition of obeying the law of the state
and the claims of duty; he had high notions of
personal dignity and a leaning to the heroic virtues.
Give him a strong, consistent, and elevating religion
and he would be normally a pious man. Stoicism
supplied him with a standard which was in keeping
with such tendencies.   About Epicureanism there was
nothing heroic or elevating.

Put briefly, and therefore crudely, the Epicurean
doctrine was that happiness is the end of life. What

men seek, and have a right to seek, is the most
pleasant existence. Our conduct should secure for us
as much real pleasure as possible. Now at first sight
this looks like what it was opprobriously called by its
enemies, "the philosophy of the pig-sty." It by no
means meant this to its founder. For what is
"pleasure"? Not by any means necessarily the
gratification of the moment, physical or otherwise.
A present pleasure may mean future pain, either of
body or of mind. Wrong actions and bestial enjoy-
ments bring their own penalty. You must choose
wisely, and so direct your life that you suffer least and
enjoy most consistently. Temperance and wisdom
are therefore virtues necessary to a true Epicurean.
You desire health; therefore you will live, as Epicurus
lived, on simple and wholesome food. You desire
tranquillity or peace of mind; therefore you will
abstain from all perverse acts and gratifications, desires
and emotions, which disturb that peace. In short the
thing to be sought is nothing else but this grateful
composure of mind — a thing which you cannot have
if you are always wanting this or that and either
abusing or misusing your bodily or mental functions,
or needlessly mortifying yourself. To the plain man
this apparently meant "Take life easily and keep
free of worry." Naturally the plain man's ideas of
taking life easily became those of taking pleasures as
they come, indolently accepting the agreeables of life
and feeling no call to make much of its duties. It
is all very well for a high-minded philosopher to avoid
a pleasure in order to avoid its pain, and to realize that

a pleasure of the mind is worth more than a pleasure of the body, but one cannot expect the ordinary pupil — the *homme moyen sensuel* — to comprehend this attitude with heartiness sufficient to put it into practice. It followed therefore that the Epicurean tended, not only to become lazy, but to become vicious, or to make light of vices. This was not indeed true Epicureanism, and Epicurus is not to blame for it; it simply shows that Epicureanism, whatever its logical or other merits, provided no sufficient stimulus to a right life. As regards theology the position of the school was that there might very well be such things as higher beings — there was nothing in physical philosophy to make them any more impossible than a man or a fish — but that, if they existed, they were not concerned with man's affairs; his moral conduct, like his sacrifices and prayers, was not matter for their consideration. No need, therefore, to let superstition worry you, or to trouble about future punishment. Conduct your life according to the same principles laid down, and let the gods — if there be any — look to themselves. Naturally the result of such a position is that ceasing to regard the gods means ceasing to believe in them, and, as a Roman writer says: "In theory it leaves us the gods, in practice it abolishes them."

The other school — that of the Stoics — is perhaps less easily comprehended, nor can it be said that its doctrines were always quite so coherent. Again we may put the position briefly, and therefore, perhaps, only approximately. The rule of life is to live as "nature" directs. Nature has its laws, which you cannot disobey with impunity. The law of nature is the mind of God. The material universe is the body, God is its soul, and He directs the workings of nature with foreknowledge and perfect wisdom. If man can only be brought to act in strict accordance with the mind of God — or law of nature — he is sure of perfect well-being, because he can do nothing as it should not be done. If he can only arrive at such perfect operation of his mental processes, he will necessarily be the perfect speaker, the perfect ruler, the perfect craftsman, the perfect performer of every task, including the securing of his own happiness. Doubtless this is logical enough, but how is one to attain to such right mental operations, and to become what was called a "sage"? Only by acting always according to reason and not according to passion. That and that alone is "virtue." The divine mind is not swayed by passion — by hope, fear, exultation, or grief — but only and always by reason. Learn therefore to obey reason and reason only. Do not permit yourself to be drawn from the true path by fear of threats, even of death, nor by grief, even for your dearest friends. Such feelings warp your reason, distract your judgment, and deflect you from the right course. When passion — feeling — comes in conflict with reason, you must drive feeling away. Your reason may not always be right; nevertheless it is the best guide you have, and you must cultivate it to act as rightly as possible. Remember that the

power to act in accordance with the divine mind —
the law of nature — lies in your own will; things
external have nothing to do with that straight-
forward proceeding — they cannot help you, and you
must not let them hinder you. The condition of
your mind is everything; as long as its operation is
right, you are living in the right way. Your mind
may act as rightly in poverty as in riches; you may
be equally wise and virtuous whether you have the
external advantages or not. You must therefore
learn to ignore these things—pain, grief, fear, joy,
and all the other perturbing influences. Cultivate,
therefore, right reason and the absence of emotions.

This, you will say, is a very high, unattainable,
if not inhuman, standard. Quite so, and therefore,
while Epicureanism often produced vicious men, this
often produced pretenders and even hypocrites.
Nevertheless it is better to set oneself a high
standard than a low one, and a Roman who endeavoured to control himself by reason, and to place
himself above fear and pain, was thereby on the way
to be brave, patient, truthful, and just. Those who
would see what high character could be associated
with Stoicism — whether as the result or as the motive
of the choice of the school — should read Epictetus,
whose text, written early in the next century, was
"sustain and abstain," and also the great-minded
gentle Emperor Marcus Aurelius. A logical outcome
of Stoicism was that you should say only the thing
which reason approved, and say it unafraid. A good
republican virtue, this, but under the emperors a

dangerous one, as an honest Stoic like Thrasea found out. In practice there was naturally much qualifying or mellowing of the rigid Stoic attitude : the exigencies of actual life had to be met part of the way, and both Greek and Roman Stoics were often only Stoics in part — the complete "sage" was of course impossible.

As for the gods, it is obvious that the Stoics were pantheists ; there was one God, and He was the soul of the universe. They also, of course, recognised His providence. What then of the gods of the state ? Some did not attempt to discuss them. Others treated the various so-called separate deities in the list as being only so many manifestations or avatars of the same divine power, and whether they were content or not with that attempt at harmonisation, who shall say ?

Meanwhile, at least in the eastern part of the empire, you might meet with another type of philosopher, the Cynic, belonging to the same school as the famous Diogenes, who had lived in that large earthenware jar commonly known as his "tub." Like the Stoic, the Cynic held that externals were of no value, and therefore he contented himself with a piece of bread, a wallet full of beans, and a jug of water. Like the Stoic, he believed in perfect freedom of speech, and therefore he spoke loudly and often abusively of all and sundry who appeared to him to deserve it. Some such men doubtless were sincere enough, like the earlier hermits or preaching friars, but many of them were simply idle and virulent impostors who thoroughly deserved that name of the "dog" which was commonly given to them, and which came to designate their school.

The mention of impostors and hypocrites brings us naturally to a point which may have been foreseen. To the ancient world the professional philosophers were the nearest approach to our professional clergy. They affected an appearance accordingly; and the philosopher was regularly known by his long beard, his coarse cloak, and his staff. But, alas! there were many who disgraced their cloth. There were Stoic teachers who practised all manner of secret vices, and whose behaviour was in outrageous contradiction to their creed of the "absence of emotions." There were not only many Honeymans, there were many Stigginses. There were idlers and vagabonds on a level with the mendicant friars and pardon-sellers of the time of Chaucer. There were pompous hypocrites. Also side by side with the serious and earnest philosopher, as deeply learned in the books of his sect as a modern divine, there were charlatans and dabblers. It is unfortunately in this last light that the Apostle Paul appeared to the professional Stoic and Epicurean teachers of Athens. They were the finished products of the philosophic schools of the most famous universities, while he was supposed by them to be teaching some new kind of philosophy. Philosophers were apt to be itinerant, and St. Paul was looked upon as but another of these new arrivals. In his language they detected what seemed to be borrowed notions not consistently bound together, and they therefore called him by a name which it is not easy to translate. Literally it is "a picker up of seeds" — that is to say, a sciolist who gathers scraps from profounder people and gives them out with an air. Perhaps the nearest, although an undignified, word is "quack." That Paul possessed a knowledge of Greek philosophy, and particularly of Stoicism, is practically certain. He came from Tarsus in Cilicia, and Cilicia was the native home of many leading Stoics, including its greatest representative in all antiquity. He had been taught by Gamaliel, who was versed in "the learning of the Greeks." His address at Athens was deliberately meant to bear a relation to the philosophy of the experts who were present, but necessarily it could only introduce a few salient allusions, such as even a dabbler could have picked up, and we can hardly blame the specialists for their erroneous judgment. As he says himself: "The Greeks demand philosophy; but we proclaim a Messiah crucified, to the Jews a stumbling-block, and to the Greeks a folly."

To discuss further the moral ideas of the Roman world would consume more space and time than can be afforded here. It may, however, be worth while to mention that suicide was commonly — and especially by the Stoics — looked upon as a natural and blameless thing, when calm reason appeared to justify the proceeding, and when due consideration was given to social claims. To seek a euthanasia in such cases was an act of wisdom. Belief in an underworld or an after life was not rare among the common people, but it certainly did not exist in any force among the cultivated classes. It was taught neither by philosophy nor by the religion of the state. Yet the sense that rewards or punishments are unfairly meted out in this world was strong in many a mind, and this is one of the facts which account for the hold taken upon such minds, first by the religion of Isis, and then in a still greater and more abiding measure by Christianity.

CHAPTER XXII

THE ROMAN PROFUSION OF ART

IT would be a more than agreeable task to deal at some length with the art of the Roman world of this period, but the subject is vast, and demands a treatise to itself. How general was the love of art — or at least the recognition of its place in life — must be obvious to those who have seen the great collections in Rome, gathered partly from the city itself and partly from the towns and country "villas" of Italy, and those in the National Museum at Naples, acquired mainly from the buried cities of Pompeii and Herculaneum. Nor are we amazed merely at the quantity of statues, statuettes, busts, reliefs, paintings, mosaic gems and cameos, and artistically wrought objects and utensils, which have been preserved while so many thousands of such productions have disappeared in the conflagrations of Rome, the vandalisms of the ignorant, or the kilns and melting-pots of the Middle Ages. The quality is still more a source of delight than the quantity. This last sentence, of course, contains a truism, since art is no delight without high quality. If we had only preserved to us such masterpieces as the Capitoline

Venus, the Dying Gaul, the Laocoon, the Dancing Faun, the so-called Narcissus, and the Resting
Mercury, we should realise something of the exquisite
skill in plastic art which had been attained in antiquity
and has never been attained since. But we might
perhaps imagine that these were altogether exceptional pieces and the choicest gems possessed by the

FIG. 114. — THE DYING GAUL.

world of the time. Yet the preservation of these is
but an accident, and there is no reason to believe
them to be more than survivals out of many equally
excellent. On the contrary, our ancient authorities —
such as the elder Pliny — prove that there was a multitude of similar creations contained in public buildings
alone. Pompeii, it has already been said more than
once, was a provincial town in no way distinguished
for the high culture of its inhabitants; yet there is

scarcely a house of any consideration which has not afforded some example of fine art in one form or another. We know that several of the Roman temples — such as those of Concord in the Forum and

FIG. 115. — A "CANDELIERA" OR MARBLE PILASTER
OF THE BASILICA AEMILIA.

of Apollo on the Palatine — were veritable galleries of masterpieces; and that the rich Romans adorned both their town houses and country villas with dozens of statues, colossal, life-size, or miniature, by distinguished masters. But still more striking is the fact that the comparatively small homes of Pompeii

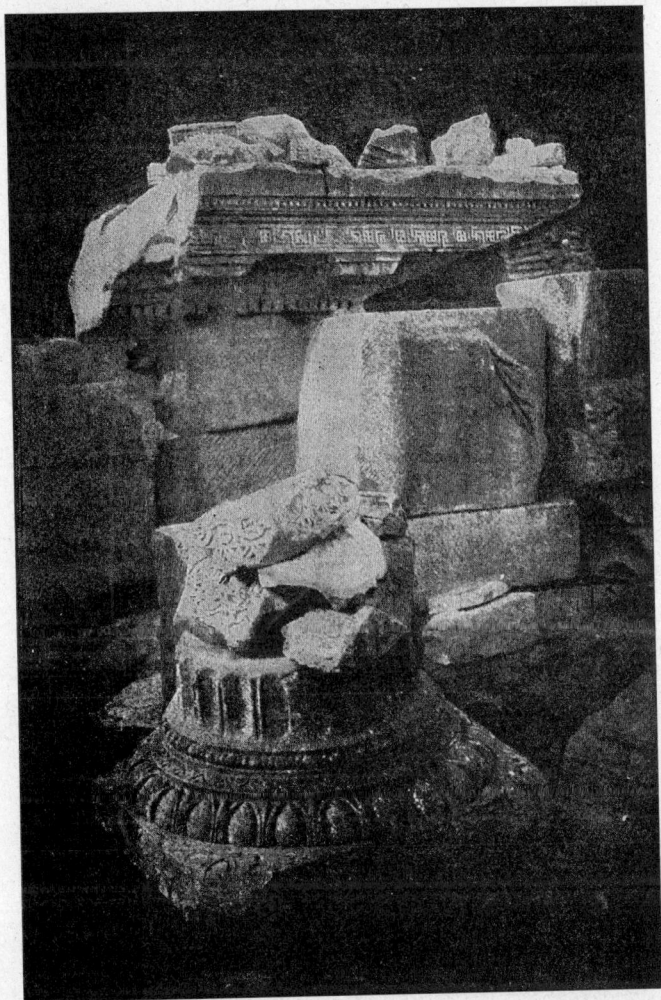

FIG. 116.—FRAGMENTS OF THE ARCHITECTURE OF THE REGIA.

often possessed a work for which no price would now be too large, and of which we are content even to obtain a tolerably good copy. At Herculaneum there

evidently lived persons of greater literary and artistic
refinement than at Pompeii, and the discoveries from
that only very partially excavated town make an in-
calculably rich show of their own. What then would
be the case with Naples, Baiae, the resorts all along
the coast as far as the Tiber, the luxurious villas on
the Alban Hills, and the great metropolis itself?

Yet the fact of this universal recognition of art
is scarcely made so impressive by these collected
specimens of perfect taste and perfect execution, as it
is incidentally by observing the delicate and graceful
finish of some moulding on a chance fragment from a
building, such as the Basilica Aemilia or the office of
the Pontifex in the Forum, or the exquisite chiselling
of trailing ivy upon a cup from Herculaneum (Fig. 56),
or the dainty pattern wrought on no more important
a thing than a bucket (Fig. 58), or the graceful shape
imparted to a household lamp (Fig. 54). Water
could hardly be permitted to spout in a peristyle or
garden without doing so from some charming statuette,
animal figure, or decorative mask or head. When
fine art is sought in things like these, we may guess
how uncompromisingly it was sought in things more
avowedly "on show."

The age with which we have been dealing fell
within the most flourishing period of Roman, or rather
Graeco-Roman, taste and craftsmanship. A hundred
years later both taste and execution were declining,
and by the age of Constantine—two centuries and a
half after Nero — not one artist could pretend to

achieve such work as had belonged to a multitude between the reigns of Augustus and Hadrian.

It is not indeed probable that, even at our date, the large and noble simplicity of the older Greek masters could be rivalled. It is not probable that most of the former creations of art still preserved could have been wrought as originals by any Greek or Roman artist living in the time of Nero. Nevertheless technical craftsmanship was still superb, and while the contemporary artist could not create a splendid original, he was at least able to create an almost perfect copy. The Roman public buildings and private houses were enriched with a host of such copies, or, when not exact copies, with modifications which, though not improvements, were at least such as could not offend by displaying a lack of technical mastery. Let us grant that it was for the most part Greeks who were the artists; nevertheless the Greek is an active member of the Roman world and of its metropolitan life, and he executes his work to the order of the Roman state or the Roman patron; and therefore the art of the time deserves to be called Roman in that sense. There is little doubt that the Romans, if left to themselves, would have developed only the solid, or the gorgeous, or the baroque. But influences which penetrate a society are part of that society, and the Greek influence accepted by the Roman becomes a Roman principle.

Perhaps it is also true that many a Roman who possessed fine works of art, and even exquisite ones, was not in reality a true connoisseur; that, even if

he were, he lacked instructive and ardent appreciation
of art for its own sake; and that, like his cultivation
of intellectual society or learning, his cultivation of
art was rather that of a man determined to be on a
level with the culture of his times. Nevertheless the
fact is palpable, that the cultivation was there, and
was displayed in public architecture and in household
embellishment in a way which puts the modern world
to shame. With us art is a luxury for the few, and a
keen enjoyment for still fewer; in the age of Nero it
penetrated the life of every class.

In architecture the native Roman gift was for the
practical combined with the massive and grandiose.
The structures in which they themselves excelled
were the amphitheatre, the public baths, the triumphal arch, the basilica, the bridge, and the aqueduct.
Their mastery of the arch, their excellent concrete,
and their engineering genius, enabled them to produce
works in this kind which had had no parallels in the
Greek world. Nor had the Greeks felt the same need
for such buildings. They had been innocent of
gladiatorial shows, and they had been unfortunately
too innocent of large conceptions in the way of water-
supply. When an amphitheatre or aqueduct of the
Roman kind was to be found in the graecized half of
the empire, it was constructed under Roman influence.
The modern may well afford to wonder at and envy
the profusion of such structures in the ancient world.
How noble and at the same time how strong was the
work of the Romans when they undertook to supply
even a provincial town with abundant and adequate

water, is manifest from such aqueducts as are still to be seen at Nîmes (Fig. 1) or at Segovia. In other architectural conceptions the Romans of the time of Nero mainly followed the Greek lead and employed Greek artists. The architectural "orders" were Greek, with sundry Graeco-Roman modifications, particularly in the way of more ornate or fantastic Corinthian capitals; the notions of sculptural decoration were equally of Hellenic origin. Their theatres also were of the Greek kind adapted in non-essentials to the somewhat different conditions of a Roman performance. The Greek taste in decoration was the simpler and purer: the Roman cultivated the sumptuous and the ornate, sometimes, with conspicuous success, often with an overloaded effect. As Friedländer (who, however, deals with a much longer period than ours) puts the matter: "Nowhere, least of all at Rome, was an important public building erected without the chiseller, the stucco-worker, the carver, the founder, the painter, and mosaic-maker being called in. Statues, single or in groups, filled gables, roofs, niches, interstices of columns, staircases in the temples, theatres, amphitheatres, basilicas, public baths, bridges, arches, portals, and viaducts. . . . Triumphal arches generally had at their summits equestrian figures, trophies, chariots of four or six horses, driven by figures of victory. Reliefs and medallions bedecked the frieze, and reliefs or paintings the walls; ceilings were gay with stucco or coloured work, and the floors with glittering mosaics. All the architectural framework, supports, thresholds, lintels, mouldings, windows, and even gutters were overloaded with decorative figures."

It was above all in plastic art that the contemporary world was enormously rich. Not only could no public building dispense with such decorations as those above mentioned; no private house of the least pretensions was without its statues, busts, statuettes, carved reliefs, and stucco-work. Never was statuary in marble or bronze so plentiful in every part of the empire, in public squares, or in the houses of representative people — in reception-hall, peristyle court, garden, or colonnade. Portrait statues in the largest towns were to be counted by hundreds, and sometimes by thousands. Men distinguished in war, in letters, in public life, and in local benefactions were as regularly commemorated by statues or busts as they are in modern times by painted portraits. Sometimes — unlike the modern portraits of course — these were paid for by the recipient of the compliment. In the comparatively unimportant Forum of Pompeii there stood five colossal statues, between seventy and eighty life-size equestrian statues, and as many standing figures, while the public buildings surrounding this open space contained their dozen or twenty each. As has been said already, most of the best work in sculpture — apart from these bronze and marble portraits of contemporaries — was reproduction of Grecian masterpieces dating from the time of Pheidias onward. Particularly did the Roman affect the more elaborate work of the period of the later "Macedonian" kings. Where the actual work was not exactly copied it at least supplied the main conception or motive. It followed naturally that there would be in existence many copies of the same piece, and, in procuring these, both the public and the householder would feel relieved of any danger of betraying the wrong taste. The workshops or studios of Greek artists turned out large numbers of a given masterpiece — a Faun, a Venus, or a Discobolus — at prices from £50 or so upwards. It followed also that there were numerous imitations passed off as originals, and many a wealthy man boasted of possessing an "original" or a genuine "old master" — a Praxiteles or a Lysippus — when he owned but a clever reproduction. The same remark applies, not only to the statues, but to the genre-groups and animal forms of which such fine examples can be seen in the Vatican Museum, and also to silver cups by "Mentor" or to bronzes of Corinth. Petronius, the coarse but witty "arbiter of taste" under Nero, mocks at the vulgar *nouveau riche* who imagined that the Corinthian bronzes were the work of an artist named Corinthus.

Next to sculpture came painting, and in this art Romans themselves appear to have often acquired a technical skill which rivalled that of the Greeks. There is also plenty of evidence that among the pictorial artists there were no few women. For us practically the only painting of the time which has been preserved is that upon the walls of private houses, and it is probable that we see some of the worst specimens of the kind as well as some of a high order of excellence. It is not difficult to distinguish between the truly artistic design and colouring of wall-pictures in the House of Vettii or of the "Tragic Poet" and the crude journeyman work in sundry other Pompeian houses which must have belonged to

FIG. 117. — WALL-PAINTING.   (Woman with Tablets.)

anything but connoisseurs. Paintings, it must be remembered, were the ancient wall-papers, as well as the ancient pictures. Here, as in sculpture, we find the same or similar motives and groupings repeated in a way which shows that the painter — or rather the collaborating painters — must have been reproducing

or adapting an original which was particularly
admired or had obtained a fashionable vogue. The
wall-pictures, done in fresco or distemper and in

Fig. 118. — Wall-Painting from Herculaneum. (Women playing
with Knuckle-Bones.)

various dimensions, fall into four main classes. There
are landscapes, from a pretty realistic garden scene
to a fantastic stretch of sea and land diversified with
woods, rocks, figures, and buildings. There are subjects from mythology and from poetical "history" or

legend, chiefly representing "moments of dramatic interest." There are genre-pictures, such as those of the Cupids acting as goldsmiths, oil-dealers, or wine-merchants. Finally there are pictures of still-life — of fishes, birds, fruits, and other objects — often admirable in their kind. Serving as frame or setting to many of the scenes there are architectural paintings — sometimes in complicated but highly skilful perspective, but often extremely unreal and confusing in conception — representing columns and pediments of buildings. It must here suffice to offer one or two characteristic examples out of the multitude of wall-paintings which have been found (see also Figs. 43, 44).

Though Romans themselves, and even persons of standing, sometimes dabbled in the fine arts, it is unquestionable that they commonly regarded the professional artist as only a superior tradesman. They admired his skill, but rendered little esteem to the man. A Roman knight or a Roman lady might occasionally paint for pleasure; Nero himself might model a figure or handle a brush; but so soon as art ceased to be dilettante and became a calling, so soon as its work was produced for payment, the artist ranked with other hirelings, however superior he might be in kind. Seneca expresses an open contempt, although he is perhaps, here as elsewhere, judging by a standard more severe than that of his contemporaries in general. To some extent this attitude is explained by the very abundance of objects of art, and by the

immense number of artists, now nameless, belonging
to the period; it is also to some extent excused by
the fact that the craftsmanship, however consummate,
was not at this period accompanied by the originality
of the great Greek times from which it borrowed.
Much of the work — particularly perhaps in painting
and metal-chasing — was done by slaves. Apart from
this consideration, the studios were so numerous and
taught so well, that there must have been thousands
of persons working either alone or co-operatively,
whose position, however excellent the performance,
became analogous to that of a house-decorator. On
a wall to be painted in fresco a number of painters
would be employed together. Throughout the Roman
world, wherever works of art were wanted, the professional would travel, often with his assistants, and
take up a contract. In modern parlance, the communities requiring some monument of art "called for
tenders" and were prone to accept the lowest.

Whatever abundance of art the Roman world
cultivated and possessed; however indispensable to a
public place was a wealth of buildings with lavish
decoration of sculptured pillars, of statues, or of
triumphal arches; however necessary to a private
house were originals, supposed originals, and copies in
the way of statuary, paintings, bronzes, mosaics, and
other means of artistic adornment; it is very doubtful whether any large number of Romans entertained
that spontaneous enjoyment of the beauty of art
which is known as genuine "artistic feeling." In
their literature we look in vain for any expression

of enthusiasm on the subject. There are many
references to works of art, but none which possess
any intense glow of warmth. Doubtless art was so
abundant that, as has already been said in reference
to the appreciation of natural beauty, the absence of
"gush" need not indicate absence of real enjoyment.
Enjoyment there was, but it was apparently for the
most part the enjoyment either of the collector or of
the man who realises that an appreciation of art
demands a large place in culture, and who is
determined to be as well supplied and as well
informed as his neighbour, while his judgment of a
piece of work, though far from unintelligent, and
often excellent in regard to principles of design and
technical execution, is mainly the result of a
deliberate training and cult, and is in consequence
somewhat chill and detached.

Of music the Romans were passionately fond, but
the music itself was of a description which perhaps
would hardly commend itself to modern notions,
particularly those of northern Europe. The instruments in use were chiefly the harp, the lyre, and the
flageolet (or flute played with a mouthpiece). To
these we may add for processions the straight trumpet
and the curved horn, and, for more orgiastic occasions
or celebrations, the panpipes, cymbals, and tambourine
or kettledrum. Performers from the East played
upon certain stringed instruments not greatly differing from the lyre and harp of Greece and Italy.
Women from Cadiz used the castagnettes. Hydraulic

organs with pipes and keys were coming into vogue,
and the bagpipes were also sufficiently familiar.   In
the use of all these instruments the ancients knew
nothing of the harmonisation of parts; to them
harmony and concerto implied no more than unison,
or a difference of octaves.   Whatever emotions may
have been evoked by
the music so produced,
it cannot be imagined
that they were of the
intensity or subtlety of
which the modern art
and instruments are
capable.   Apart from
the professionals, many
Roman youths and the
majority of Roman girls
learned both to play
and sing, the instru-

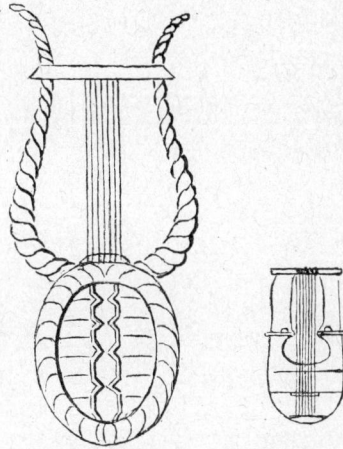

FIG. 119. — LYRE AND HARP.

ment most affected being the harp, and the teacher of
harp-playing being held in the highest esteem and
receiving the highest emoluments.   Sacrifices were
regularly accompanied by the flageolet; processions by
this and the trumpet; the rites of Bacchus by pipes,
tambourines, and cymbals; performances in the theatre
by an immense orchestra of various instruments; the
more elaborate dinners by flute, harp, concerto of the
two, singing, and such coarser and more exciting
performances as were to the taste of the host or his
company.   The greatest houses kept their own choir
and orchestra of slaves; the less wealthy hired

musicians as they needed them. As for the Romans themselves, certain religious ceremonies called for singing of boys and girls in chorus; and in a purely domestic way the women of the house played on the harp and sang. Where there was singing, the words dominated the music and not the contrary, but snatches from recent popular pieces were sung and hummed in the streets for the sake of their taking air, just as they are in modern times. We cannot conceive of any Roman festivity without abundance of music. When in spring at Baiae on the Bay of Naples the holiday frequenters of that resort were rowed about the Lucrine Lake in their flower-bedecked gondolas or boats with coloured sails, the musicians were no less in evidence than they are now at every opportunity on the waters of the same bay or in the evening on the Grand Canal at Venice. In the truly Greek portion of the empire music, though no more advanced in method, was for the most part of a finer and severer kind; but at Alexandria — where it amounted to a mania — the influence of the native Egyptian style, blent with the more passionate among the Greek modes, had produced a music extremely exciting and highly demoralising.

On the whole, it may reasonably be held that music played at least as important a part both in the houses and the public entertainments of the ancient Romans as it plays in modern Italy. The artists were as carefully trained, the audiences as critical or as receptive, the personal affectations of the musicians as characteristic, and their effect on emotional admirers of the opposite sex as great, as they are at the present day. The difference between the two ages consists in the nature of the music itself, and in the instruments through which it is respectively delivered; and in these respects the advantage is entirely with the modern world.

CHAPTER XXIII

THE LAST SCENE OF ALL — BURIAL AND TOMBS

WHATEVER conceptions may have been entertained as to existence beyond the grave, there was no doubt in the Roman mind as to the claim of the dead to a proper burial and a worthy monument. It had once on a time been a matter of universal belief that the spirit which had departed from an unburied corpse could find no admittance to the company in the realms of Hades. It could not join "the majority" below. Originally no doubt the notion was simply that, as the body had not been consigned to the earth, the spirit also remained homeless above ground. Gradually this fancy shifted to the notion that, through neglect of burial, the dead man was dishonoured — he had no friends — and that his spirit was thereby disgraced and unworthy of reception by the powers beneath. It must therefore remain shivering on the near side of the river across which the grim Charon ferried the more fortunate souls. Even when the body had been decently buried, the spirit, though received into the gloomy realm, called for continued respect on the part of its friends on earth. Unless it received its periodical honours and was commemorated by a fitting sepulchre, it would meet with slights from other ghosts and would feel its position keenly. Naturally it would then do its best, by some form of haunting, to punish the living for their disregard and forgetfulness. From such considerations there arose in very ancient days in Italy, as in Greece, a great anxiety to perform scrupulously "the dues" of the defunct. Even if the body could not be found, it was obligatory to perform the obsequies and to build a cenotaph. If a stranger came across a dead body he must not pass it by without throwing at least three handfuls of dust or earth upon it and bidding it "Farewell."

Though the burial customs still employed sprang from old fancies like these, we are not to suppose that such notions were in full life in the Roman world of our period. Poets might play with them, and some ignorant folk might still vaguely entertain them. The mere belief in ghosts was doubtless general, and even the learned argued the question of their existence. Here are parts of another letter culled from Pliny already several times quoted. He writes to his friend Sura: "I should very much like to know whether you think that apparitions actually exist, with a real shape of their own and a kind of supernatural power, or that it is only our fear which gives an embodiment to vain fancies. My own inclination is to believe in them, and chiefly because of an experience which, I am told, befell Curtius Rufus." He then speaks of a phantom form which prophesied that person's fortune. "Another

occurrence, quite as wonderful and still more terrify-
ing, I will relate as I was told it. There was at
Athens a house which was roomy and commodious,
but which bore an ill-name and was plague-stricken.
In the silence of the night there was heard a sound
of iron. On closer attention it proved to be a
rattling of chains, first at a distance and then close
at hand. Soon there appeared the spectre of an old
man, miserably thin and squalid, with a long beard
and unkempt hair. On his legs were fetters, and
on his hands chains, which he kept shaking. In
consequence the inhabitants spent horrible and
sleepless nights; the sleeplessness made them ill,
and, as their terror increased, the illness was followed
by death. . . . As a result the house was deserted
and totally abandoned to the ghost. Nevertheless
it was advertised, on the chance that some one ignorant
of all this trouble" (note the commercial morality)
"might choose to buy it or rent it. To Athens there
comes a philosopher named Athenodorus, who reads
the placard. On hearing the price and finding it so
cheap, he has his suspicions" (the ancient philosopher
had his practical side), "makes enquiry, and learns
the whole story. So far from being less inclined to
hire it, he is only the more willing. On the approach
of evening he gives orders for his couch to be made
up in the front part of the house, and asks for his
tablets, pencils, and a light. After dismissing his
attendants to the back rooms, he applies all his
attention, as well as his eyes and hand, steadily to
his writing, for fear his mind, if unoccupied, might

conjure up imaginary sounds and causeless fears. At first there was the same silence of the night as elsewhere; then there was a shaking of iron, a movement of chains. The philosopher refused to lift his eyes or stop his pencil; instead he braced up his mind so as to overcome his hearing. The noise grew louder; it approached; it sounded as if on the threshold; then as if within the room. He looks behind him; sees and recognises the apparition of which he has been told. It was standing and beckoning to him with its finger, as if calling him. In answer our friend makes it a sign with his hand to wait a while, and once more applies himself to tablet and pencil. The ghost began to rattle its chains over his head while he was writing. He looks behind him again, sees it making the same signal as before, and promptly picks up the light and follows. It goes at a slow pace, as if burdened with chains, then, after turning into the open yard of the house, it suddenly vanishes and leaves him by himself. At this he gathers some grass and leaves, and marks the spot with them. The next day he goes to the magistrates and urges them to dig up the spot in question; and they find bones tangled with chains through which they were passed. . . . These they put together and bury at the public charge. The spirit being thus duly laid, the house was henceforward free of them."

Whatever the Roman beliefs on this point, so far as funeral rites and ceremonies were concerned, they were carried out simply in accordance with custom

and tradition. The Romans of this date no more
analysed their motives and sentiments than we do
ours in dealing with such matters They honoured
the dead with funeral pomp and conspicuous monument ; but, at the bottom, it was often more out of
respect for themselves than because they imagined
that it made any difference to the departed. In a
very early age it had been considered that the spirit
led in the underworld a feeble replica of human
existence : it required food, playthings, utensils,
money, as well as consideration. Hence food was
periodically poured into the ground, playthings and
utensils were burned on the pyre or laid in the coffin,
and money was placed in that most primitive of
purses, the mouth. Conservatism is nowhere so
strong as in rites and ceremonies, and therefore the
Romans continued to burn and bury articles along
with the remains of the dead, and they continued to
put a coin in the mouth before the burial. But it
would be absurd to suppose that an intelligent
Roman of our date would have offered the original
and ancient motives for this conduct as rational
motives still actuating himself. Enough that convention expected certain proceedings as "due"
and "proper" : a true Roman would not fail to
perform what convention decreed.

Our friend the elder Silius dies a natural death,
after completing the fullest public career. His
family has its full share of both affection and pride,
and therefore his obsequies will be worthy of his

character and standing. When his Greek physician
Hermogenes assures the watching family that life is
departing, Marcia or Publius or Bassa will endeavour
to catch the last breath with a kiss, and will then
close the eyelids. Upon this all those who are
present will call "Silius! Silius! Silius!" The original
motive of this cry — which has its modern parallel
in the case of a dead Pope — was to make sure that

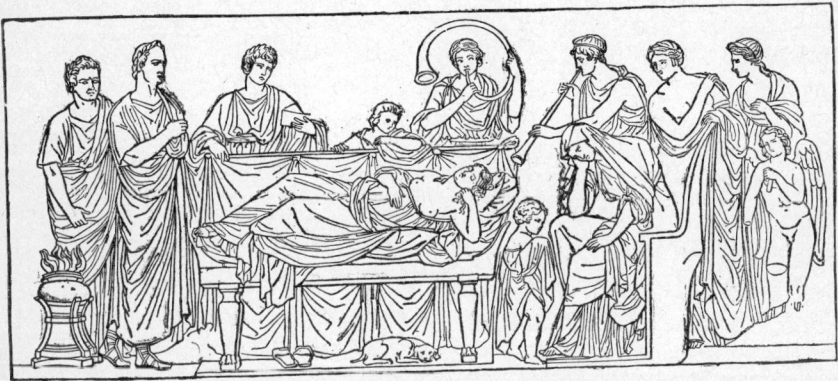

FIG. 120. — "CONCLAMATIO" OF THE DEAD.

the man was actually dead and beyond reply. This
point made certain, the professional undertaker is
called in and instructed to take charge of all the proceedings usual in such cases. It is he who will provide
the persons who are to wash and anoint the body and
lay it in state, and also, on the day of the procession,
the musicians, the wailing-women, the builders of the
funeral pyre, and others who may be necessary, together with the proper materials and accessories. He
will further see that the name of Quintus Silius Bassus
is registered in the death-roll in the temple of "Juno

the Death-Goddess," and that the registration fee is paid. The name will also appear in the next issue of the "Daily News." The body, anointed so as to preserve it till the third day, and dressed in the toga — which will be that of the highest position he ever occupied — is laid in state in the high reception-hall, with the feet pointing to the door. On the bier are wreaths, by it is burning a pan of incense, in or before the vestibule is placed a cypress tree or a number of cypress branches for warning information to the public.

On the day next but one after death the contractor, attended by subordinates dressed in black, marshals his procession. Though it is daytime, the procession will be accompanied by torches — another piece of conservatism reminiscent of the time when funerals took place at night, as they still did with children and commonly with the lower orders. First go the musicians, playing upon flageolet, trumpet, or horn; behind these, professional wailing-women, who raise loud lamentation and beat their breasts. Next come the wax-masks, already mentioned, of the distinguished ancestors of the Silii. These, which are life-like portraits, have been taken out of their cupboards in the wing of the reception-hall, and are worn over their faces by men of a build as nearly as possible resembling that of the ancestors represented. Each man also wears the insignia of the character for whom he stands. The more of such "effigies" a house could produce, the greater its glory. Such, however, was not the original purpose of this part of the procession, for — though it had doubtless been generally forgotten — the intention was to represent the deceased as being conducted into the underworld by an honourable company already established there. After the effigies comes that which would correspond to our hearse. It is, however, no hearse of the modern kind, but a bier or couch with the usual embellishment of ivory and with covers of purple worked with gold. On this the body lies, open to the sky, like that of Juliet. The bearers are either relatives or such slaves as have been set free under Silius's last will. Behind come the nearest relatives or heirs, the freedmen, friends, and clients, all clothed in black, except the women, who are in white, without colour or gold upon their dress. Young Publius will walk with his head covered by his toga; Bassa with her hair loose and dishevelled. The whole party will utter lamentations, though under more restraint than those of the professional women in front.

Silius having been a senator and a man of other official standing, the procession passes from the Caelian Hill along the Sacred Way to the Forum, as far as the Rostra or speaking-platform. There the bier is set down, the "ancestors" seat themselves on the folding-stools which were the old-fashioned chairs of the higher officers, and one of the relatives delivers an oration in praise, not only of Silius, but of his family as represented in the ancestors.

The procession then forms again, and the party proceeds to whatever place outside the walls may

contain the family tomb of the Silii. No burial is
allowed within the city proper, and for our purposes
we will assume that the place is distant nearly a

Fig. 121. — Tomb of Caecilia Metella.

mile along the Appian Way. We will assume also
that Silius is to be cremated, and not simply buried
in a coffin or a marble sarcophagus. Few persons
of the higher classes, except certain of the Cornelii,

FIG. 122. — STREET OF TOMBS. (Pompeii.)

443

are buried at this date, although there is nothing in
law or custom to prevent the choice. There exists
no "crematorium," and the Silii are regularly burned
at their own sepulchral allotment beside the "Queen
of Roads."

If you were with the procession on this day you
would find yourself before one of an almost continuous
chain of monuments, built in all manner of shapes
and sizes — such as great altars, small shrines, pyramids (like that of Cestius on another road), or round
towers like the beautiful tomb of Caecilia Metella.
The exterior of these structures is often adorned with
commemorative or symbolic carvings, and the inside,
which may be wholly above the surface or partly
sunk beneath — is a chamber surrounded by niches,
in which are placed the urns containing the ashes
of the dead. Perhaps an illustration of the present
state of the "Street of Tombs" at Pompeii will afford
some notion, although the sepulchres of that provincial
place by no means matched those upon the various
roads outside the Roman gates. Often the monumental chamber stands somewhat back from the
road, leaving space for a large semicircular seat of
stone open to public use, its back wall being inscribed
with some statement of honour to the family.
Round the sepulchre — "where all the kindred of the
Silii lie" is a space of ground, planted with shrubs
and trees, and surrounded by a low wall. Somewhere
near, on an open level, the funeral pile has been
built of pine-logs, with the interstices stuffed with
pitch, brushwood, or other inflammable material.

It is natural that the pyre should take the shape of an altar and that cypress branches should lean against the sides.

Upon the summit of this pile is laid Silius on his bier; incense and unguents are shed over him; wreaths and other offerings, often of no little value, are cast upon the heap. While loud cries of lamentation are being raised by the company present, a near kinsman approaches the pile with a torch, and, turning his face away, sets fire to the whole structure. It speedily burns down, the last embers are quenched with wine, the general company thrice cries "farewell," and, except for the nearest relatives, the procession returns to the city. The relatives who stay take off their shoes, wash their hands, and proceed to gather up the bones — which they cleanse in wine and milk — and the ashes, which they mix with perfume. These remains are then placed in the urn of bronze, marble, alabaster, or maybe of coloured glass, and the urn fills one more niche in the chamber of the monument.

Now and then there were more magnificent obsequies than those of Silius. A "public" funeral might be decreed to a man who had deserved conspicuously well of the state. On such an occasion the crier would go round, calling "Oyez, come all who choose to the funeral of So-and-So." The invitation meant, not merely participation in a solemn procession, but also in the funeral feast, and probably an exhibition of gladiators. On the other hand the majority of burials were naturally of a far more simple and inexpensive kind. The poor could not afford to use unguents and keep their dead till the third day; they could not afford real cypress trees, but must use cheaper substitutes, if anything at all. They could not afford all the processionists and paraphernalia of the undertaker, but must be satisfied

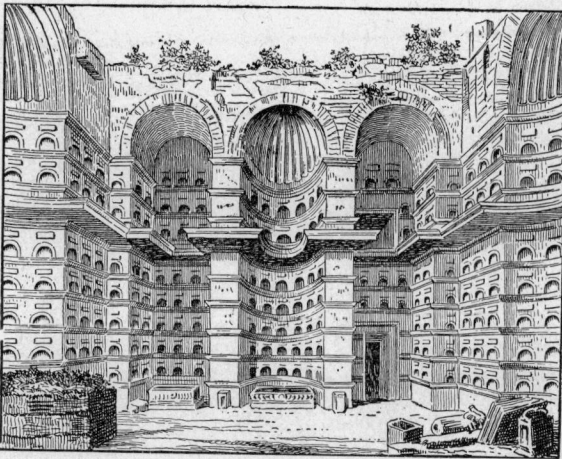

Fig. 123.— Columbarium.

with four commonplace bearers, who hurried away the corpse in the evening, not on a couch but in a cheap box, and carried it out to the common necropolis beyond the Esquiline Gate. Seldom could they afford the fuel to burn the body, and in many cases it must simply be thrown into a pit roughly dug and there left without monument. To secure more respect and decency there were many burial clubs, whether connected with the trade-guilds or not, and these procured a joint tomb of the kind known as a "dovecote," or columbarium, from the resemblance of its niches to so many pigeon-holes. These cooperative sepulchres were underground vaults, and it is perhaps hardly necessary to point out their direct relation to the Christian catacombs. Similar tombs were sometimes used by the great Roman families for the remains of the freedmen and slaves of their house.

FIG. 124. — TEMPLE OF JUPITER ON THE CAPITOL (Platform omitted).

INDEX

Actors, contempt for, 268
Advertisements, 257
Aemilia, Basilica, 108
Africa, 45
Age, coming of, 332
Agriculture, implements of, 252
Alexander the Great, 34
Alexandria, 14, 25, 34, 44
Amphitheatres, 280; performances, 282
Amulets, 318
Andalusia, 36
Antioch, 14, 43
Appian Way, 22, 118
Aqueducts, 136
Architecture, 112, 422–424
Argiletum, the, 108
Aristocrat, clients of, 206; daily life of, 193; dress of, 196; as pleader in law-courts, 216; social duties of, 217
Army, the, 12, 52, 338–358; artillery, 356; auxiliaries, 352; camping arrangements, 349; cavalry, 339, 353, 356; composition, 339; dress and equipment, 342; Imperial Guards, 353; infantry, 339, 352; legionaries, 339; pay and rations, 344; promotion, 347; terms of service, 340; training, 340, 345; typical soldier's life, 342–350
Art, 416–433; apparent lack of artistic feeling, 429; contempt for professional artists, 428; influence of Greece, 421; profession and quality of, 416–420; statues, 418, 424; wall-paintings, 425–428
Artemis, temple of, 42
Artillery, 356
Asia Minor, towns of, 42
Astronomy, 397
Athens, 40
Athletics, 263
Auctioneers, receipt tablets of, 250
Augustus, title of emperor, 55

Augustus, Forum of, 118; mausoleum of, 120
Authors, amateur, 219, 235

Baetica (see Andalusia)
Bakers, 248
Bandits, 24
Banking, 216, 239
Basilica Aemilia, 108; of Julius, 106
Baths, 122, 224
Beard, method of wearing, 195
Beds, 182
Beggars, 243
Betrothal ceremony, 296
Boadicea, 39
Books, size and shape of, 335–337
Booksellers, 109, 247
Boots (see Shoes)
Boxing-gloves, 265
Breakfast, 200
Britain, 39
Burial, 434–447; funeral rites, 439–445; offerings to the dead, 438; tombs, 444, 446

Caligula, 73, 95, 115, 234
Camps, military, 349
Campus Martius, the, 120
Carpets, absence of, 180
Carriages, 19 : regulation of traffic, 131
Cavalry, 339, 353, 356
Census of Augustus, 85
Chariot-races, 263, 274, 280; colours in, 274, 278; horses, 275; prizes, 278; procession of chariots, 277
Charts, 18
Chemistry, 402
Children : ceremony at birth and naming, 317; coming of age, 332; early life, 319; education, 320–335; parental power over, 315–317; privileges of parents, 314; registration, 318
Christians, earlier tolerance towards,

WILLIAM STEARNS DAVIS'S HISTORICAL NOVELS

A Victor of Salamis

A TALE OF THE DAYS OF XERXES, LEONIDAS, AND THEMISTOCLES

Cloth, 12mo, $1.50

"A really moving narrative, with figures of flesh and blood in it, and a broad vitality that touches the reader's imagination. The thing is astonishingly human . . . and as unaffectedly dramatic as though he had drawn his material from the modern world." — *The New York Tribune.*

"The novel reproduces Greek life, and the events of the Persian invasion brilliantly and with correctness. . . . Mr. Davis has even surpassed his previous efforts in highly imaginative work." — *Boston Budget.*

A Friend of Cæsar

A TALE OF THE FALL OF THE ROMAN REPUBLIC

Cloth, 12mo, $1.50

"As a story . . . there can be no question of its success. . . . While the beautiful love of Cornelia and Drusus lies at the sound sweet heart of the story, to say so is to give a most meagre idea of the large sustained interest of the whole. . . . There are many incidents so vivid, so brilliant that they fix themselves in the memory." — *The Bookman.*

"God Wills It"

A TALE OF THE FIRST CRUSADE

With Illustrations by Louis Betts.   Cloth, 12mo, $1.50

"Not since Sir Walter Scott cast his spell over us with 'Ivanhoe,' 'Count Robert of Paris,' and 'Quentin Durward' have we been so completely captivated by a story as by 'God Wills It,' by William Stearns Davis. It grips the attention of the reader in the first chapter and holds it till the last. . . . It is a story of strenuous life, the spirit of which might well be applied in some of our modern Crusades. While true to life in its local coloring, it is sweet and pure, and leaves no after-taste of bitterness. The author's first book, 'A Friend of Cæsar,' revealed his power, and 'God Wills It' confirms and deepens the impression made." — *Christian Endeavor World.*

PUBLISHED BY

THE MACMILLAN COMPANY

64-66 Fifth Avenue, New York

An Outline History of the Roman Empire

By WILLIAM STEARNS DAVIS, Professor of
History in the University of Minnesota

Cloth, 65 cents net

A comprehensive review of the progress and fall of the
Roman Empire such as is a necessary pre-requisite to an
intelligent study of the history of the Middle Ages. The
volume is brief and, considering its condensation, of un-
usually interesting style.

A History of Rome to the Battle of Actium

By EVELYN S. SHUCKBURGH

Cloth, $1.75 net

The author has presented in a vivid manner the story of the
gradual extension of power of a single city over a large part
of the known world. The countries conquered and the
details of the conquest, the internal development of the state,
and the constitutional changes that resulted, are all clearly
set forth in the narrative along with a discussion of the
development of literature and the social life. The book is
grounded throughout upon the old writers.

A History of Greece

By J. B. BURY, Regius Professor of
Greek in the University of Dublin

Cloth, $1.90 net

" Excellence in a historical work by this scholar was to be
expected, but the charm of his literary style and clearness of
expression have placed this volume at the head of single
volume texts. The history of Greece is considered in great
detail from the political and constitutional sides, but special
emphasis is laid on the literature, art, and social life."

A Student's History of Greece

By J. B. BURY. Revised by EVERETT KIMBALL

Cloth, $1.10 net

"This volume, a condensation of Professor Bury's larger work,
presents in a scholarly manner, such details of Greek history,
life, letters, and art as are necessary for an elementary understanding of the subject."

PUBLISHED BY
THE MACMILLAN COMPANY
64–66 Fifth Avenue, New York

Roman Society from Nero
to Marcus Aurelius
$2.50 net (by mail $2.67)

Roman Society in the Last Century
of the Western Empire
$1.75 net (by mail $1.90)

By SAMUEL DILL, M.A., Hon. Litt.D. (Dublin) ; Hon. LL.D.
(Edinburgh) ; Professor of Greek in Queens College, Belfast

"The most important contribution yet made in English to
our knowledge of the way in which all classes of Roman
society lived." — M. W. H., in *The Sun*, New York.

Social Life at Rome
in the Age of Cicero

By W. WARDE FOWLER

Cloth, $2.25 net (by mail $2.40)

A notable example of the kind of history that deals with men
rather than with institutions and events. This is the only
book in the English language that supplies a picture of life
and manners, of education, morals, and religion, in the intensely interesting period of the Roman Republic. The age
of Cicero is one of the most important periods of Roman
history, and the Ciceronian correspondence, of more than
nine hundred contemporary letters, is the richest treasure
house of social life that has survived from any period of
classical antiquity.

The Monuments of Christian Rome

By ARTHUR L. FROTHINGHAM

Cloth, *Fully Illustrated*, $2.25 net (by mail $2.44)

"The first part gives an historical sketch of Rome from the
times of Constantine and Honorius to that of 1305, when the
popes were in exile at Avignon. The second part is an
exhaustive classification of the monuments, together with an
index of illustrations and of churches. . . . The book is
interestingly written, and as its author was at one time asso-
ciate director of the American School at Rome, it has the
authority of first-hand knowledge to give it standing." —
Boston Transcript.

PUBLISHED BY

THE MACMILLAN COMPANY

64-66 Fifth Avenue, New York

By THOMAS G. TUCKER

Life in Ancient Athens

The Social and Public Life of a Classical Athenian
from Day to Day

By T. G. TUCKER, Litt.D. (Camb.), Hon. Litt.D. (Dublin),
Professor of Classical Philology in the University of Melbourne

323 pages, with illustrations, $1.25 net

"Professor Tucker has looked at Greek life in Athens exactly
as we should look at it to-day with our Anglo-Saxon predilections
and modes of expression, without in any way destroying the
Athenian tone. The method is a very attractive one, and enables
us to compare Greek life with that of our own day without any
of that glamour and mystery which is but too apt to be thrown
over everything from which the veil of antiquity is withdrawn.
The period chosen is that of Socrates, Sophocles, Euripides,
Thucydides and later, Plato, Xenophon, and Demosthenes.

"After giving us a picture of Athens and its environment, its
public buildings, streets, and places where citizens congregate, the
various classes of inhabitants, citizens, women, outlanders, slaves ;
its homes and the way in which they were arranged and furnished
— Professor Tucker takes an ordinary citizen and traces out the
daily routine of his social, family, and public life. He then supposes the citizen has a daughter who must be trained at home and
then married. She has a son, who must be nursed as a baby, sent
to school under the charge of his 'pedagogue,' and when of age
must serve in the army and the navy. We are allowed to examine
him in religious matters, to be told what festivals he observes,
what dramas he sees in the theatre, and his way of fulfilling his
citizen duties. He has a lawsuit, and so we accompany him to
court, and, lastly we are present at his burial.

"There is a chapter on Athenian art, and another of special
importance which shows that, although the Athenian is separated
from us chronologically by many centuries, he was an un-
commonly 'modern' man in his habits, tastes, and aims in life.
The volume is beyond doubt one which brings the Athenian of
old very vividly before us and gives us a picture of his life full
of touches of nature common to him and us. There are many
excellent illustrations, maps, and plans which add to the value
of the book." — *The Philadelphia Public Ledger.*

PUBLISHED BY

THE MACMILLAN COMPANY

64-66 Fifth Avenue, New York